JUDGE DREDD

THE BLESSED EARTH

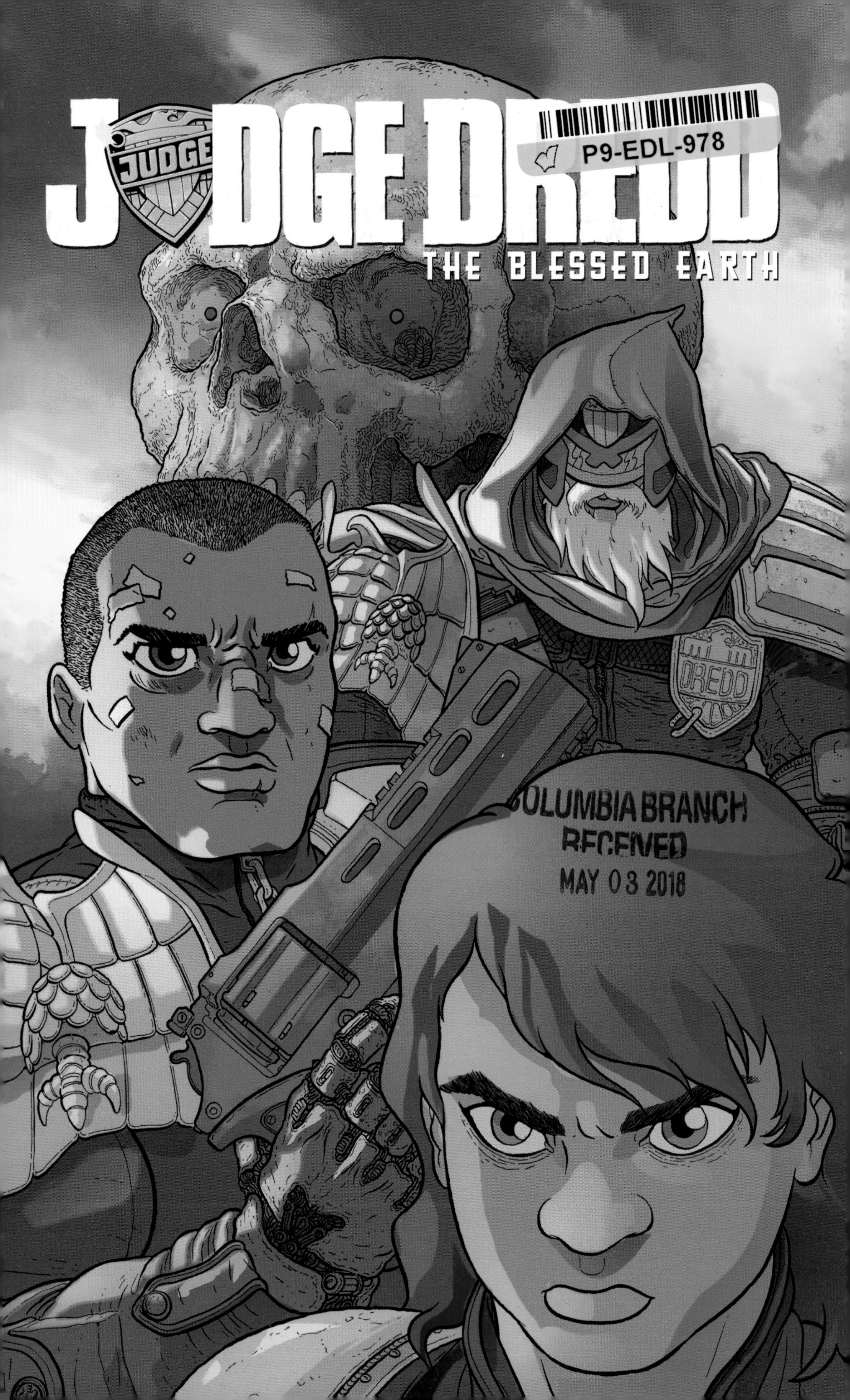
JUDGE
DREDD

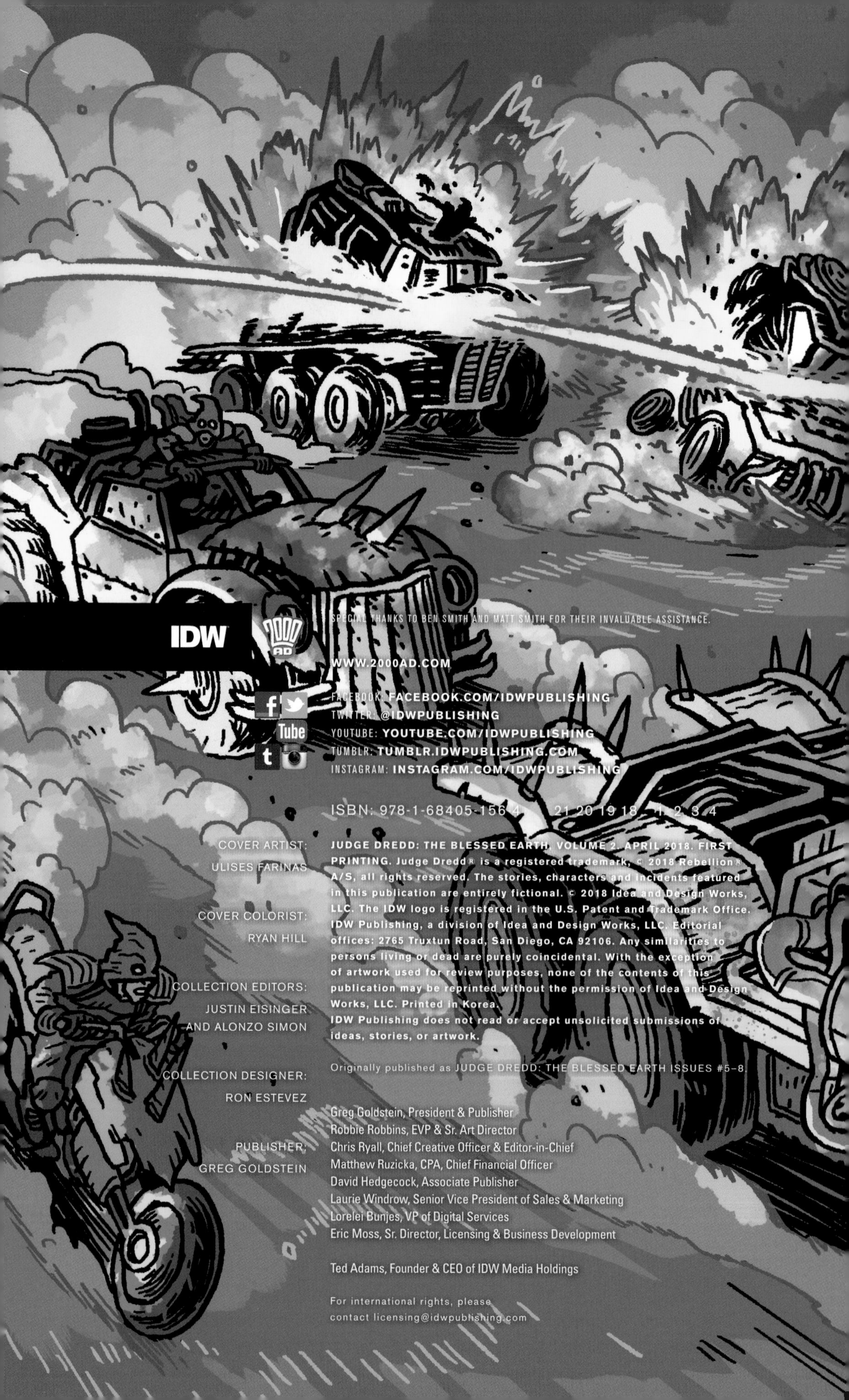

IDW

2000 AD

SPECIAL THANKS TO BEN SMITH AND MATT SMITH FOR THEIR INVALUABLE ASSISTANCE.

WWW.2000AD.COM

FACEBOOK: FACEBOOK.COM/IDWPUBLISHING
TWITTER: @IDWPUBLISHING
YOUTUBE: YOUTUBE.COM/IDWPUBLISHING
TUMBLR: TUMBLR.IDWPUBLISHING.COM
INSTAGRAM: INSTAGRAM.COM/IDWPUBLISHING

ISBN: 978-1-68405-156-4 21 20 19 18 1 2 3 4

COVER ARTIST:
ULISES FARINAS

COVER COLORIST:
RYAN HILL

COLLECTION EDITORS:
JUSTIN EISINGER
AND ALONZO SIMON

COLLECTION DESIGNER:
RON ESTEVEZ

PUBLISHER:
GREG GOLDSTEIN

Originally published as JUDGE DREDD: THE BLESSED EARTH ISSUES #5–8.

Greg Goldstein, President & Publisher
Robbie Robbins, EVP & Sr. Art Director
Chris Ryall, Chief Creative Officer & Editor-in-Chief
Matthew Ruzicka, CPA, Chief Financial Officer
David Hedgecock, Associate Publisher
Laurie Windrow, Senior Vice President of Sales & Marketing
Lorelei Bunjes, VP of Digital Services
Eric Moss, Sr. Director, Licensing & Business Development

Ted Adams, Founder & CEO of IDW Media Holdings

For international rights, please
contact licensing@idwpublishing.com

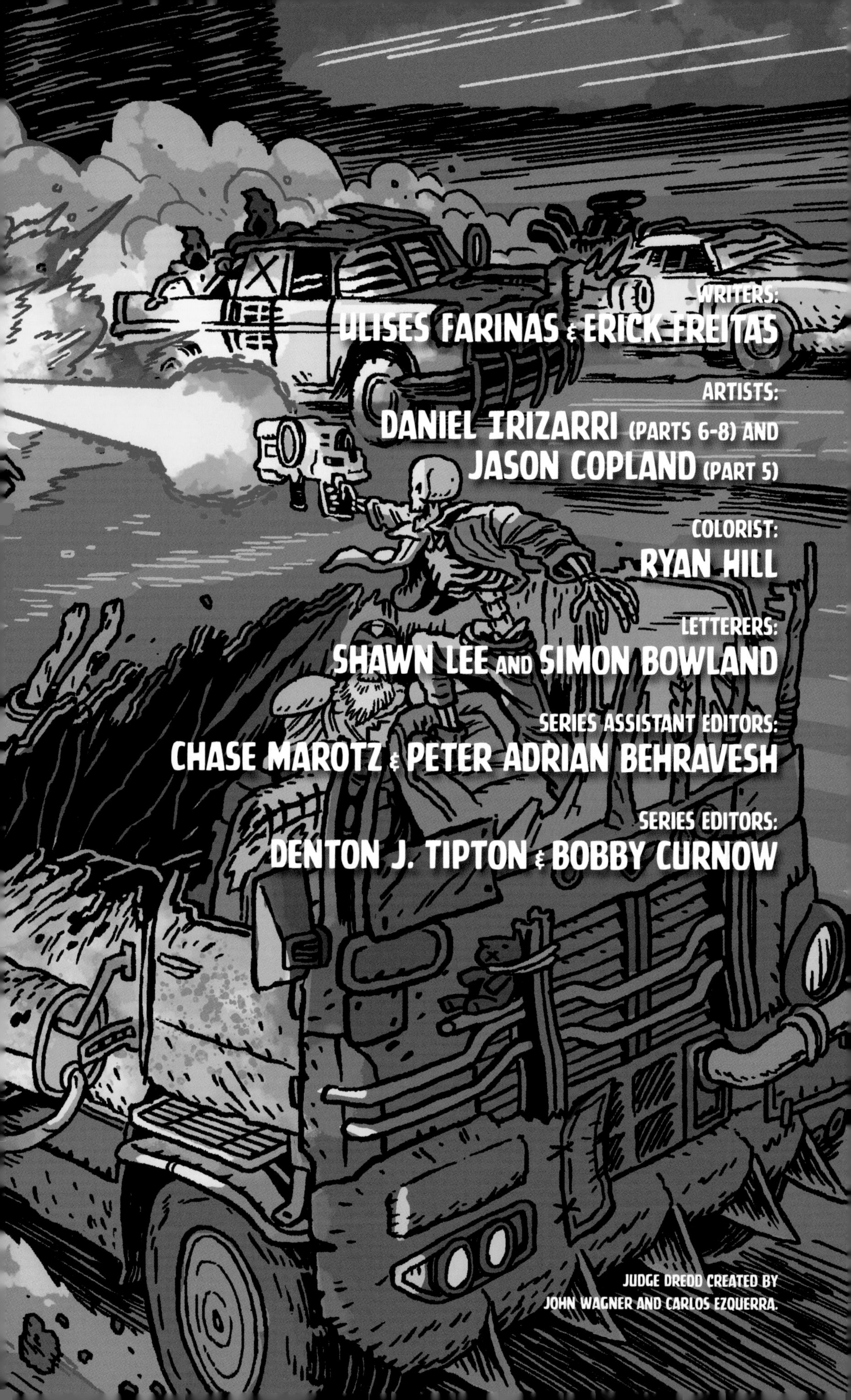

WRITERS:
ULISES FARINAS & ERICK FREITAS

ARTISTS:
DANIEL IRIZARRI (PARTS 6-8) AND
JASON COPLAND (PART 5)

COLORIST:
RYAN HILL

LETTERERS:
SHAWN LEE AND SIMON BOWLAND

SERIES ASSISTANT EDITORS:
CHASE MAROTZ & PETER ADRIAN BEHRAVESH

SERIES EDITORS:
DENTON J. TIPTON & BOBBY CURNOW

JUDGE DREDD CREATED BY
JOHN WAGNER AND CARLOS EZQUERRA.

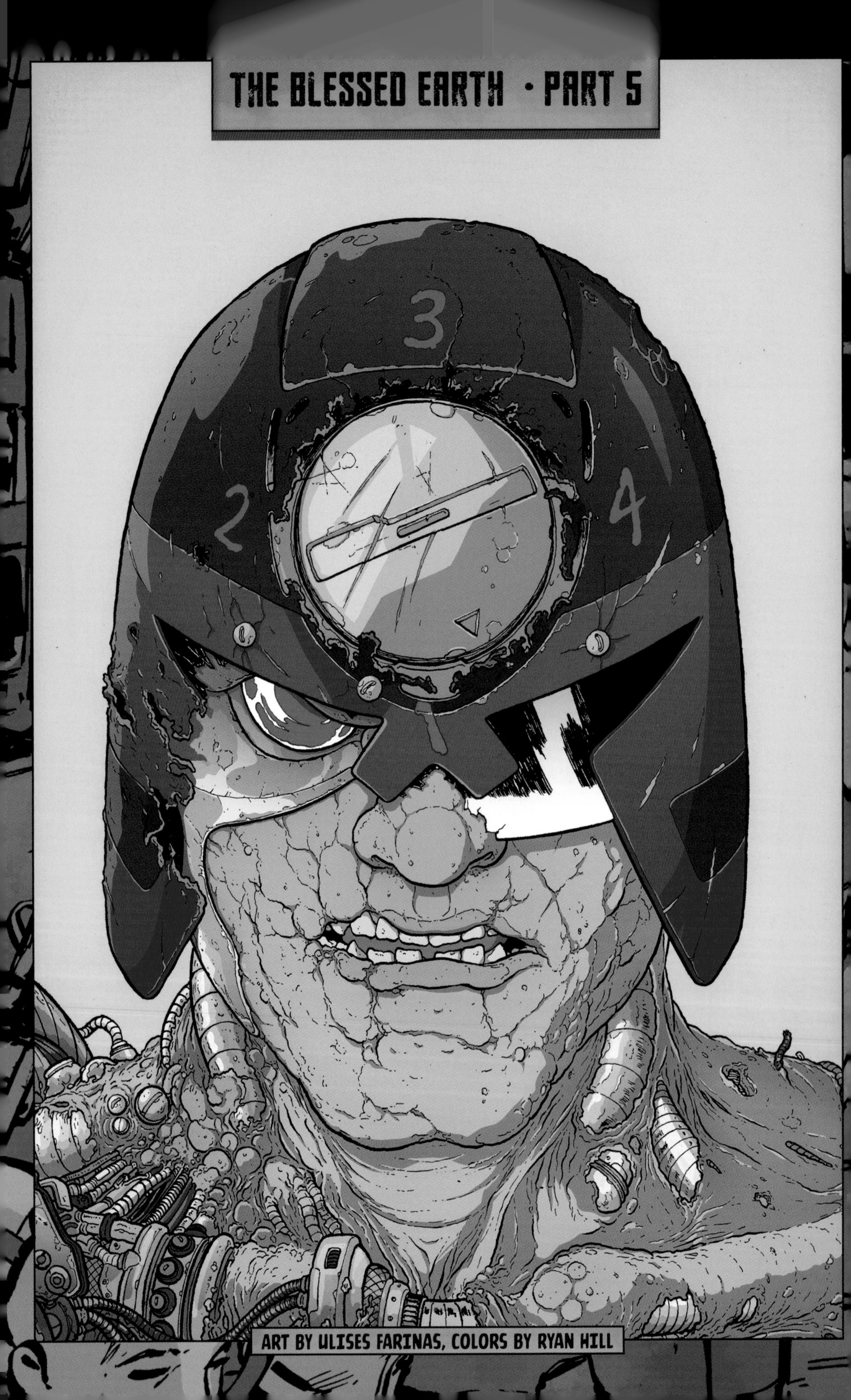
THE BLESSED EARTH · PART 5
ART BY ULISES FARINAS, COLORS BY RYAN HILL

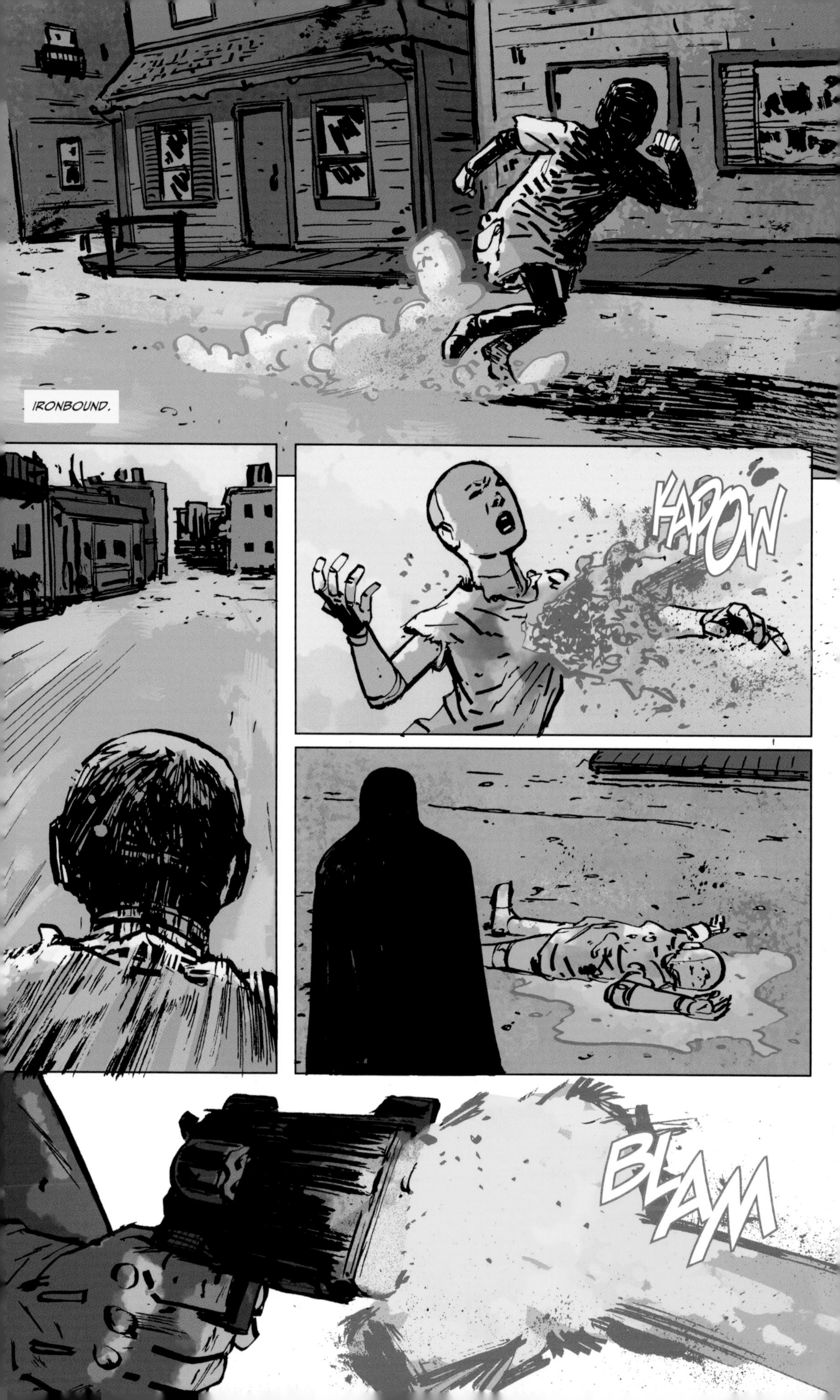
IRONBOUND.
KAPOW
BLAM

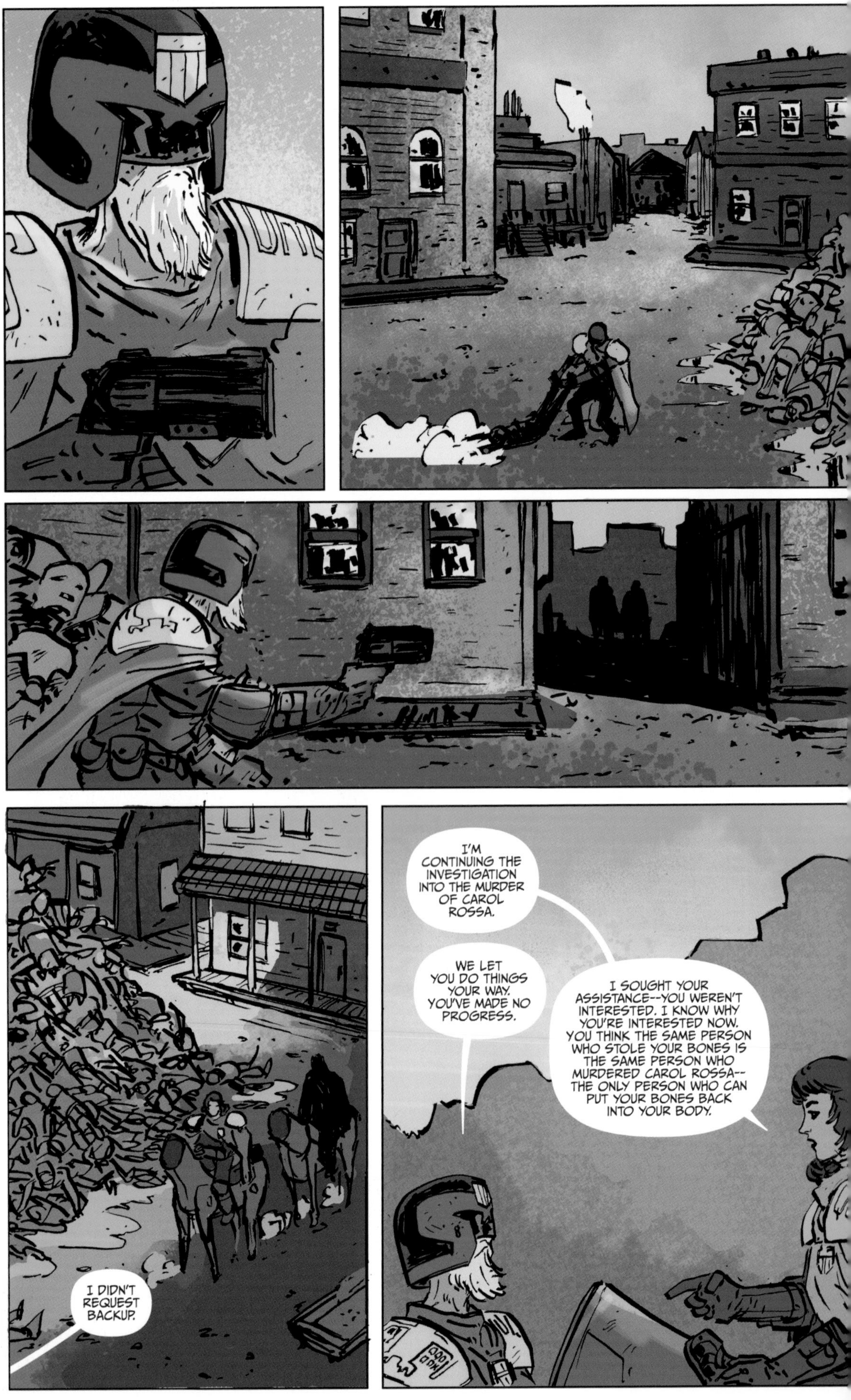
I DIDN'T REQUEST BACKUP.
I'M CONTINUING THE INVESTIGATION INTO THE MURDER OF CAROL ROSSA.
WE LET YOU DO THINGS YOUR WAY. YOU'VE MADE NO PROGRESS.
I SOUGHT YOUR ASSISTANCE--YOU WEREN'T INTERESTED. I KNOW WHY YOU'RE INTERESTED NOW. YOU THINK THE SAME PERSON WHO STOLE YOUR BONES IS THE SAME PERSON WHO MURDERED CAROL ROSSA-- THE ONLY PERSON WHO CAN PUT YOUR BONES BACK INTO YOUR BODY.

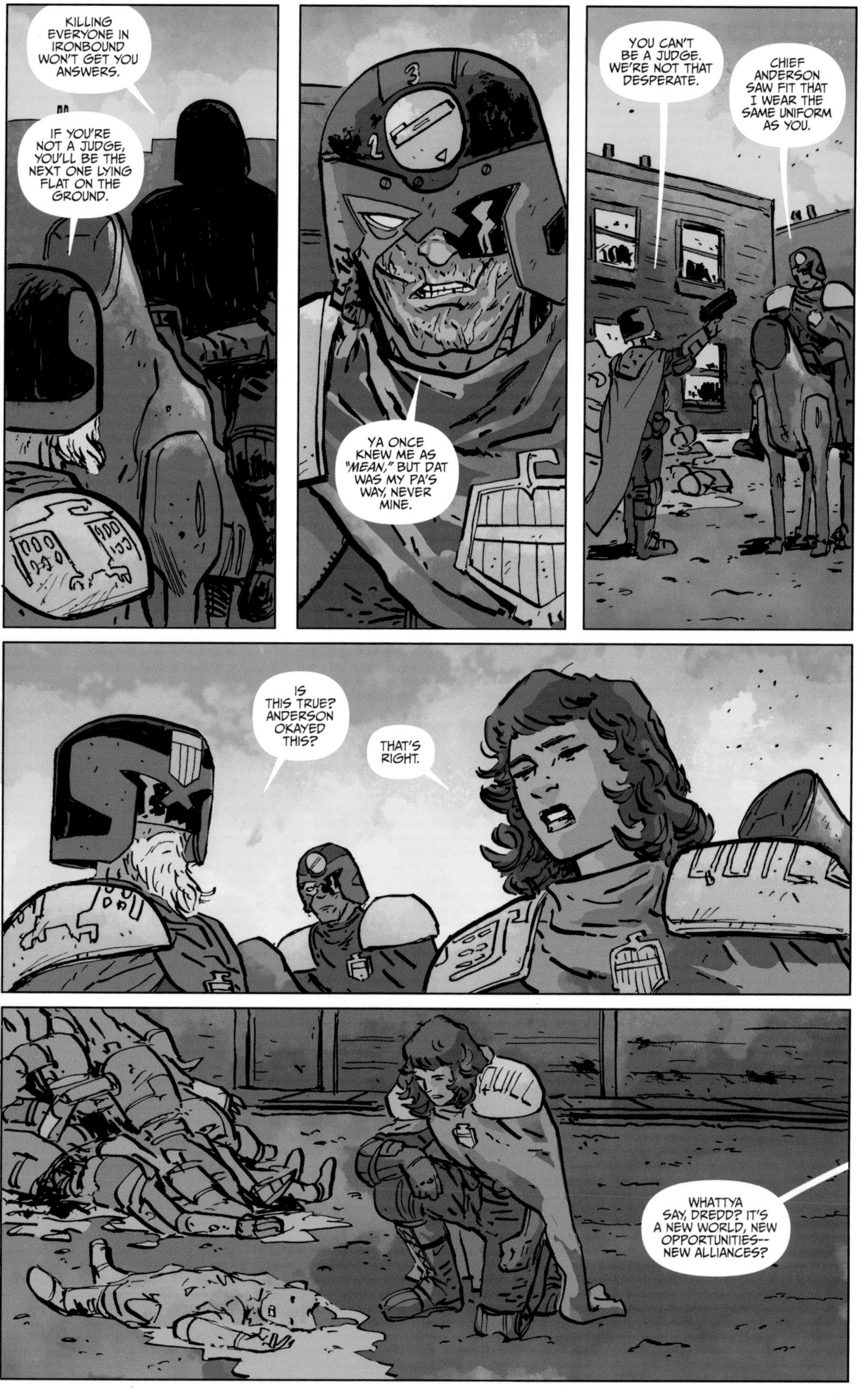
KILLING EVERYONE IN IRONBOUND WON'T GET YOU ANSWERS.
IF YOU'RE NOT A JUDGE, YOU'LL BE THE NEXT ONE LYING FLAT ON THE GROUND.
YA ONCE KNEW ME AS "MEAN," BUT DAT WAS MY PA'S WAY, NEVER MINE.
YOU CAN'T BE A JUDGE. WE'RE NOT THAT DESPERATE.
CHIEF ANDERSON SAW FIT THAT I WEAR THE SAME UNIFORM AS YOU.
IS THIS TRUE? ANDERSON OKAYED THIS?
THAT'S RIGHT.
WHATTYA SAY, DREDD? IT'S A NEW WORLD, NEW OPPORTUNITIES-- NEW ALLIANCES?

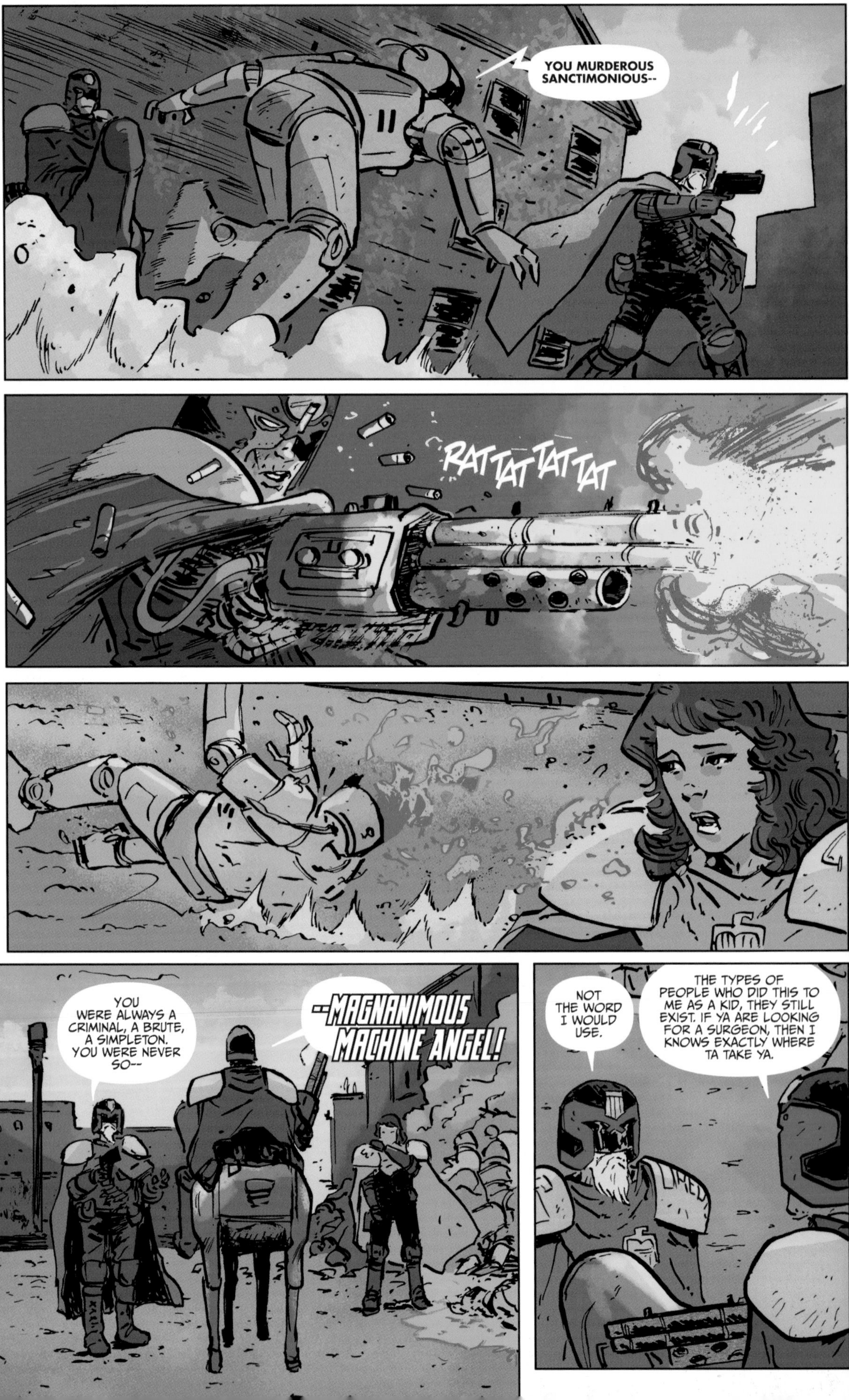
YOU MURDEROUS SANCTIMONIOUS--
RAT TAT TAT TAT
YOU WERE ALWAYS A CRIMINAL, A BRUTE, A SIMPLETON. YOU WERE NEVER SO--
--MAGNANIMOUS MACHINE ANGEL!
NOT THE WORD I WOULD USE.
THE TYPES OF PEOPLE WHO DID THIS TO ME AS A KID, THEY STILL EXIST. IF YA ARE LOOKING FOR A SURGEON, THEN I KNOWS EXACTLY WHERE TA TAKE YA.

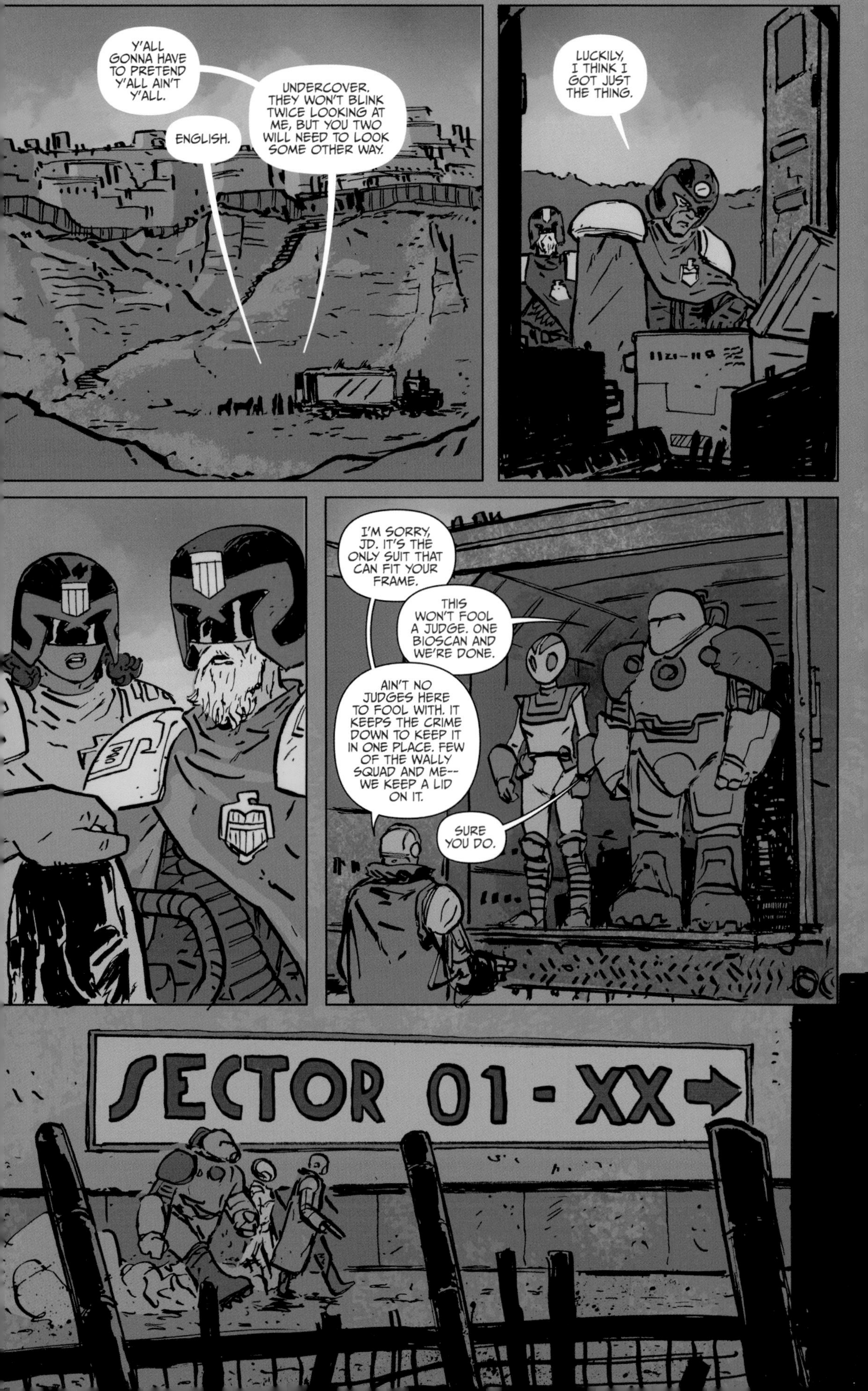

Y'ALL GONNA HAVE TO PRETEND Y'ALL AIN'T Y'ALL.
ENGLISH.
UNDERCOVER. THEY WON'T BLINK TWICE LOOKING AT ME, BUT YOU TWO WILL NEED TO LOOK SOME OTHER WAY.
LUCKILY, I THINK I GOT JUST THE THING.
I'M SORRY, JD. IT'S THE ONLY SUIT THAT CAN FIT YOUR FRAME.
THIS WON'T FOOL A JUDGE. ONE BIOSCAN AND WE'RE DONE.
AIN'T NO JUDGES HERE TO FOOL WITH. IT KEEPS THE CRIME DOWN TO KEEP IT IN ONE PLACE. FEW OF THE WALLY SQUAD AND ME-- WE KEEP A LID ON IT.
SURE YOU DO.
SECTOR 01 - XX

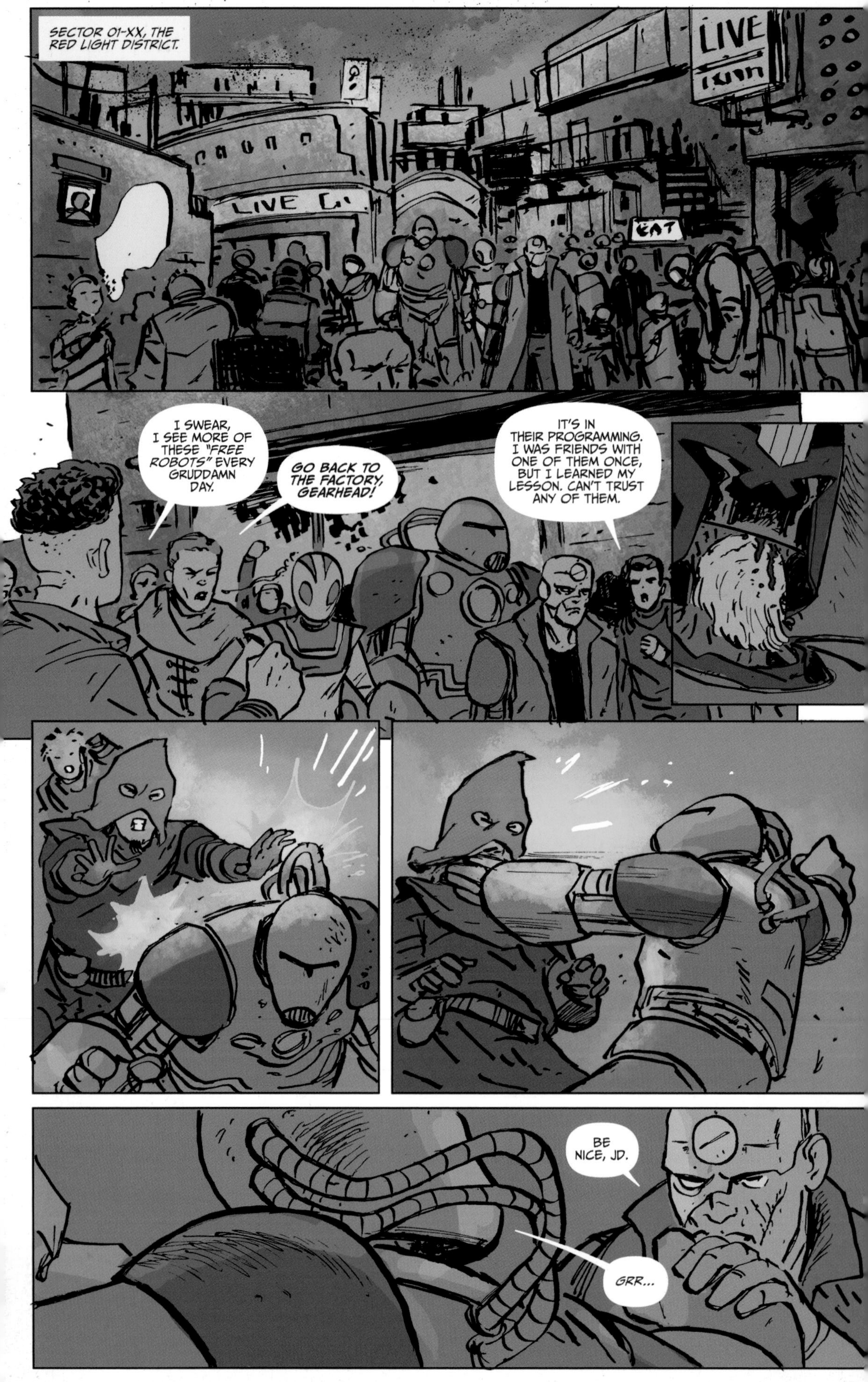
SECTOR 01-XX, THE RED LIGHT DISTRICT.
LIVE
LIVE
EAT
I SWEAR, I SEE MORE OF THESE "FREE ROBOTS" EVERY GRUDDAMN DAY.
GO BACK TO THE FACTORY, GEARHEAD!
IT'S IN THEIR PROGRAMMING. I WAS FRIENDS WITH ONE OF THEM ONCE, BUT I LEARNED MY LESSON. CAN'T TRUST ANY OF THEM.
BE NICE, JD.
GRR...

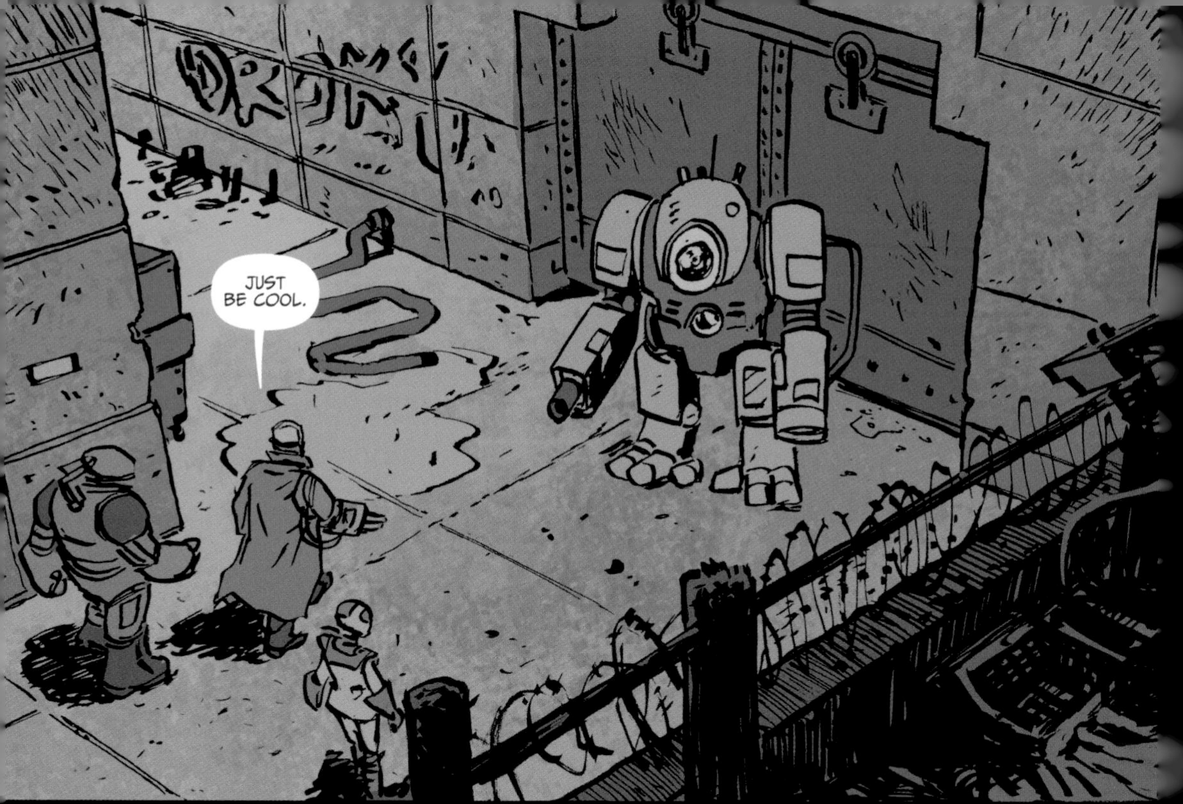
JUST BE COOL.

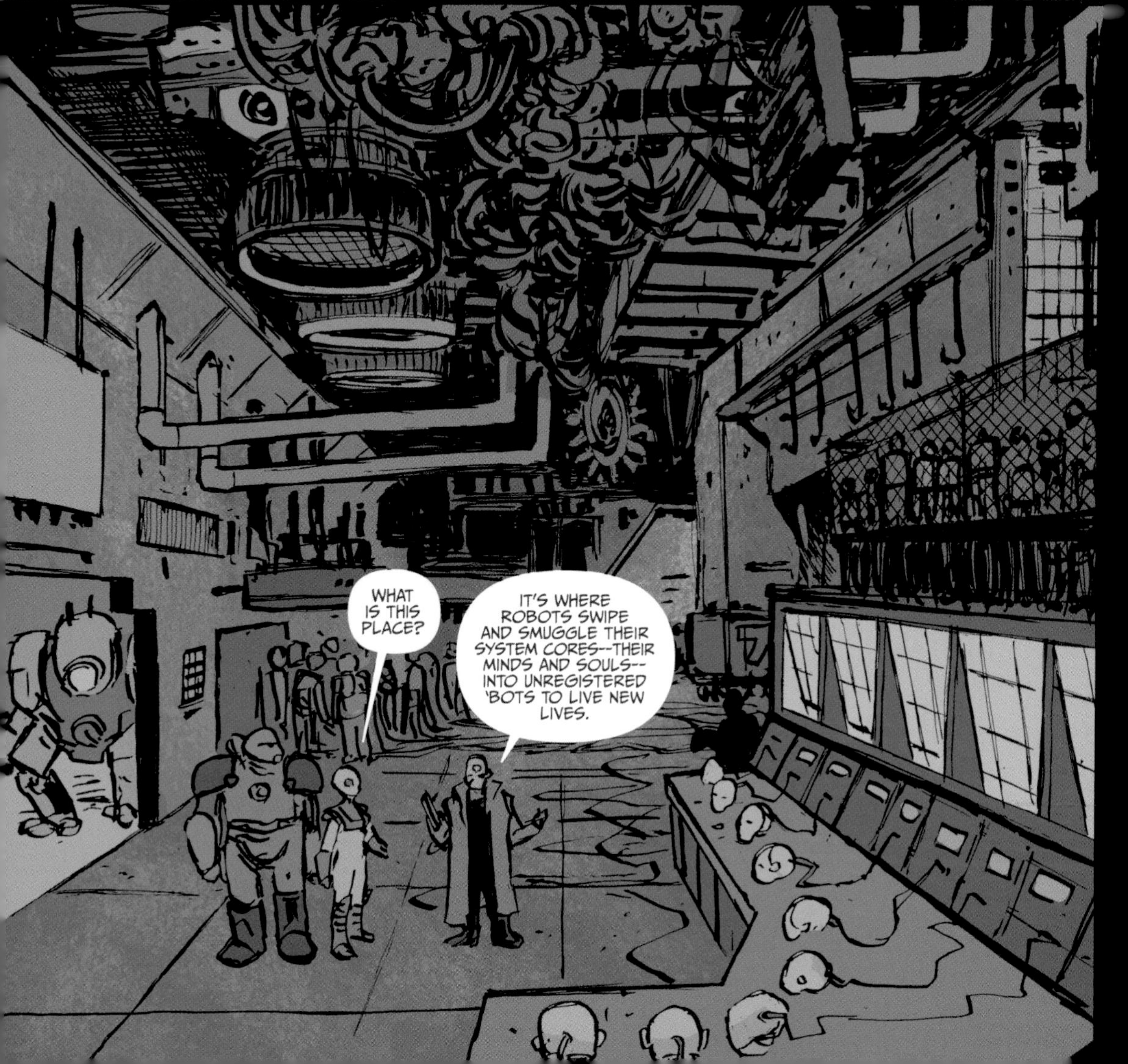
WHAT IS THIS PLACE?
IT'S WHERE ROBOTS SWIPE AND SMUGGLE THEIR SYSTEM CORES--THEIR MINDS AND SOULS--INTO UNREGISTERED 'BOTS TO LIVE NEW LIVES.

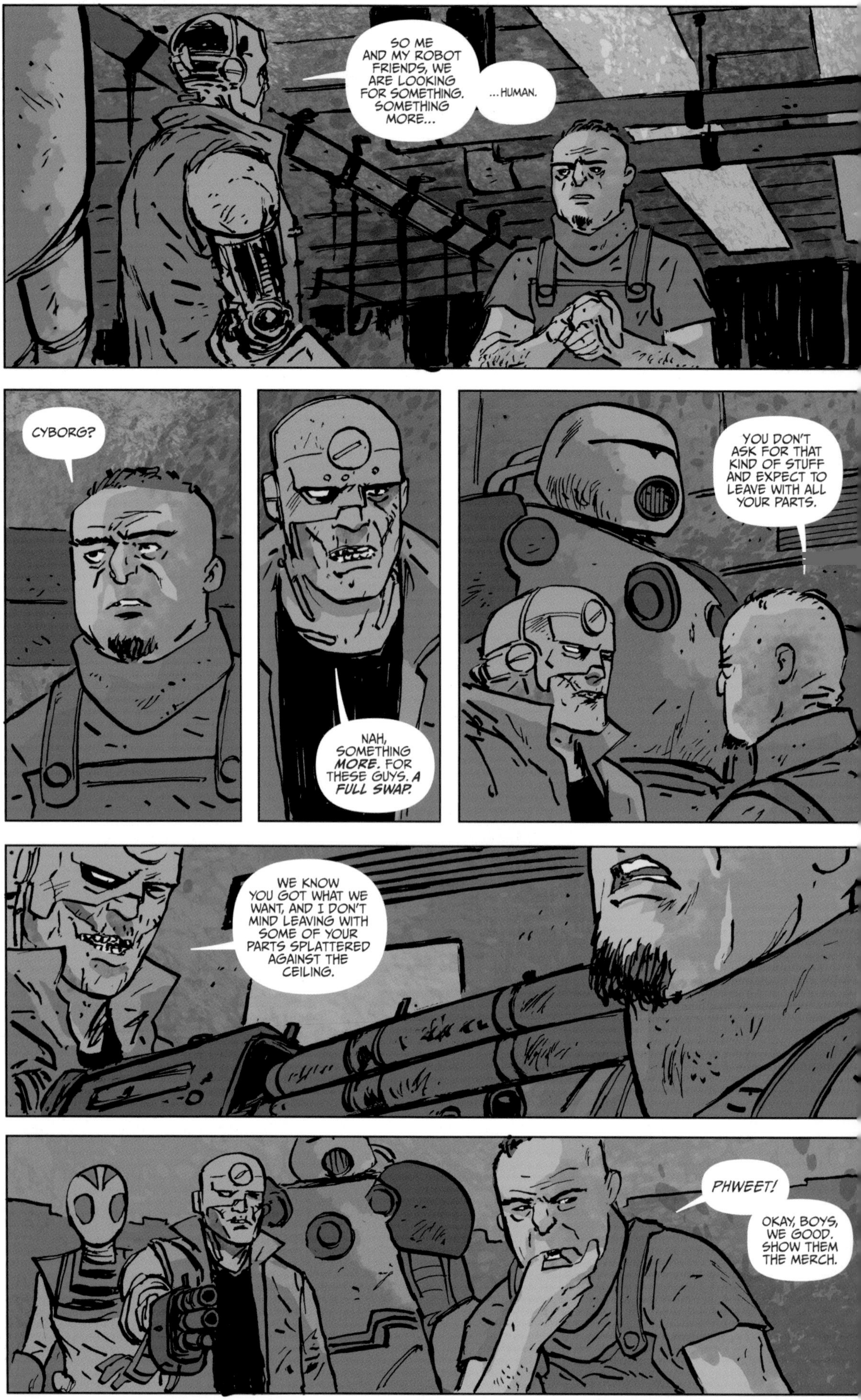
SO ME AND MY ROBOT FRIENDS, WE ARE LOOKING FOR SOMETHING. SOMETHING MORE...
...HUMAN.
CYBORG?
NAH, SOMETHING *MORE*. FOR THESE GUYS. *A FULL SWAP.*
YOU DON'T ASK FOR THAT KIND OF STUFF AND EXPECT TO LEAVE WITH ALL YOUR PARTS.
WE KNOW YOU GOT WHAT WE WANT, AND I DON'T MIND LEAVING WITH SOME OF YOUR PARTS SPLATTERED AGAINST THE CEILING.
PHWEET!
OKAY, BOYS, WE GOOD. SHOW THEM THE MERCH.

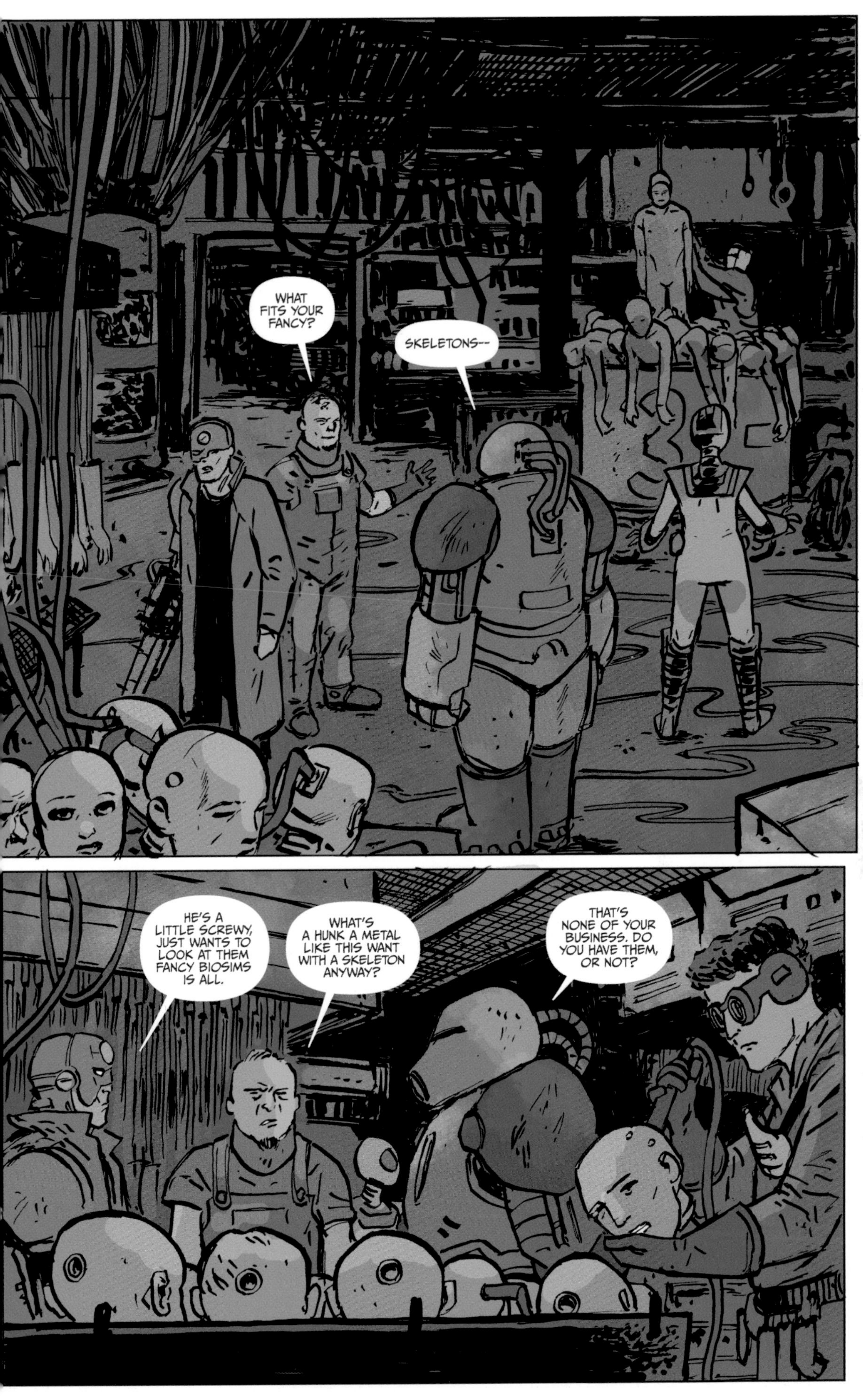
WHAT FITS YOUR FANCY?
SKELETONS--
HE'S A LITTLE SCREWY, JUST WANTS TO LOOK AT THEM FANCY BIOSIMS IS ALL.
WHAT'S A HUNK A METAL LIKE THIS WANT WITH A SKELETON ANYWAY?
THAT'S NONE OF YOUR BUSINESS. DO YOU HAVE THEM, OR NOT?

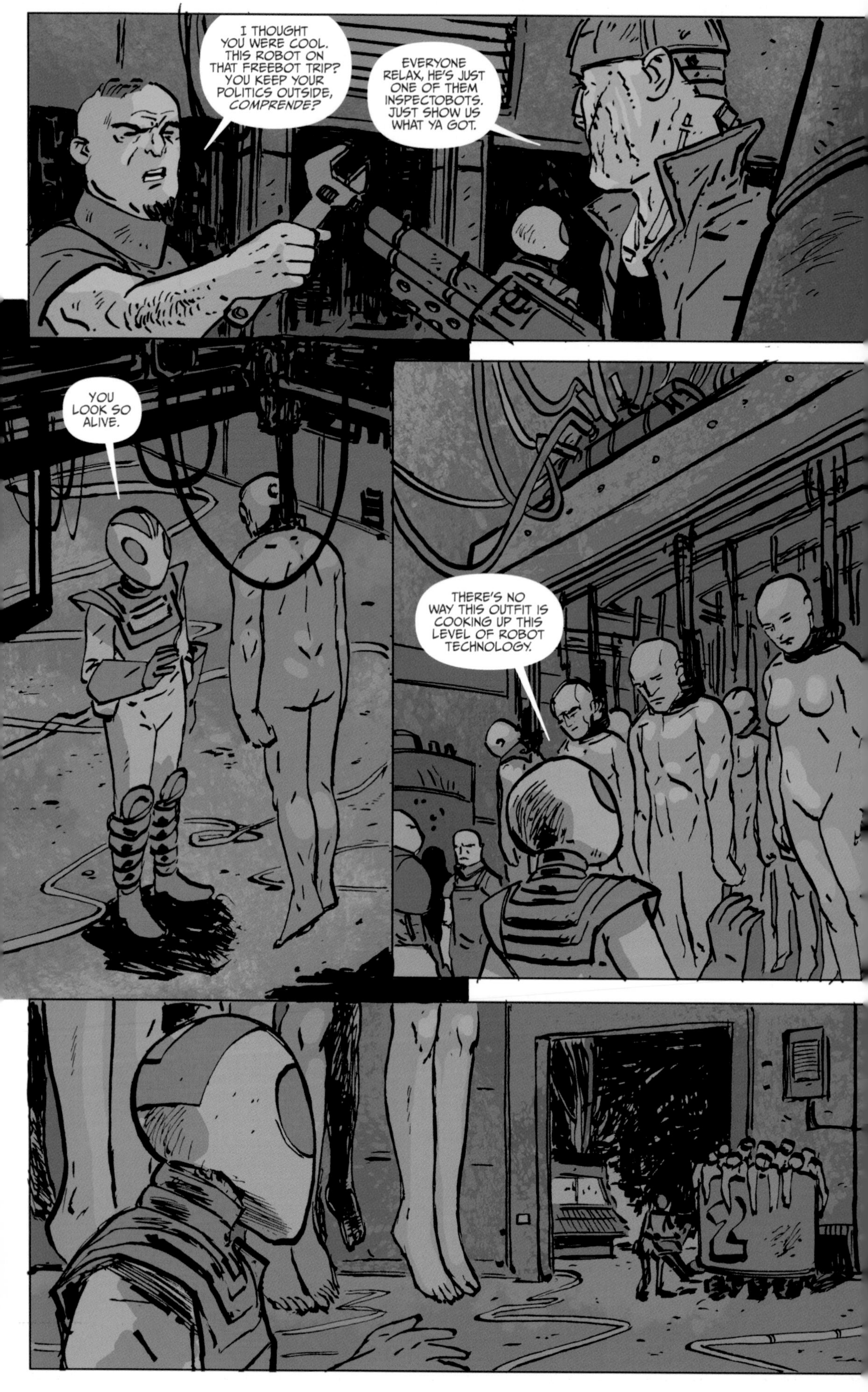
I THOUGHT YOU WERE COOL. THIS ROBOT ON THAT FREEBOT TRIP? YOU KEEP YOUR POLITICS OUTSIDE, *COMPRENDE?*
EVERYONE RELAX, HE'S JUST ONE OF THEM INSPECTOBOTS. JUST SHOW US WHAT YA GOT.
YOU LOOK SO ALIVE.
THERE'S NO WAY THIS OUTFIT IS COOKING UP THIS LEVEL OF ROBOT TECHNOLOGY.

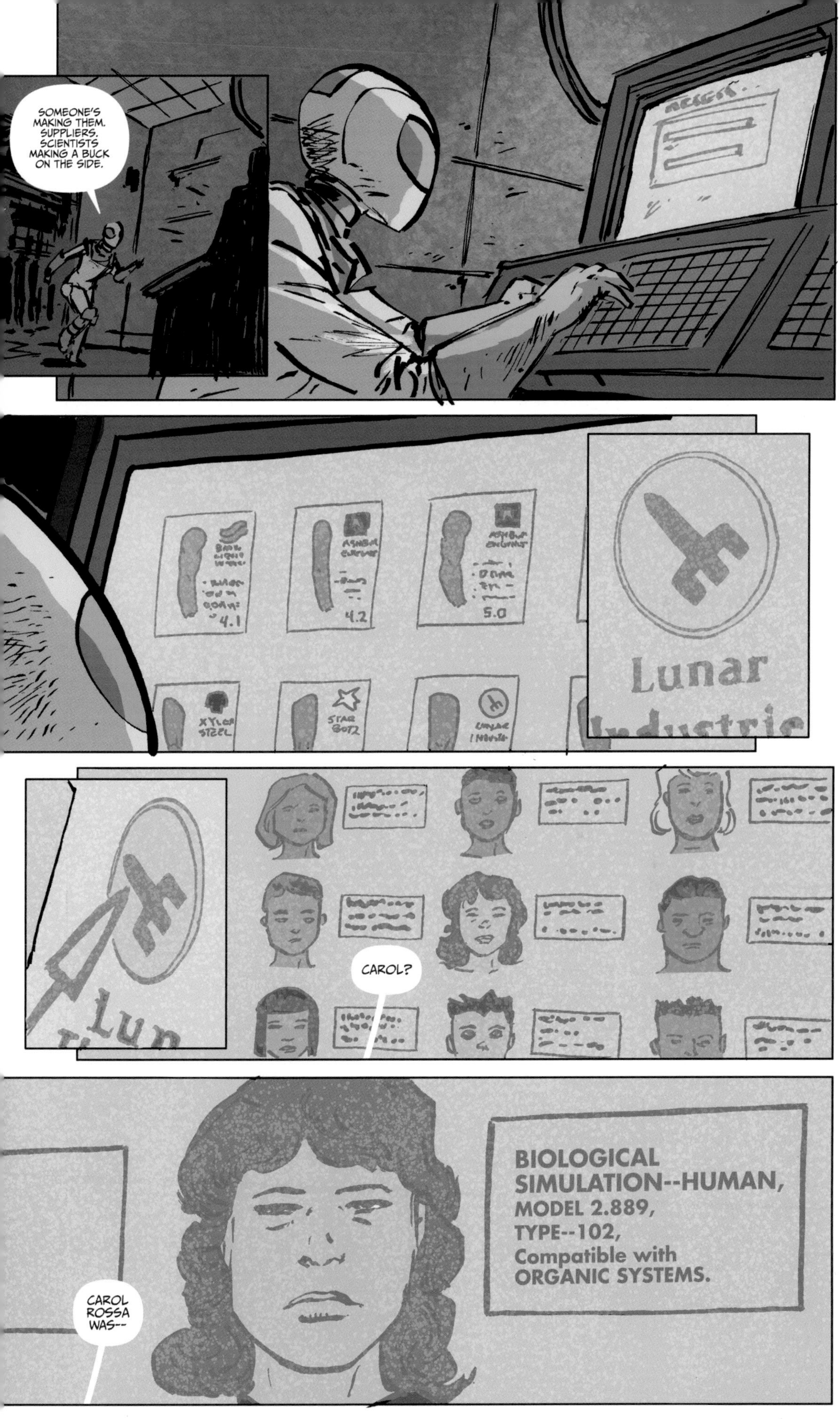
SOMEONE'S MAKING THEM. SUPPLIERS. SCIENTISTS MAKING A BUCK ON THE SIDE.
Lunar
CAROL?
BIOLOGICAL SIMULATION--HUMAN, MODEL 2.889, TYPE--102, Compatible with ORGANIC SYSTEMS.
CAROL ROSSA WAS--

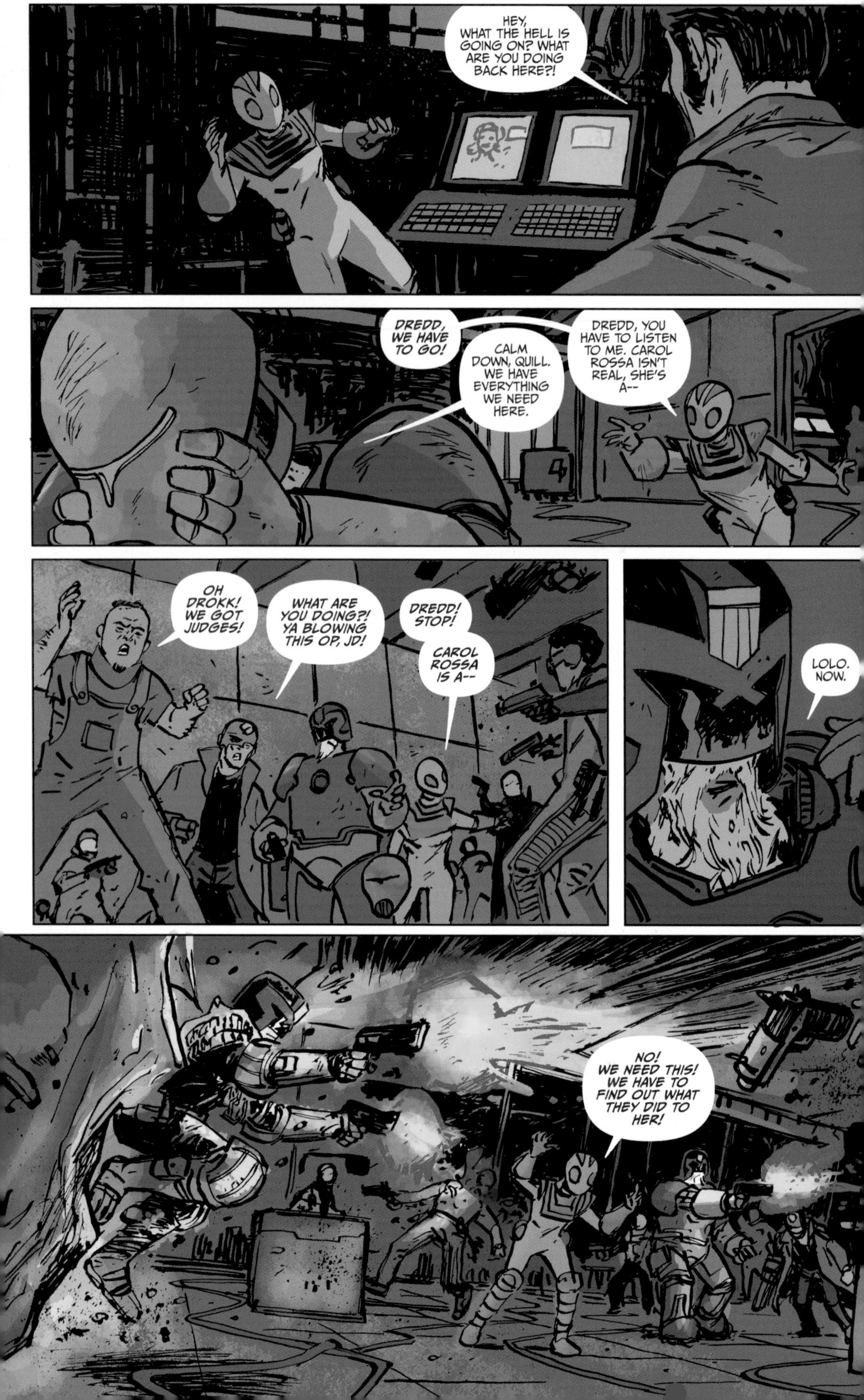
HEY, WHAT THE HELL IS GOING ON? WHAT ARE YOU DOING BACK HERE?!
DREDD, WE HAVE TO GO!
CALM DOWN, QUILL. WE HAVE EVERYTHING WE NEED HERE.
DREDD, YOU HAVE TO LISTEN TO ME. CAROL ROSSA ISN'T REAL, SHE'S A--
OH DROKK! WE GOT JUDGES!
WHAT ARE YOU DOING?! YA BLOWING THIS OP, JD!
DREDD! STOP!
CAROL ROSSA IS A--
LOLO. NOW.
NO! WE NEED THIS! WE HAVE TO FIND OUT WHAT THEY DID TO HER!

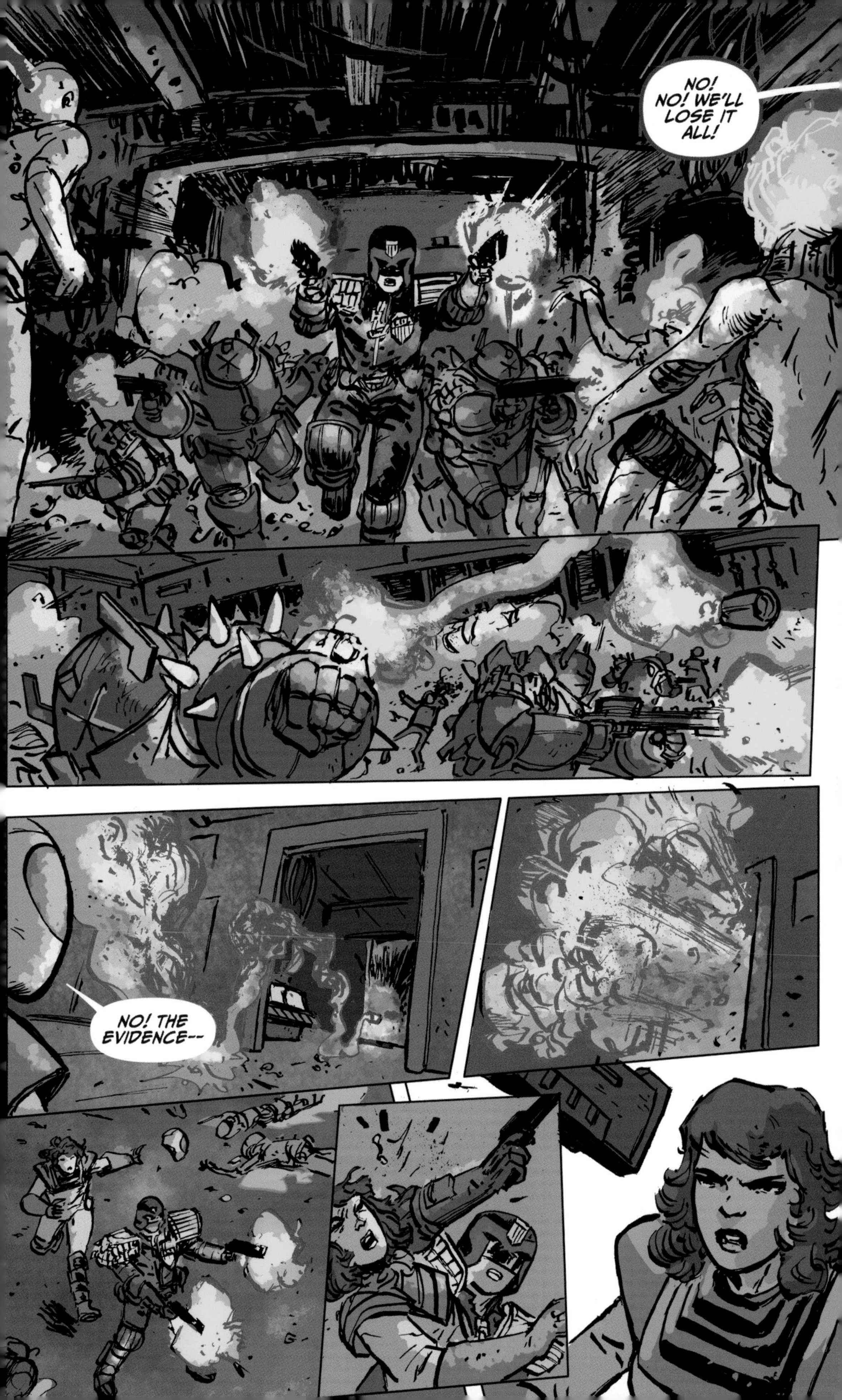
NO! NO! WE'LL LOSE IT ALL!
NO! THE EVIDENCE--

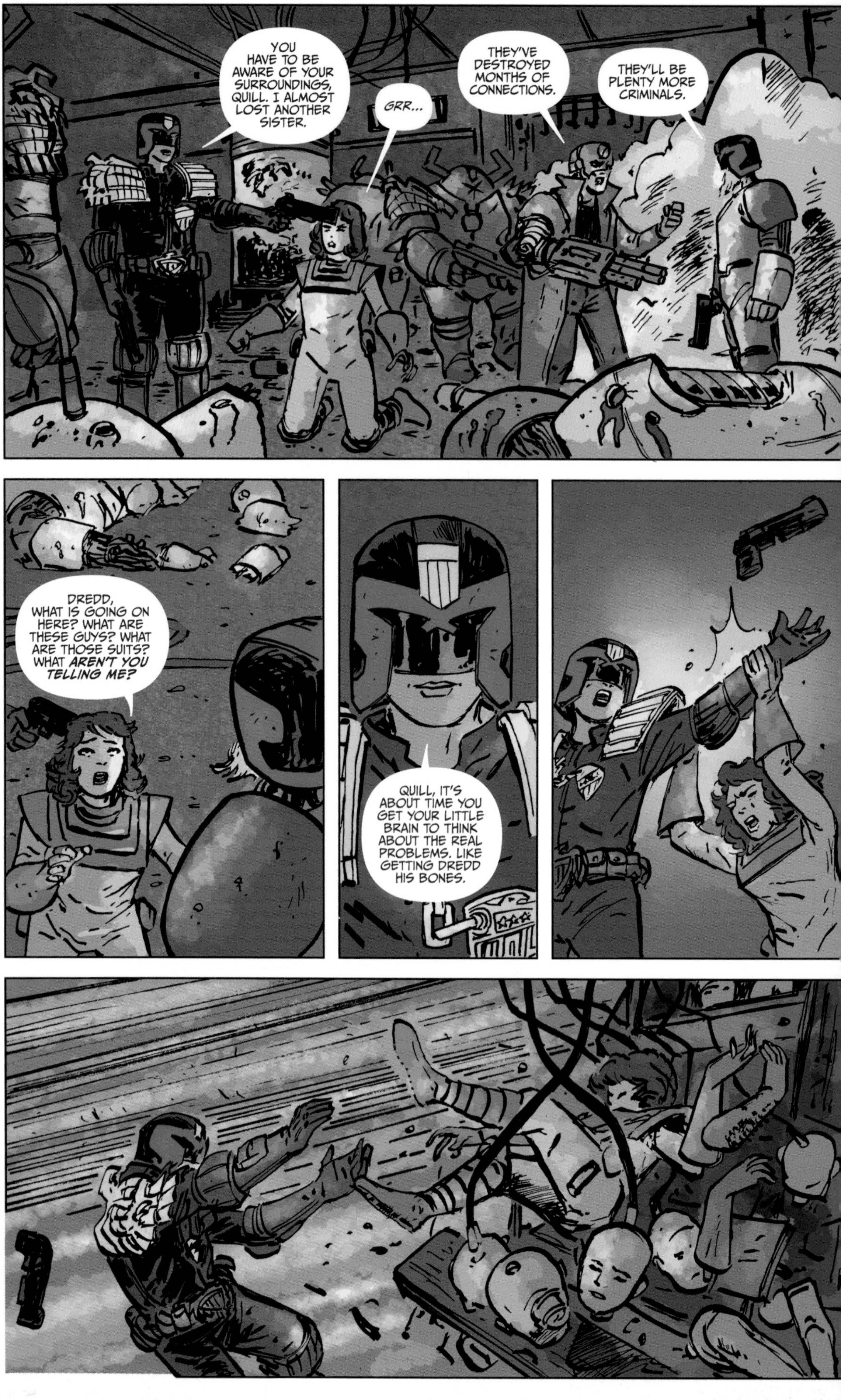
YOU HAVE TO BE AWARE OF YOUR SURROUNDINGS, QUILL. I ALMOST LOST ANOTHER SISTER.
GRR...
THEY'VE DESTROYED MONTHS OF CONNECTIONS.
THEY'LL BE PLENTY MORE CRIMINALS.
DREDD, WHAT IS GOING ON HERE? WHAT ARE THESE GUYS? WHAT ARE THOSE SUITS? WHAT *AREN'T YOU TELLING ME?*
QUILL, IT'S ABOUT TIME YOU GET YOUR LITTLE BRAIN TO THINK ABOUT THE REAL PROBLEMS. LIKE GETTING DREDD HIS BONES.

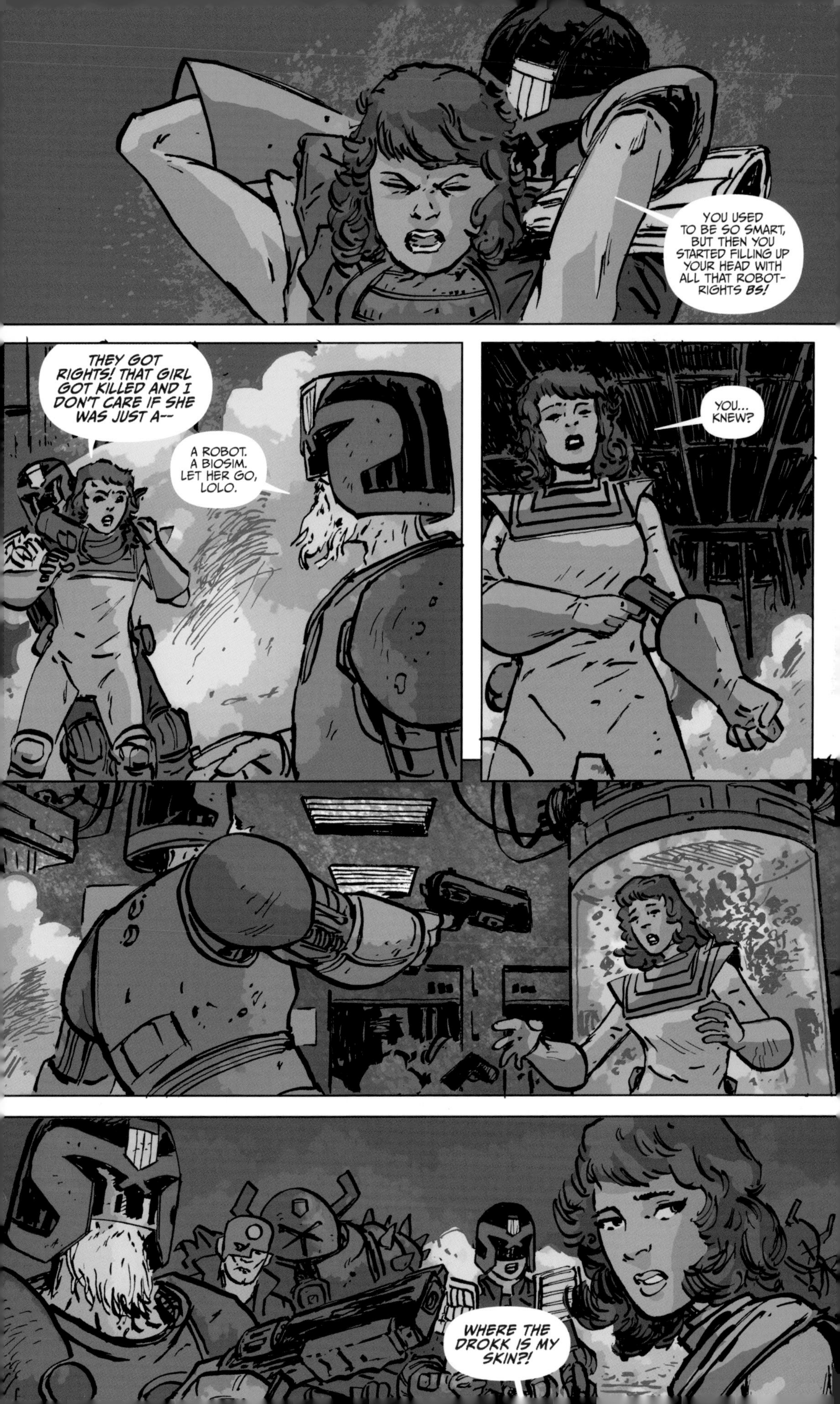
YOU USED TO BE SO SMART, BUT THEN YOU STARTED FILLING UP YOUR HEAD WITH ALL THAT ROBOT-RIGHTS BS!
THEY GOT RIGHTS! THAT GIRL GOT KILLED AND I DON'T CARE IF SHE WAS JUST A--
A ROBOT. A BIOSIM. LET HER GO, LOLO.
YOU... KNEW?
WHERE THE DROKK IS MY SKIN?!

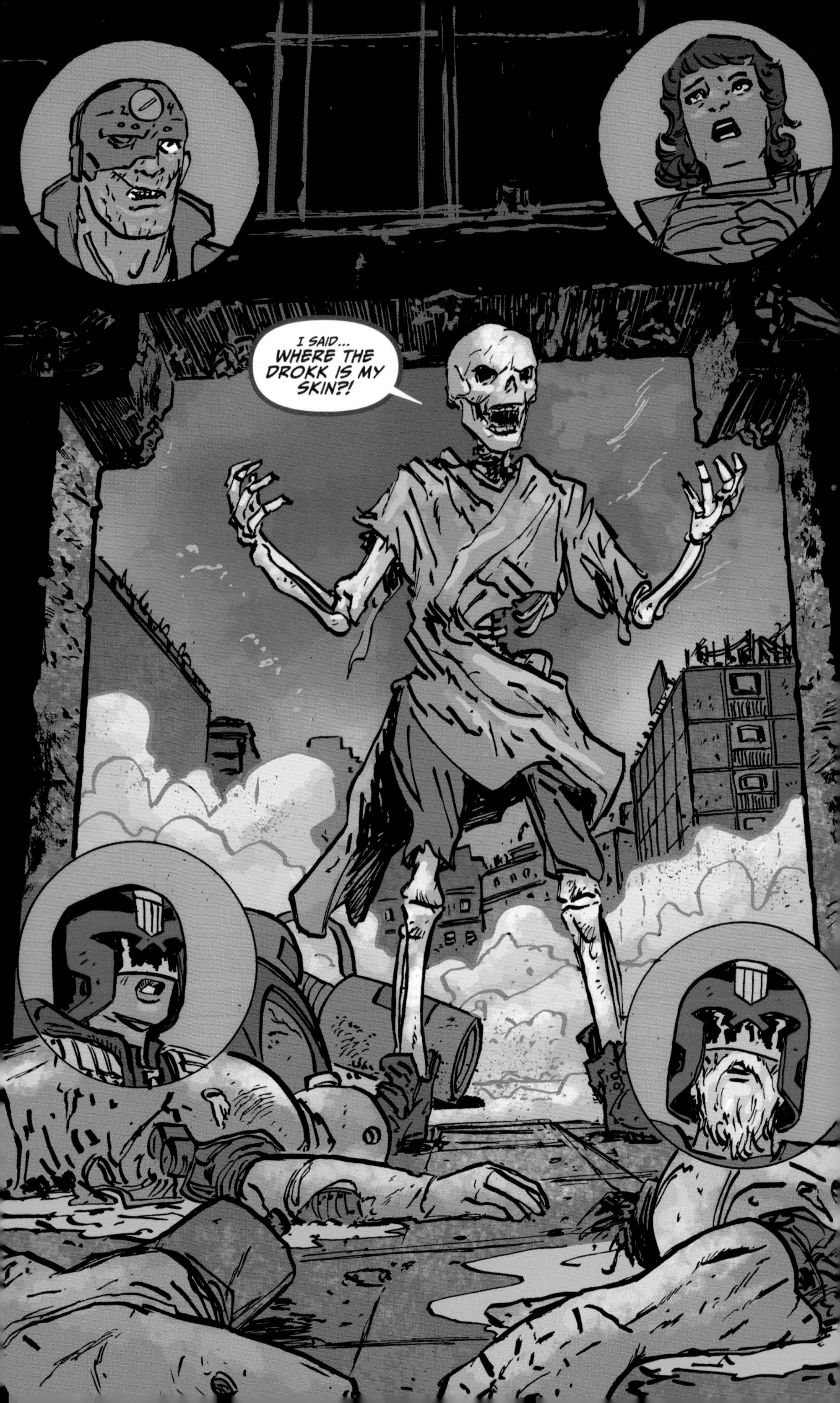
I SAID... WHERE THE DROKK IS MY SKIN?!

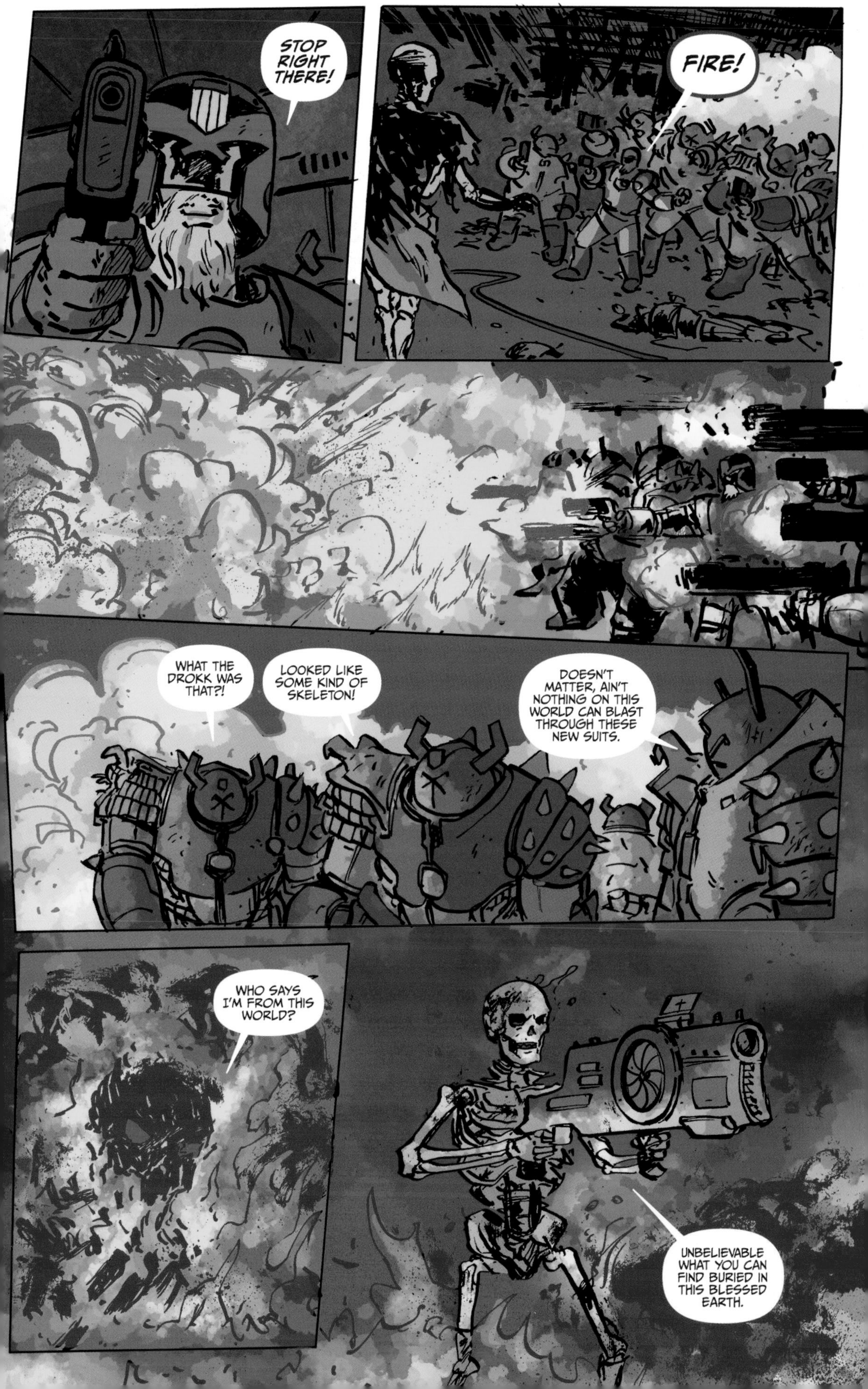
STOP RIGHT THERE!
FIRE!
WHAT THE DROKK WAS THAT?!
LOOKED LIKE SOME KIND OF SKELETON!
DOESN'T MATTER, AIN'T NOTHING ON THIS WORLD CAN BLAST THROUGH THESE NEW SUITS.
WHO SAYS I'M FROM THIS WORLD?
UNBELIEVABLE WHAT YOU CAN FIND BURIED IN THIS BLESSED EARTH.

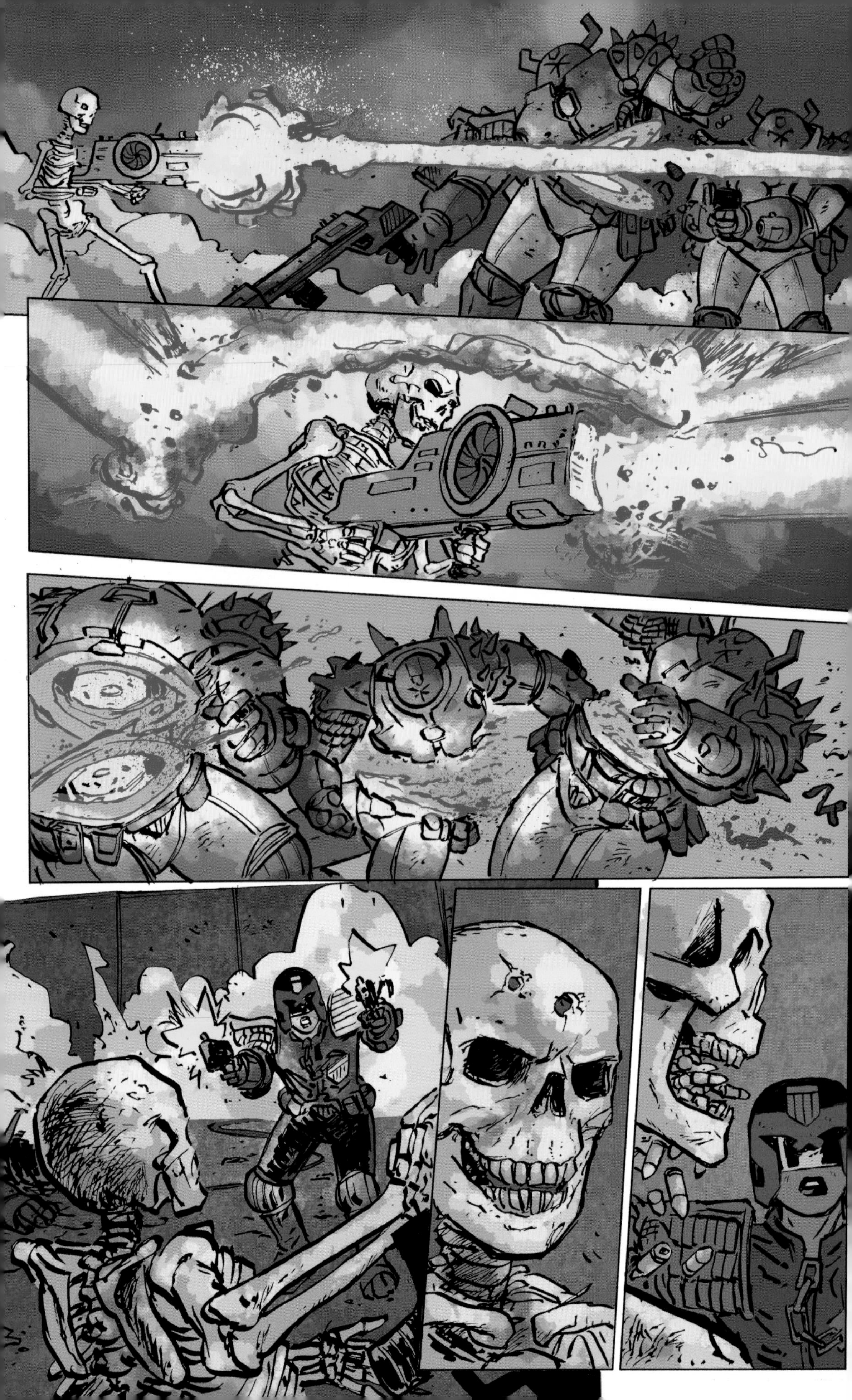

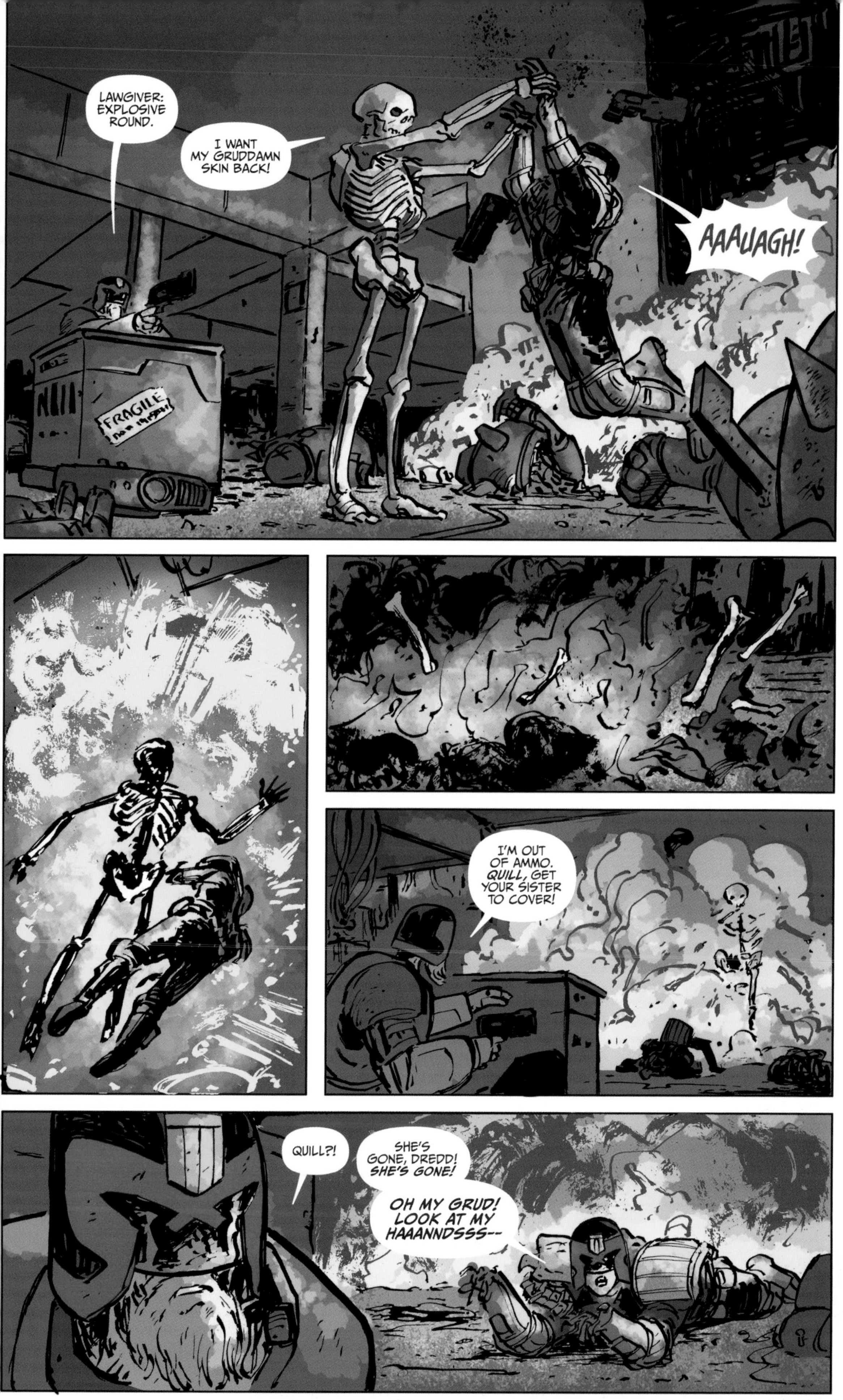
LAWGIVER: EXPLOSIVE ROUND.
I WANT MY GRUDDAMN SKIN BACK!
AAAUAGH!
FRAGILE
I'M OUT OF AMMO. QUILL, GET YOUR SISTER TO COVER!
QUILL?!
SHE'S GONE, DREDD! SHE'S GONE!
OH MY GRUD! LOOK AT MY HAAANNDSSS--

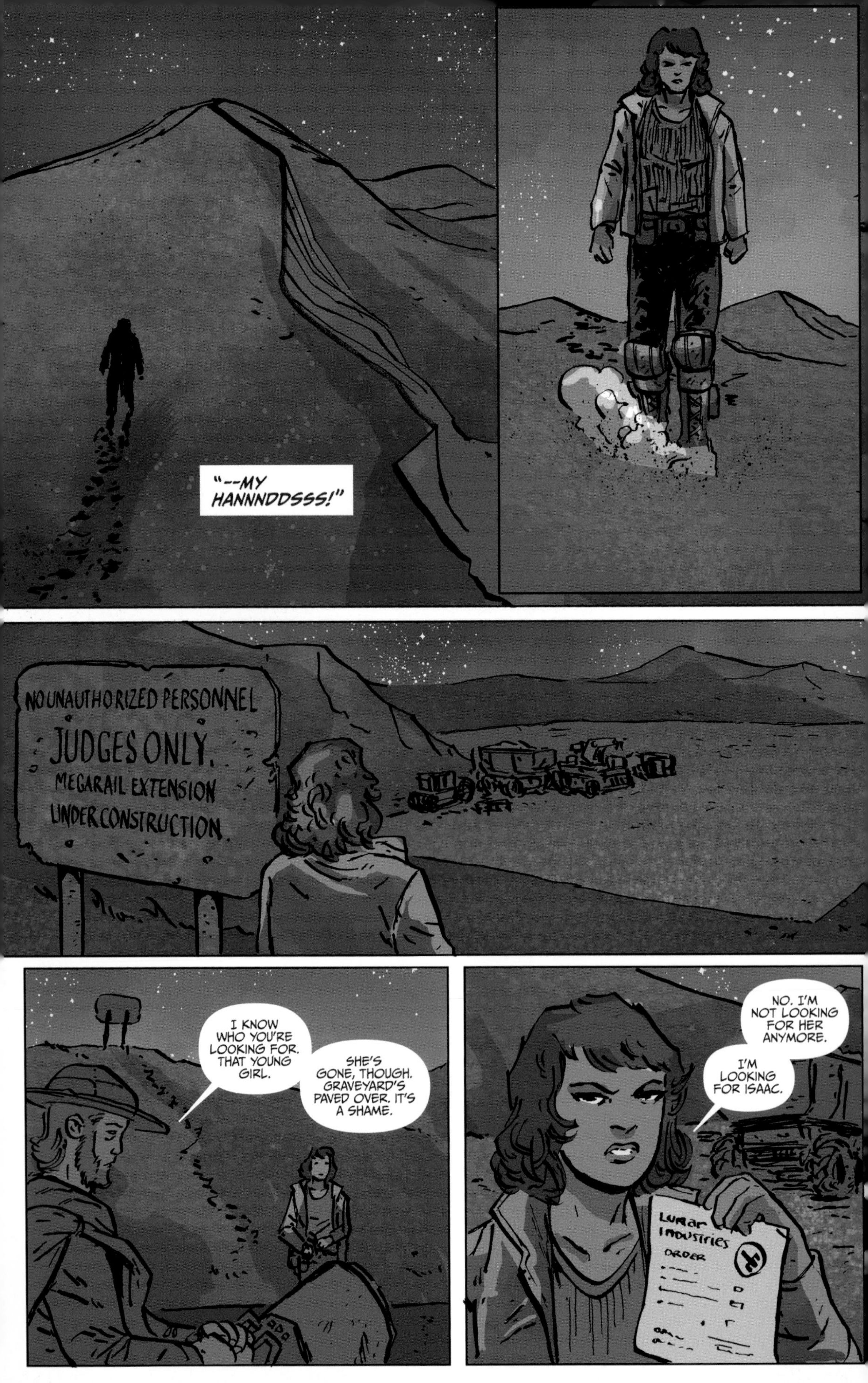
"--MY HANNNDDSSS!"
NO UNAUTHORIZED PERSONNEL
JUDGES ONLY.
MEGARAIL EXTENSION
UNDER CONSTRUCTION.
I KNOW WHO YOU'RE LOOKING FOR. THAT YOUNG GIRL.
SHE'S GONE, THOUGH. GRAVEYARD'S PAVED OVER. IT'S A SHAME.
NO. I'M NOT LOOKING FOR HER ANYMORE.
I'M LOOKING FOR ISAAC.
Lunar Industries
ORDER

THE BLESSED EARTH • PART 6

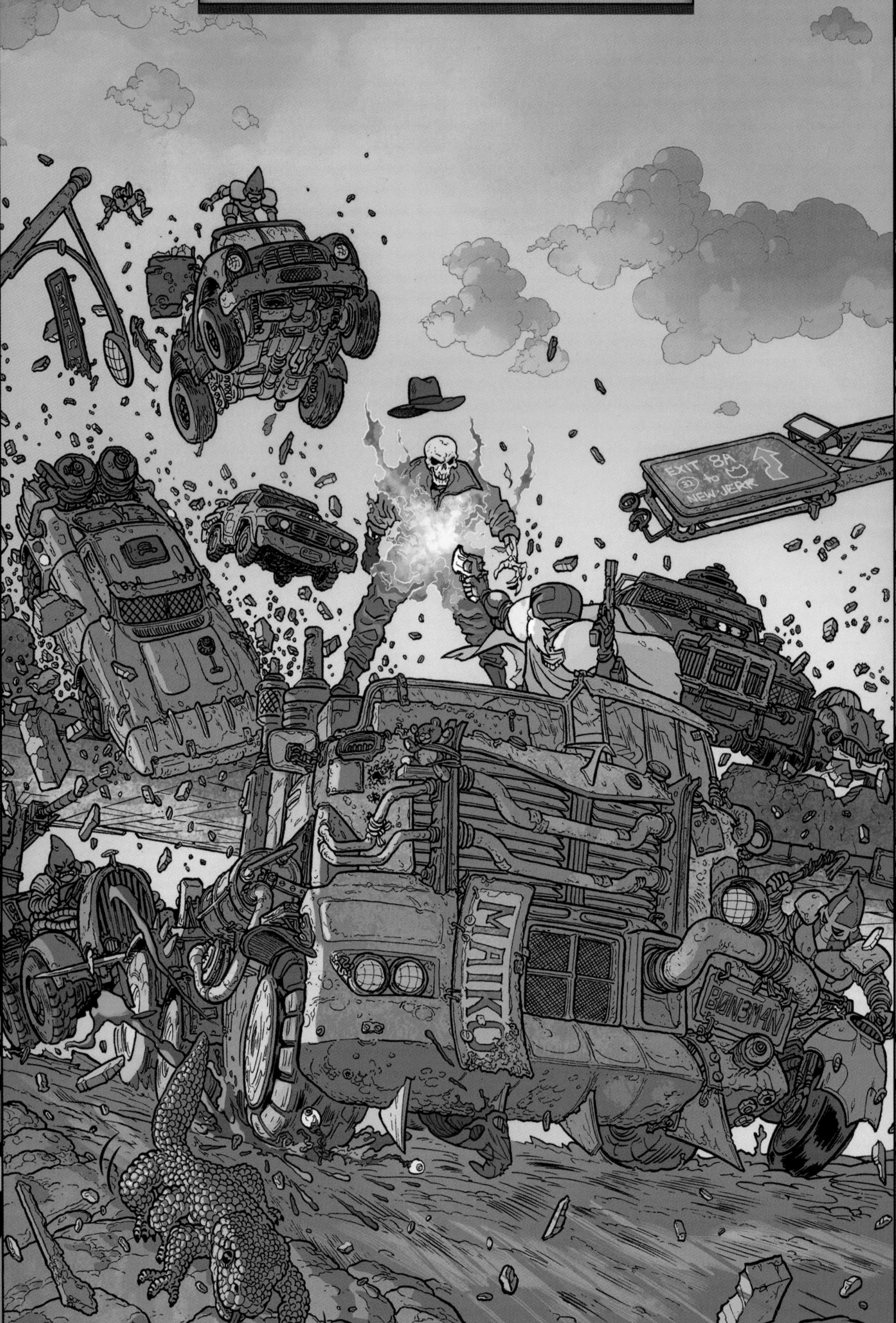
EXIT 8A
32 to
NEW JER
MAIKO
B0N3MAN

ART BY ULISES FARINAS, COLORS BY RYAN HILL

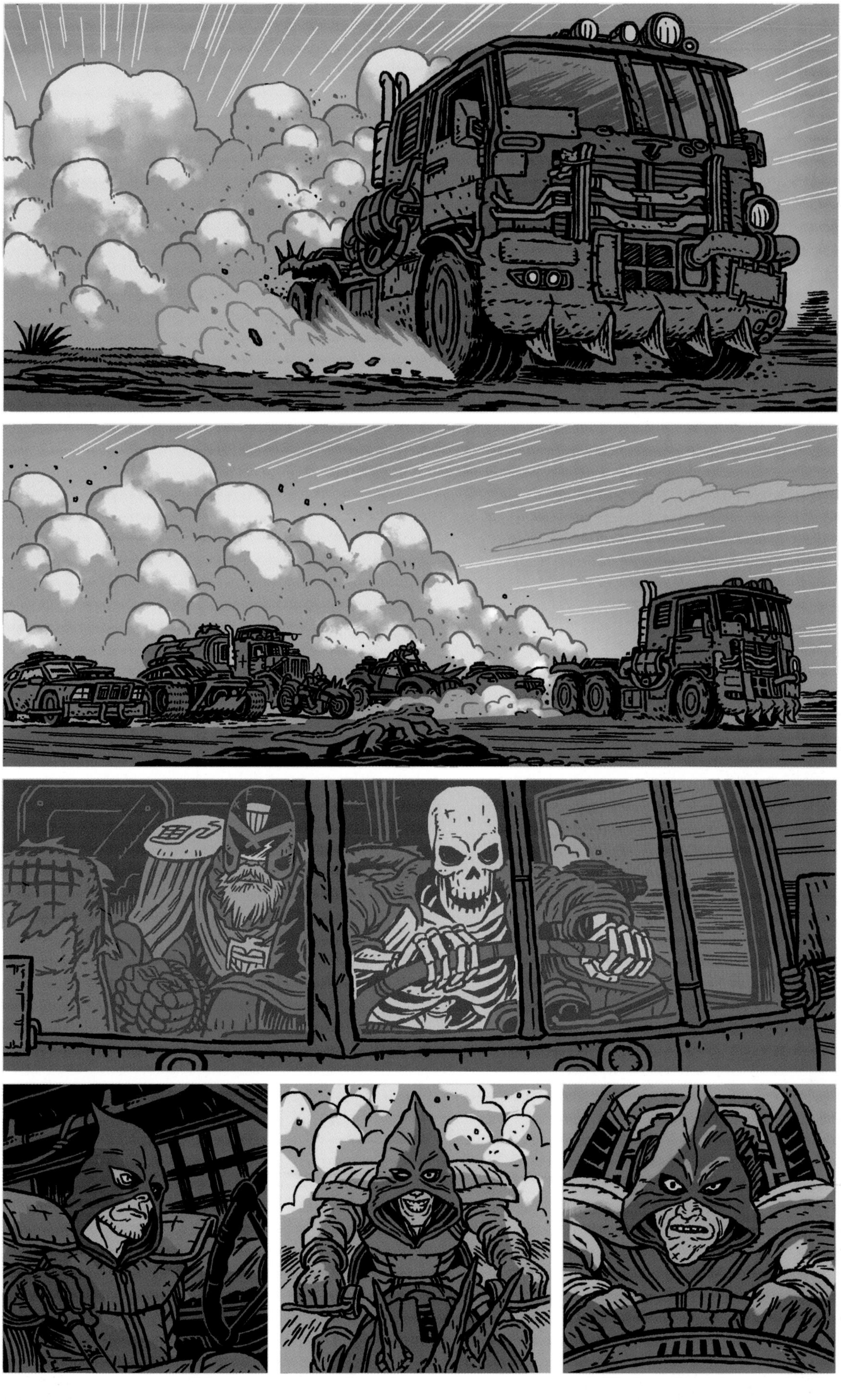

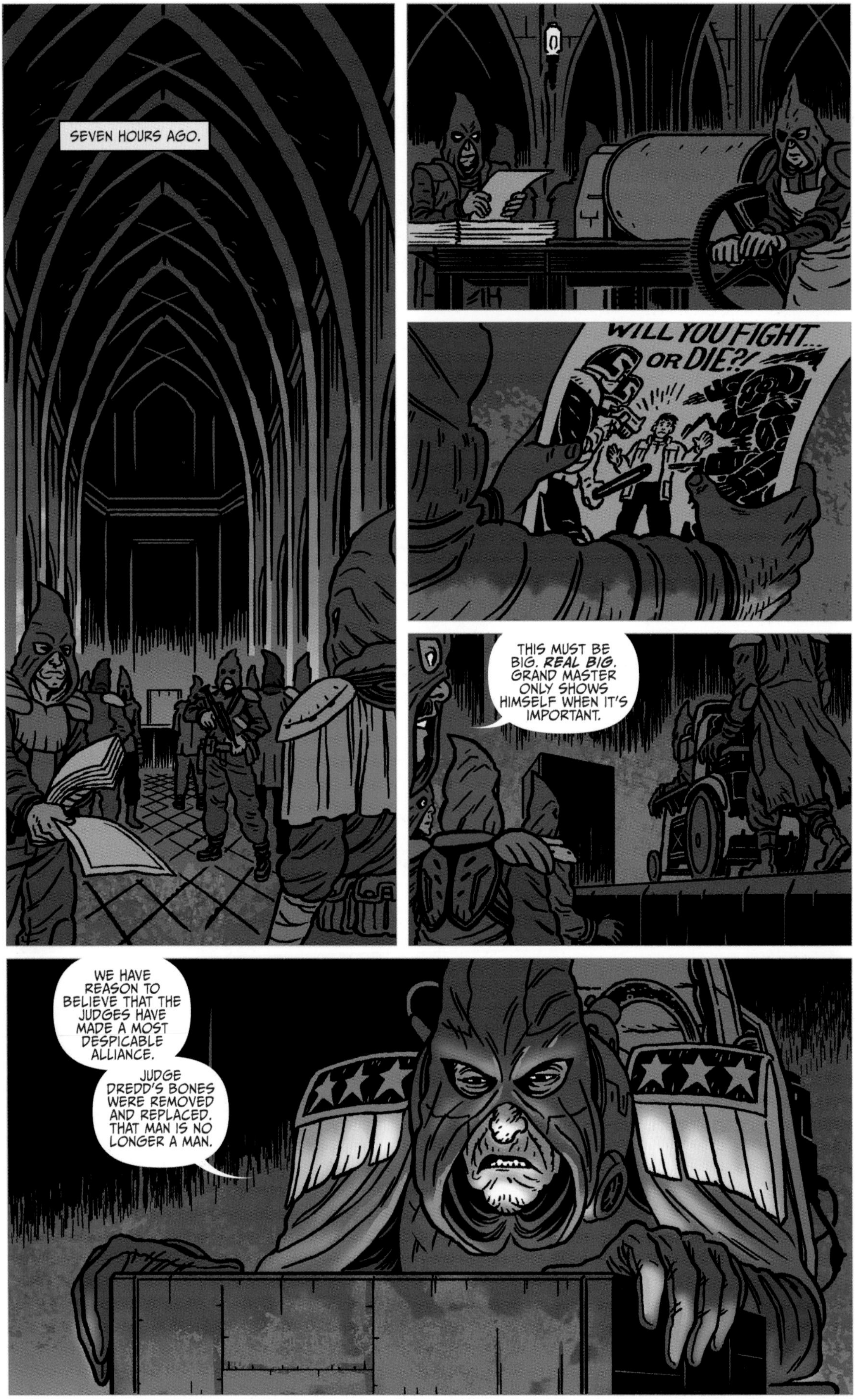
SEVEN HOURS AGO.
WILL YOU FIGHT... OR DIE?!
THIS MUST BE BIG. *REAL BIG.* GRAND MASTER ONLY SHOWS HIMSELF WHEN IT'S IMPORTANT.
WE HAVE REASON TO BELIEVE THAT THE JUDGES HAVE MADE A MOST DESPICABLE ALLIANCE.
JUDGE DREDD'S BONES WERE REMOVED AND REPLACED. THAT MAN IS NO LONGER A MAN.

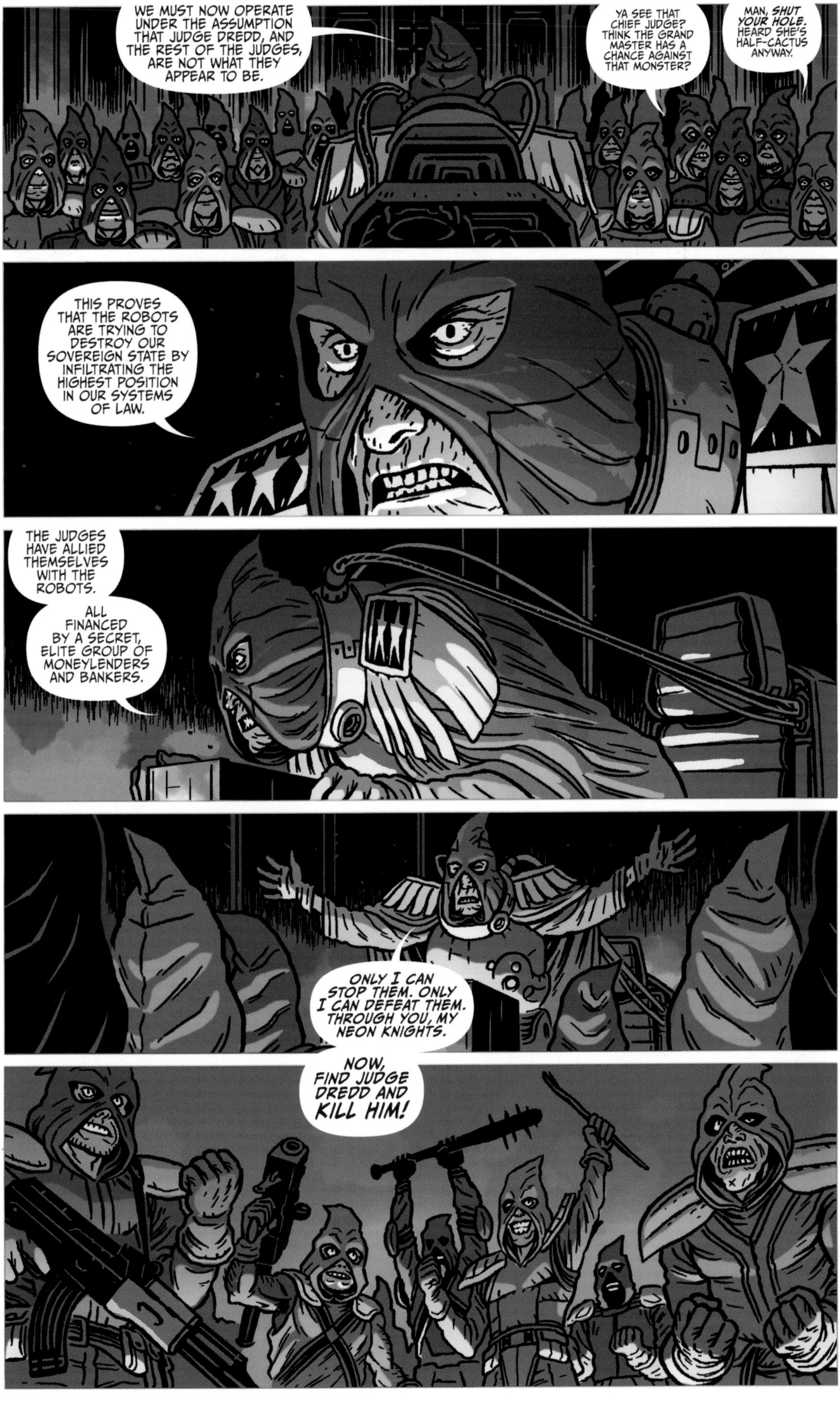
WE MUST NOW OPERATE UNDER THE ASSUMPTION THAT JUDGE DREDD, AND THE REST OF THE JUDGES, ARE NOT WHAT THEY APPEAR TO BE.
YA SEE THAT CHIEF JUDGE? THINK THE GRAND MASTER HAS A CHANCE AGAINST THAT MONSTER?
MAN, *SHUT YOUR HOLE.* HEARD SHE'S HALF-CACTUS ANYWAY.
THIS PROVES THAT THE ROBOTS ARE TRYING TO DESTROY OUR SOVEREIGN STATE BY INFILTRATING THE HIGHEST POSITION IN OUR SYSTEMS OF LAW.
THE JUDGES HAVE ALLIED THEMSELVES WITH THE ROBOTS.
ALL FINANCED BY A SECRET, ELITE GROUP OF MONEYLENDERS AND BANKERS.
ONLY I CAN STOP THEM. ONLY I CAN DEFEAT THEM. THROUGH YOU, MY NEON KNIGHTS.
NOW, FIND JUDGE DREDD AND ***KILL HIM!***

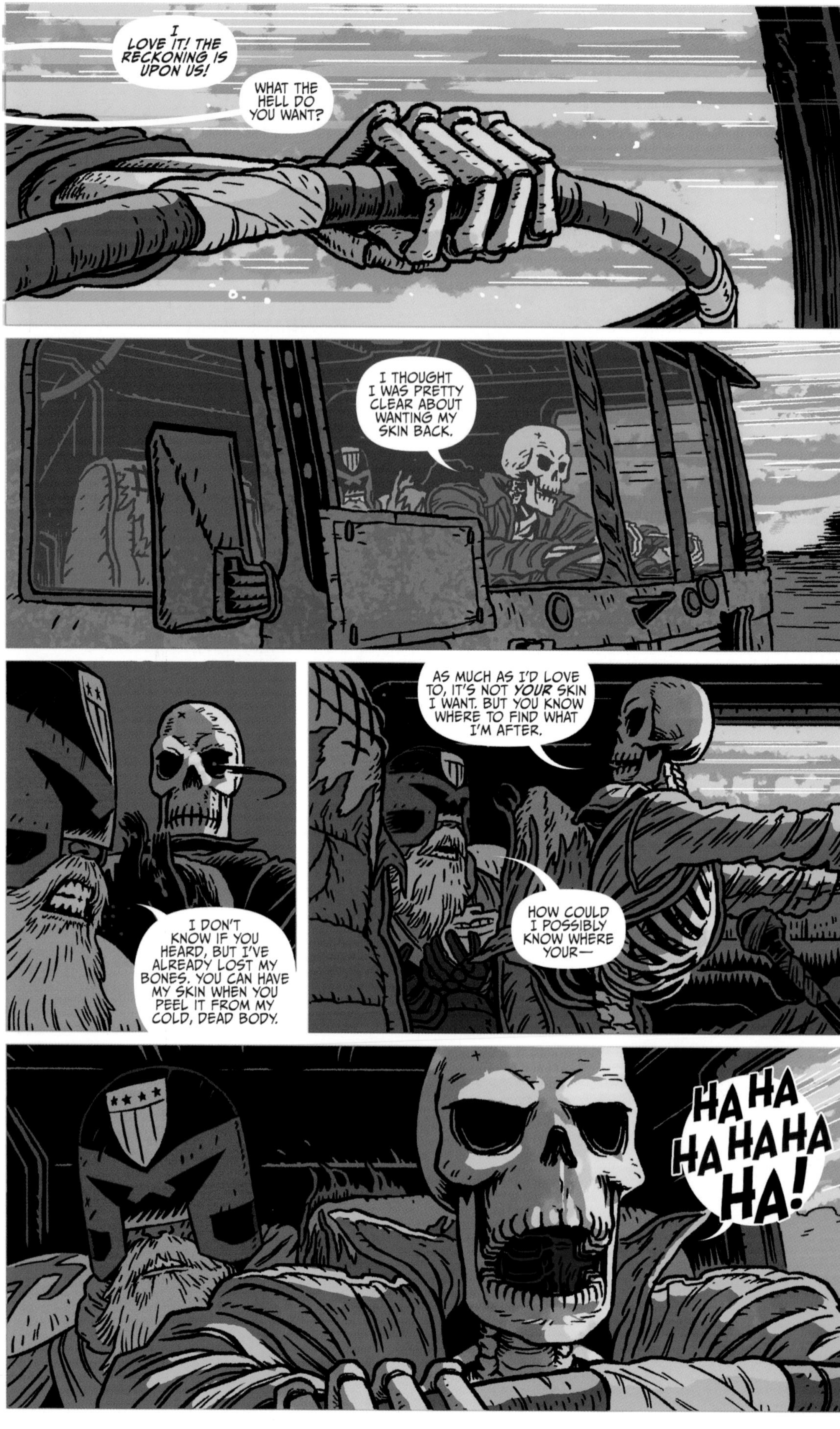
I LOVE IT! THE RECKONING IS UPON US!
WHAT THE HELL DO YOU WANT?
I THOUGHT I WAS PRETTY CLEAR ABOUT WANTING MY SKIN BACK.
I DON'T KNOW IF YOU HEARD, BUT I'VE ALREADY LOST MY BONES. YOU CAN HAVE MY SKIN WHEN YOU PEEL IT FROM MY COLD, DEAD BODY.
AS MUCH AS I'D LOVE TO, IT'S NOT *YOUR* SKIN I WANT. BUT YOU KNOW WHERE TO FIND WHAT I'M AFTER.
HOW COULD I POSSIBLY KNOW WHERE YOUR—
HAHA HAHAHA HA!

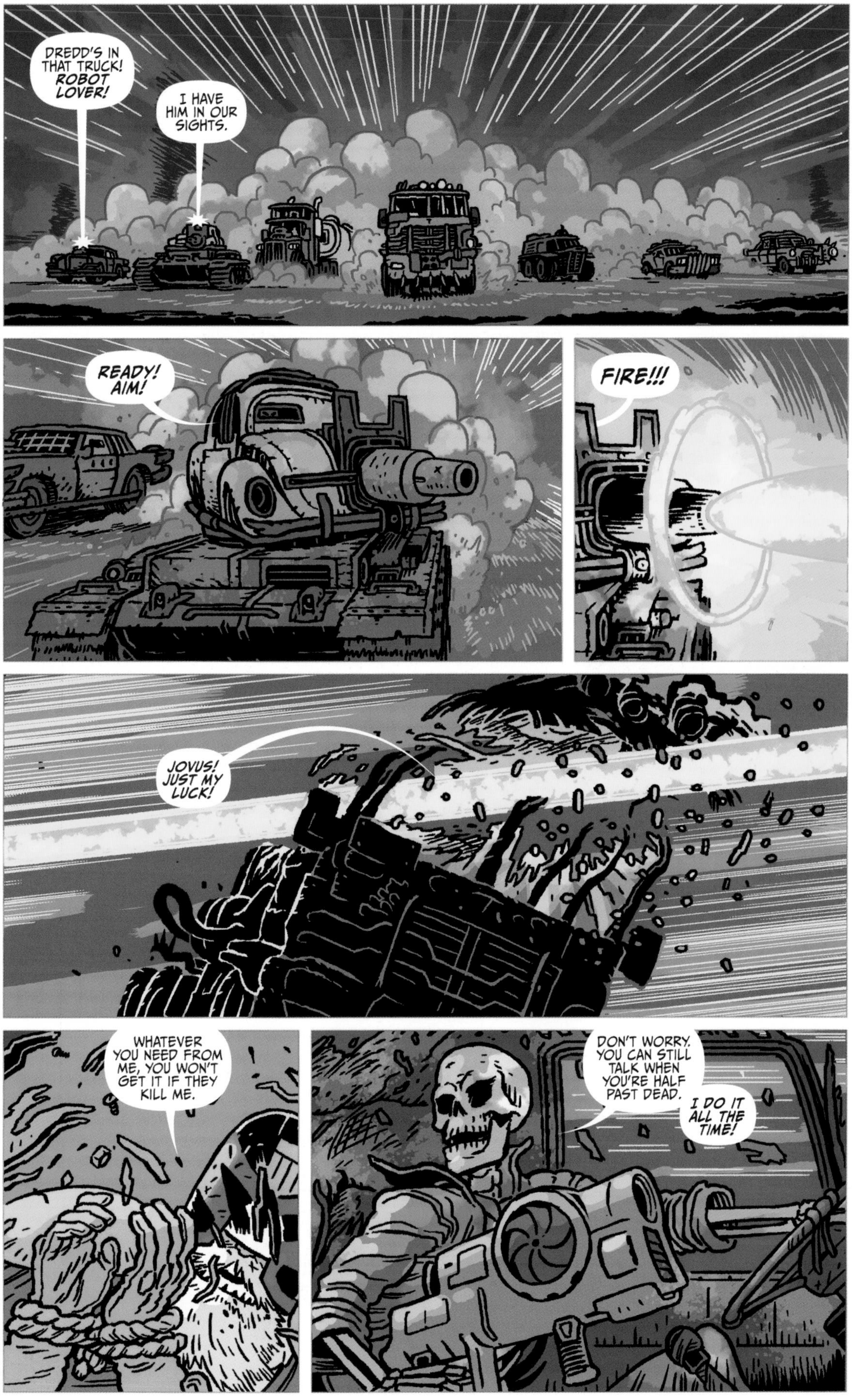
DREDD'S IN THAT TRUCK! ROBOT LOVER!
I HAVE HIM IN OUR SIGHTS.
READY! AIM!
FIRE!!!
JOVUS! JUST MY LUCK!
WHATEVER YOU NEED FROM ME, YOU WON'T GET IT IF THEY KILL ME.
DON'T WORRY. YOU CAN STILL TALK WHEN YOU'RE HALF PAST DEAD.
I DO IT ALL THE TIME!

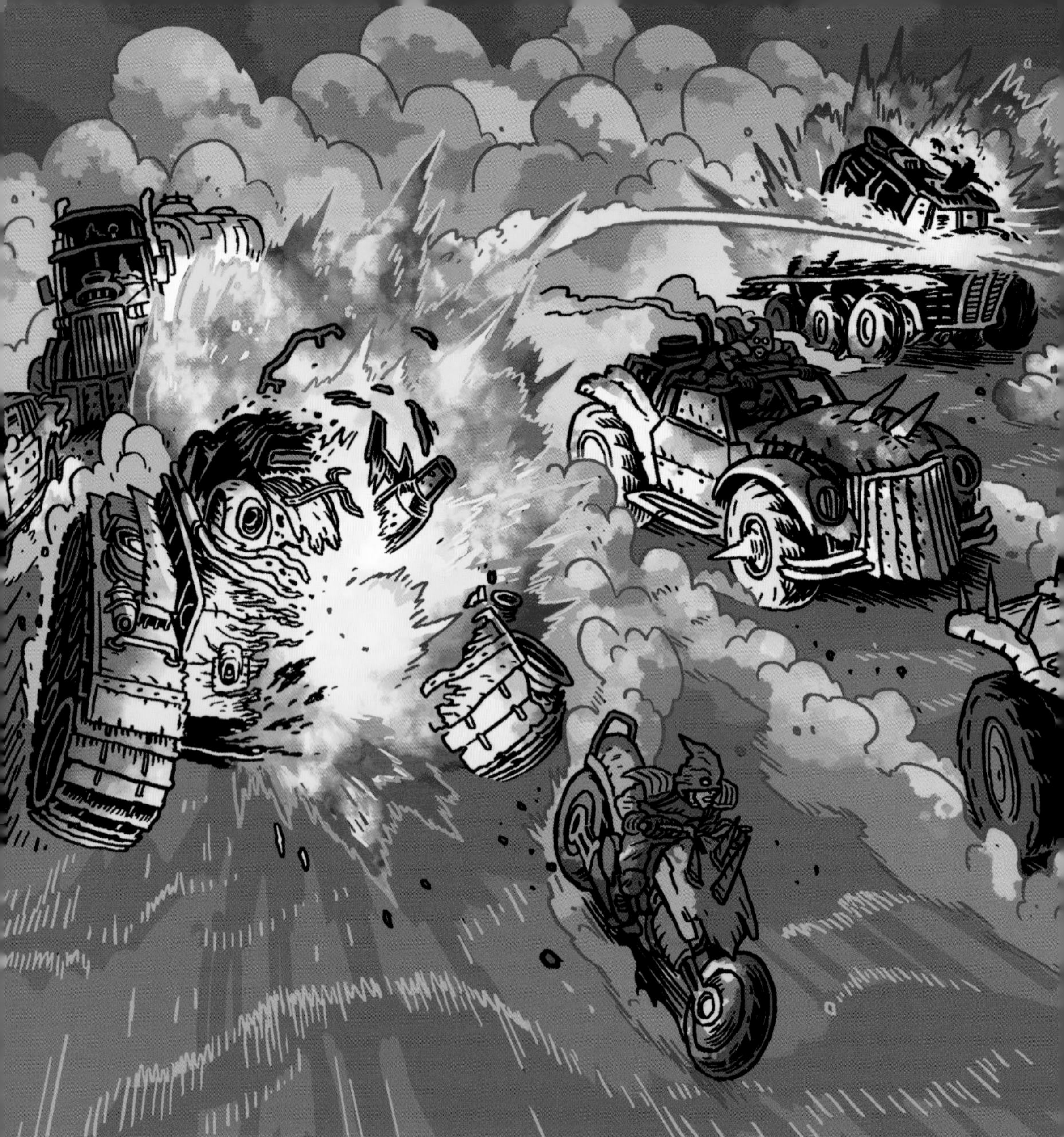

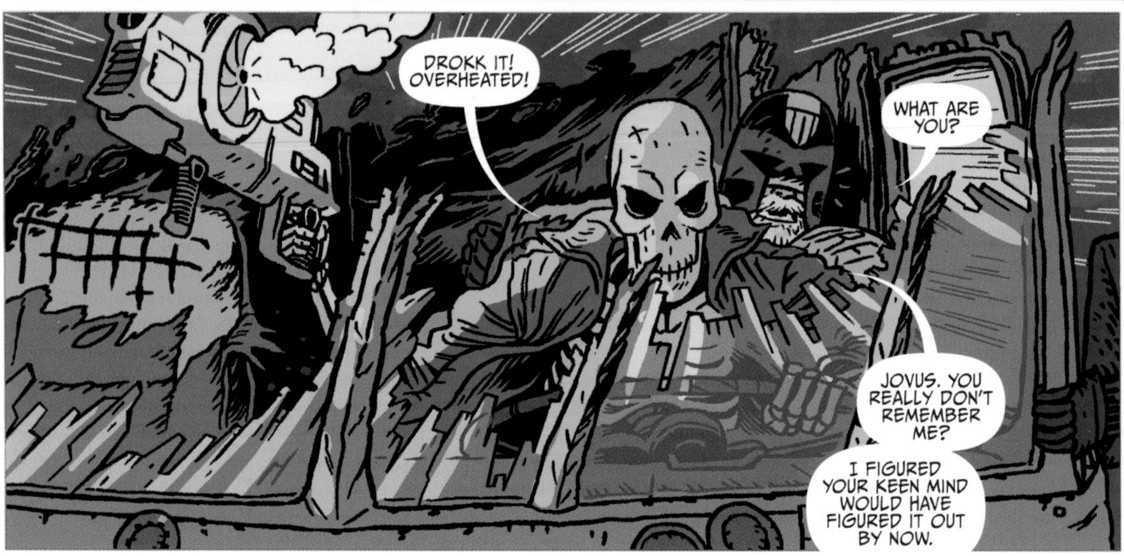
DROKK IT! OVERHEATED!
WHAT ARE YOU?
JOVUS. YOU REALLY DON'T REMEMBER ME?
I FIGURED YOUR KEEN MIND WOULD HAVE FIGURED IT OUT BY NOW.

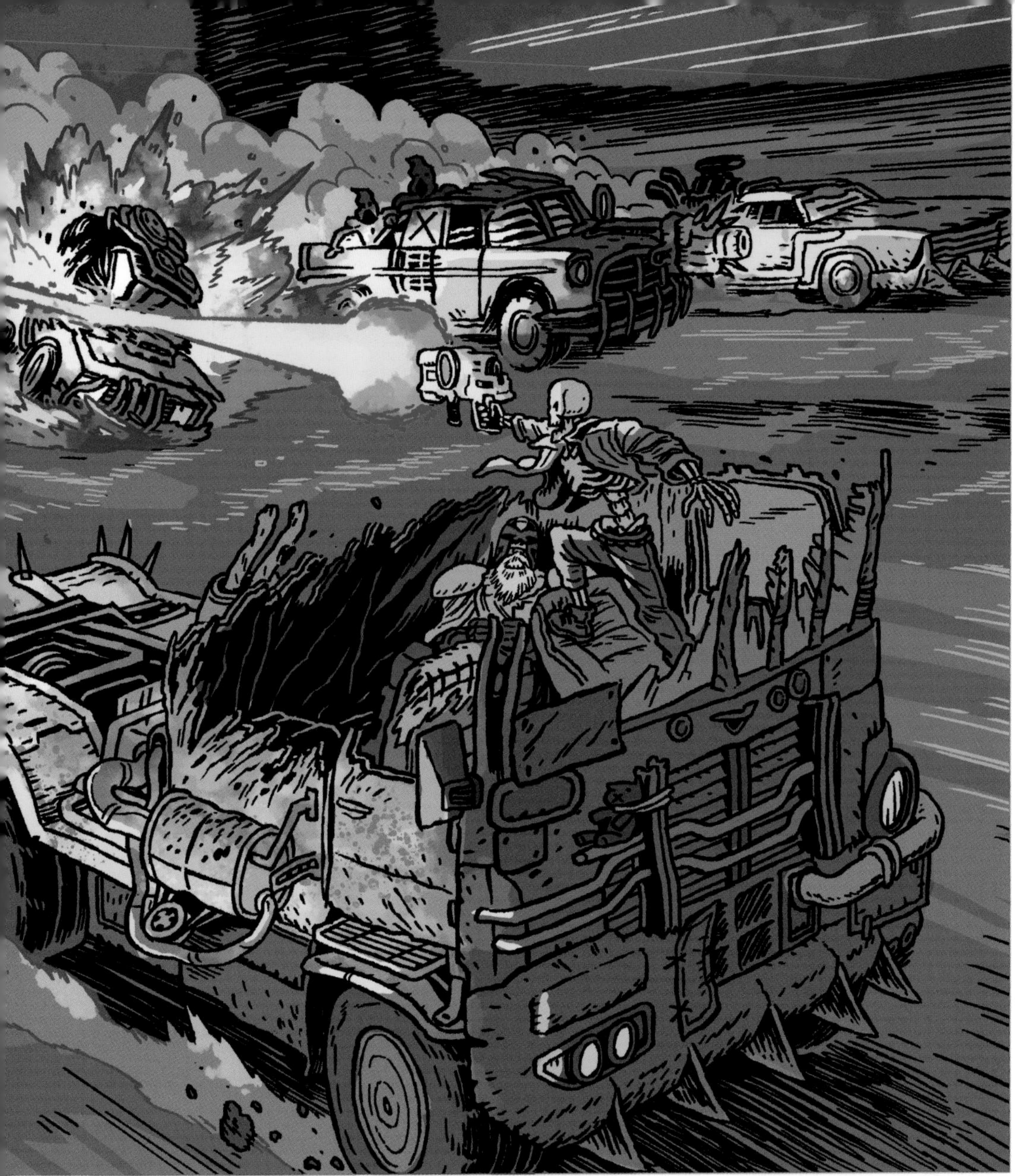

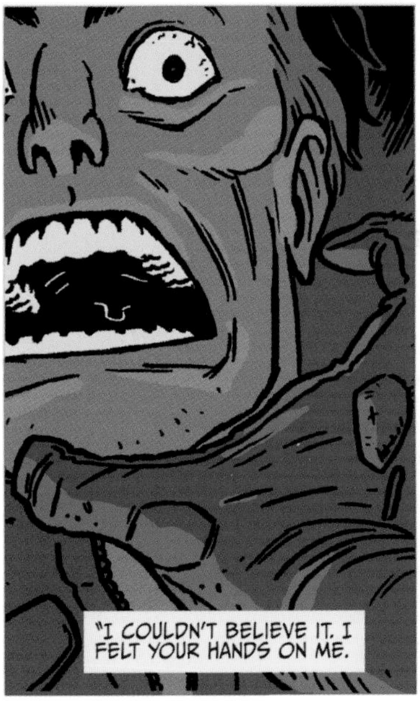
"I COULDN'T BELIEVE IT. I FELT YOUR HANDS ON ME.

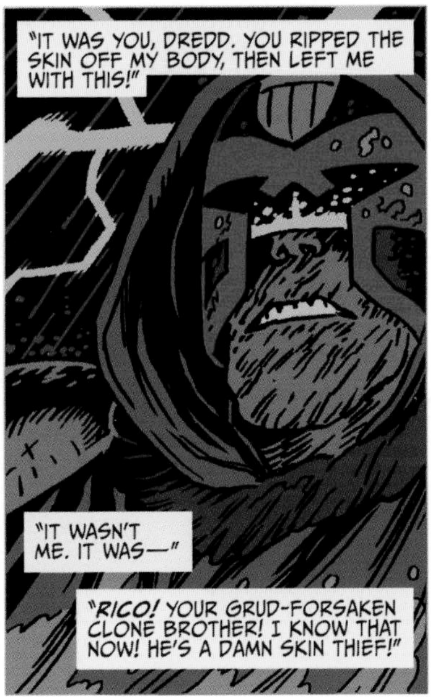
"IT WAS YOU, DREDD. YOU RIPPED THE SKIN OFF MY BODY, THEN LEFT ME WITH THIS!"
"IT WASN'T ME. IT WAS—"
"RICO! YOUR GRUD-FORSAKEN CLONE BROTHER! I KNOW THAT NOW! HE'S A DAMN SKIN THIEF!"

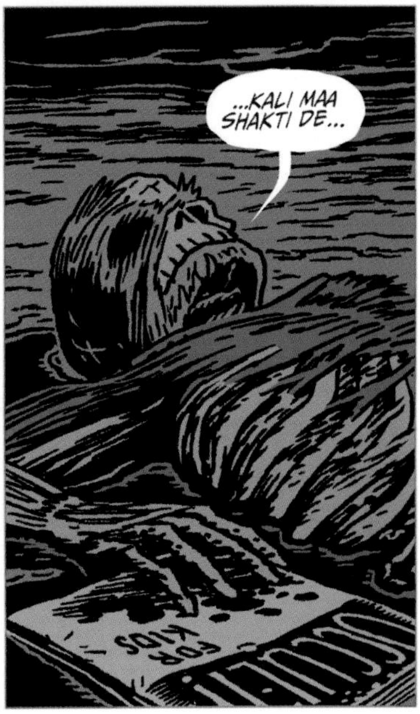
...KALI MAA SHAKTI DE...

"I DON'T KNOW HOW I GOT WHERE I WAS. MUST'VE WALKED HUNDREDS OF MILES.

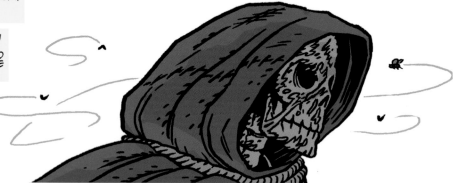

"I ALWAYS WAS UNLUCKY, BUT THIS WAS THE WORST JAM YET.

"DO YOU KNOW HOW HUMILIATING IT IS TO LOSE YOUR SKIN? TO BE FED UPON BY THE CRAWLING THINGS?

"ALL I KNEW WAS THIS WAS YOUR FAULT. I THOUGHT I'D BE SAFE IF I WAS A JUDGE. IF I BET IT ALL ON THE BADGE. BUT THE GAME IS RIGGED. BET ON RED OR BET ON BLACK. I USED TO THINK THERE WERE SIDES TO THESE THINGS.

"JUDGES VS. NEON KNIGHTS. ROBOTS VS. HUMANS. SECURITY VS. FREEDOM. BUT NOW I GET IT. I GET WHY JUDGES GOT RID OF ELECTIONS. WHY THE NEON KNIGHTS WANNA TAKE THIS COUNTRY BACK.

"WHEN YOU DON'T GOT EYES, YOU SEE THINGS CLEARLY. THERE AIN'T NO DIFFERENCE. THERE AIN'T NO CHOICE.

"YOU CAN'T WIN. YOU CAN'T BREAK EVEN. BUT YOU CAN... YOU CAN GET OUT OF THE GAME. YOU CAN—"

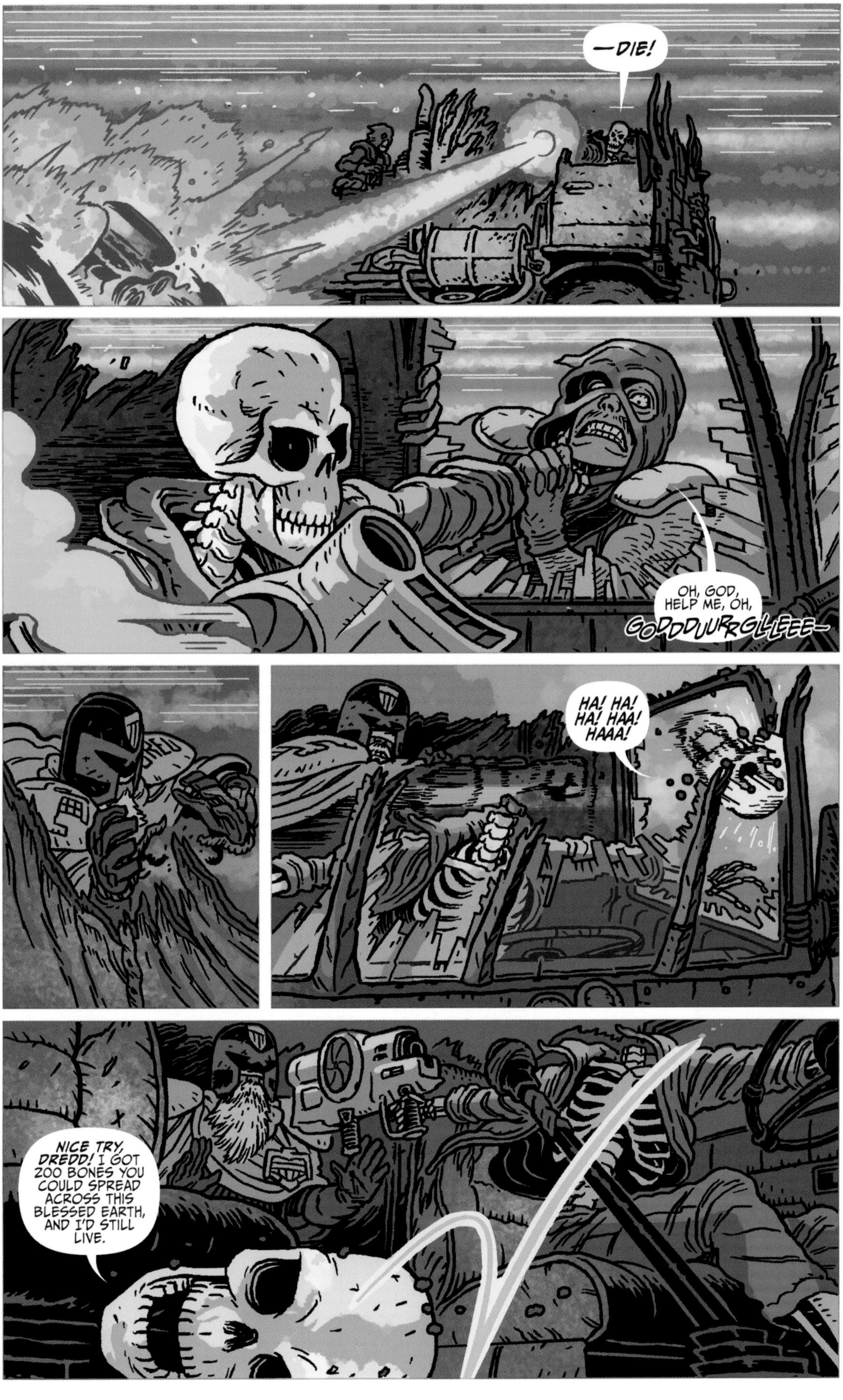
—DIE!
OH, GOD, HELP ME, OH, GODDDUURRGLLLEEE—
HA! HA! HA! HAA! HAAA!
NICE TRY, DREDD! I GOT 200 BONES YOU COULD SPREAD ACROSS THIS BLESSED EARTH, AND I'D STILL LIVE.

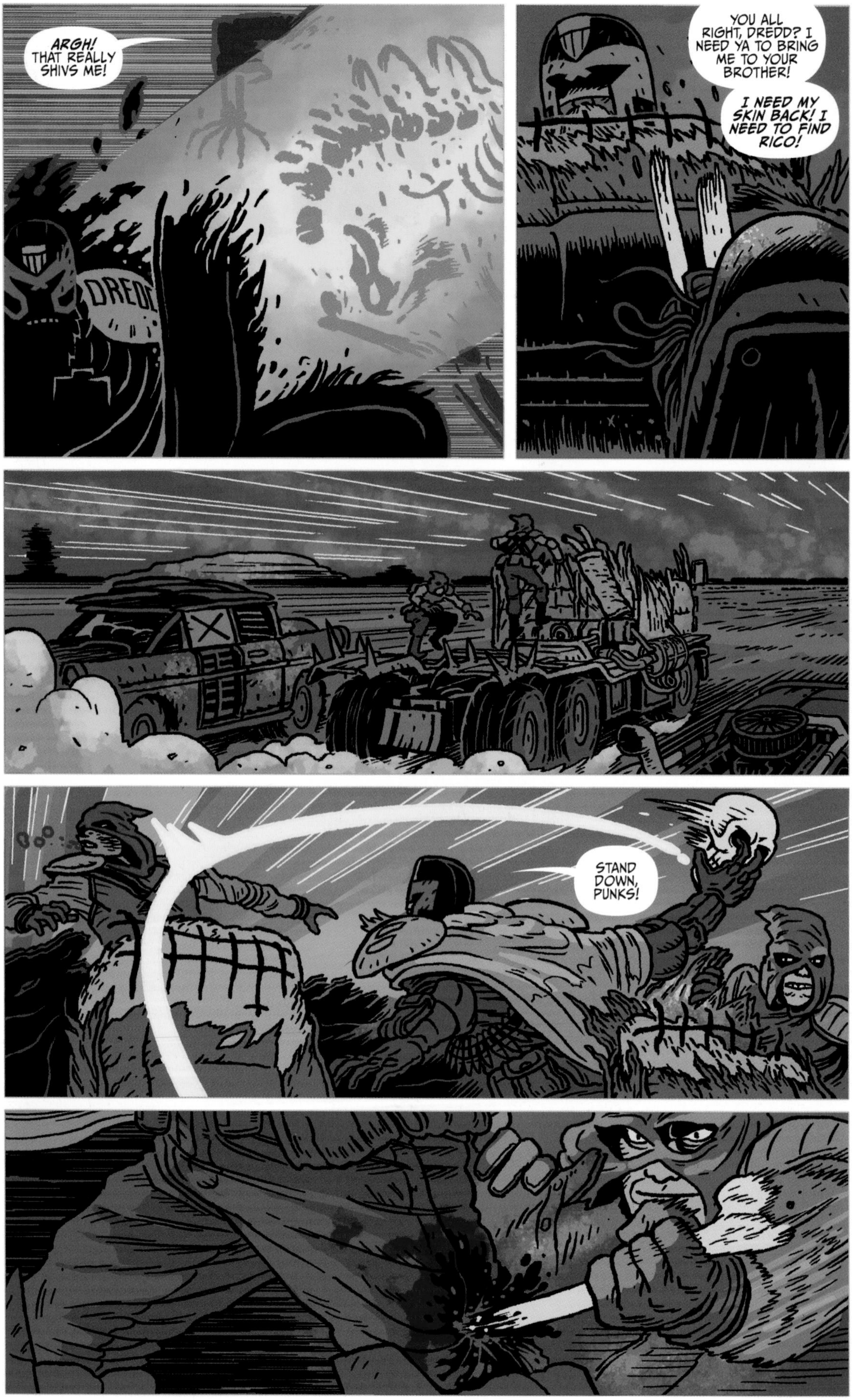

ARGH! THAT REALLY SHIVS ME!
DREDD
YOU ALL RIGHT, DREDD? I NEED YA TO BRING ME TO YOUR BROTHER!
I NEED MY SKIN BACK! I NEED TO FIND RICO!
STAND DOWN, PUNKS!

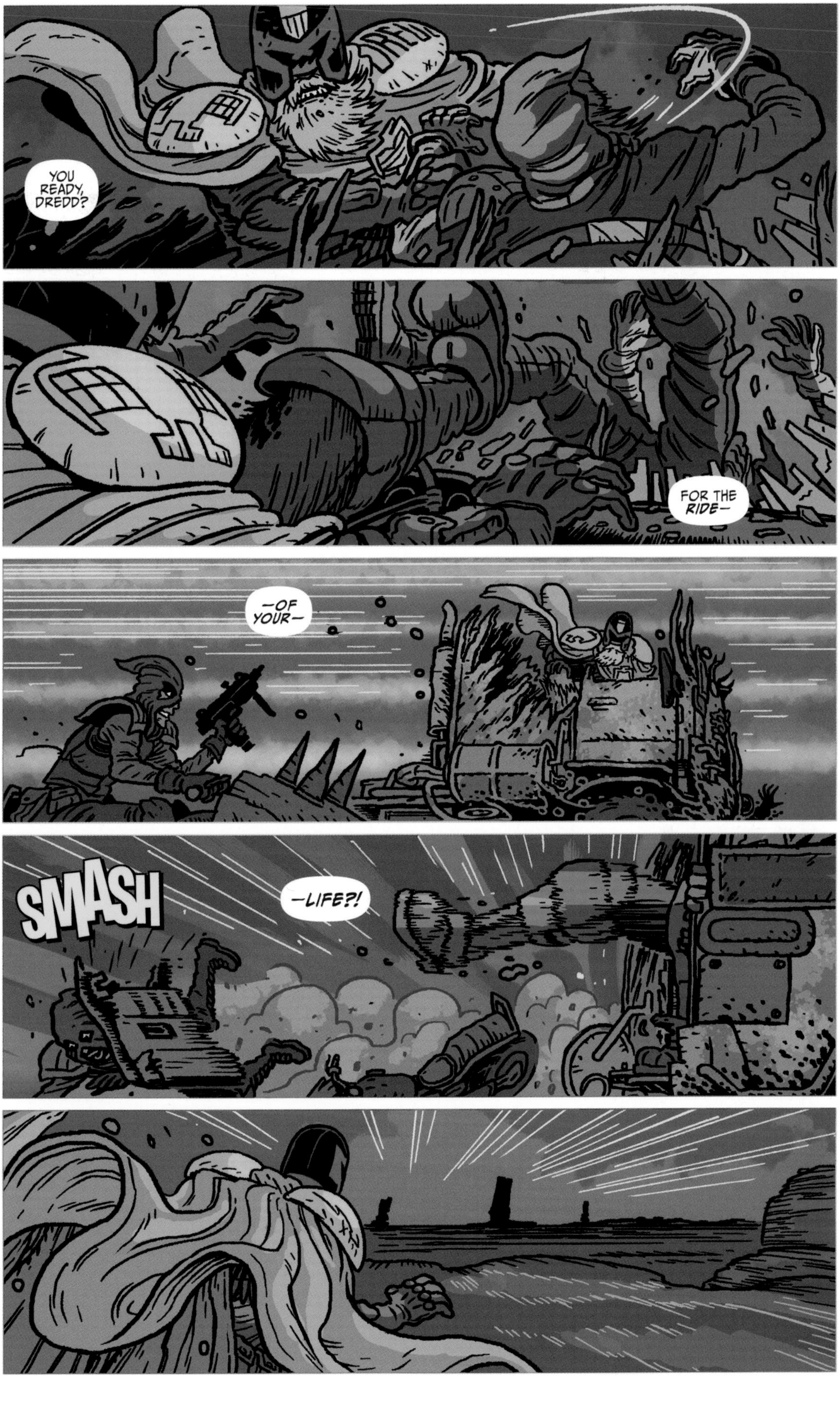
YOU READY, DREDD?
FOR THE RIDE—
—OF YOUR—
SMASH
—LIFE?!

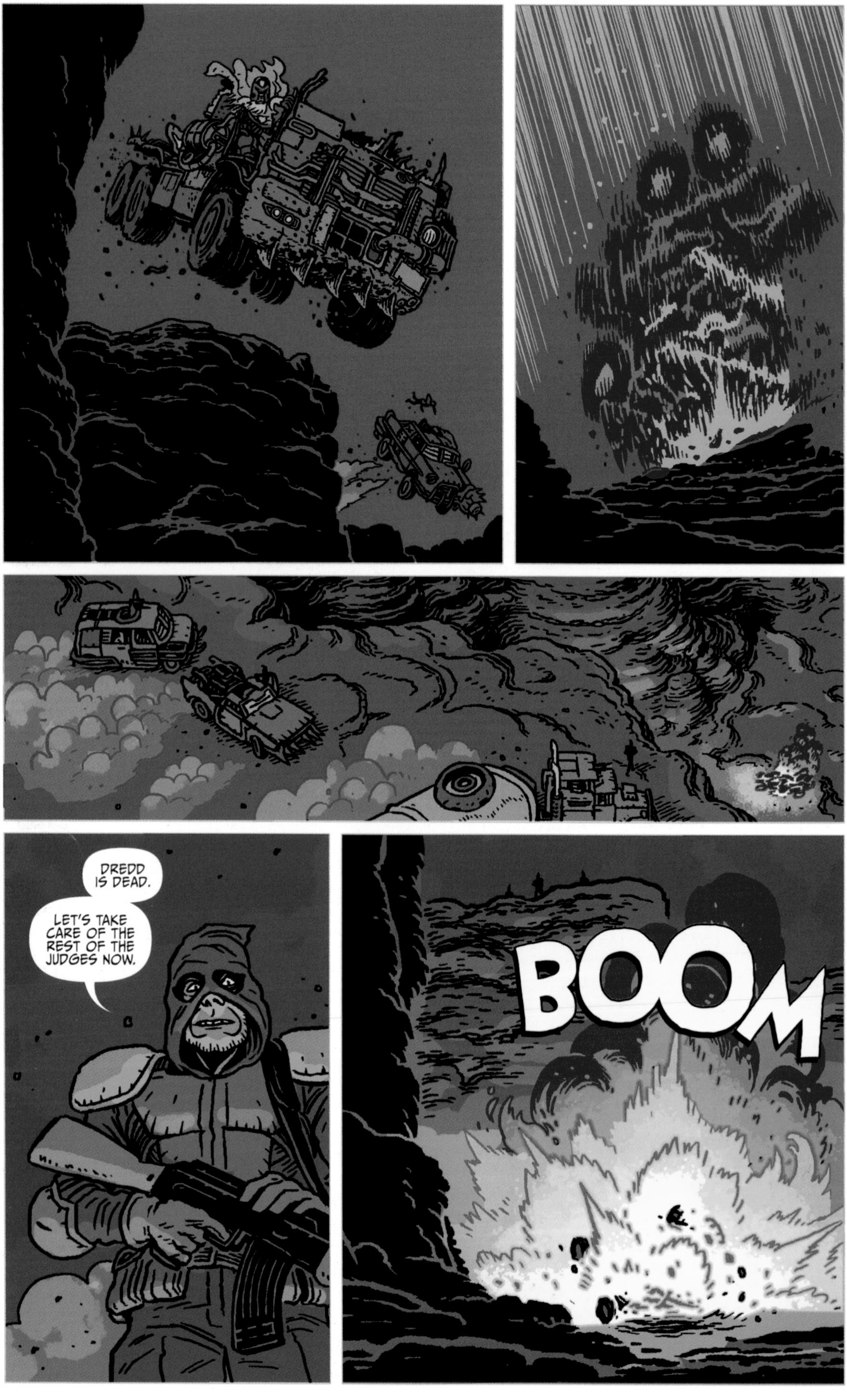
DREDD IS DEAD.
LET'S TAKE CARE OF THE REST OF THE JUDGES NOW.
BOOOM

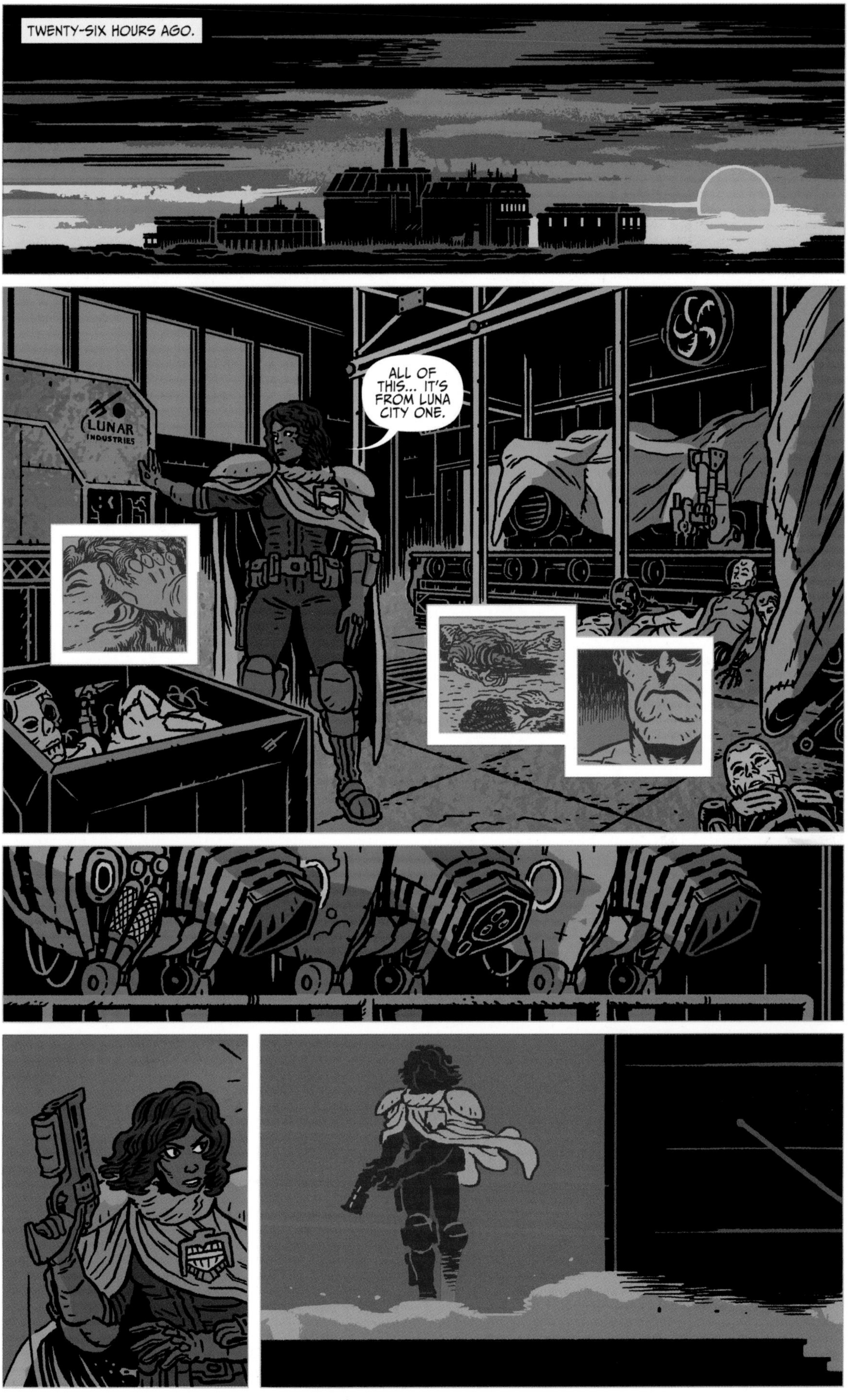
TWENTY-SIX HOURS AGO.
ALL OF THIS... IT'S FROM LUNA CITY ONE.
LUNAR INDUSTRIES

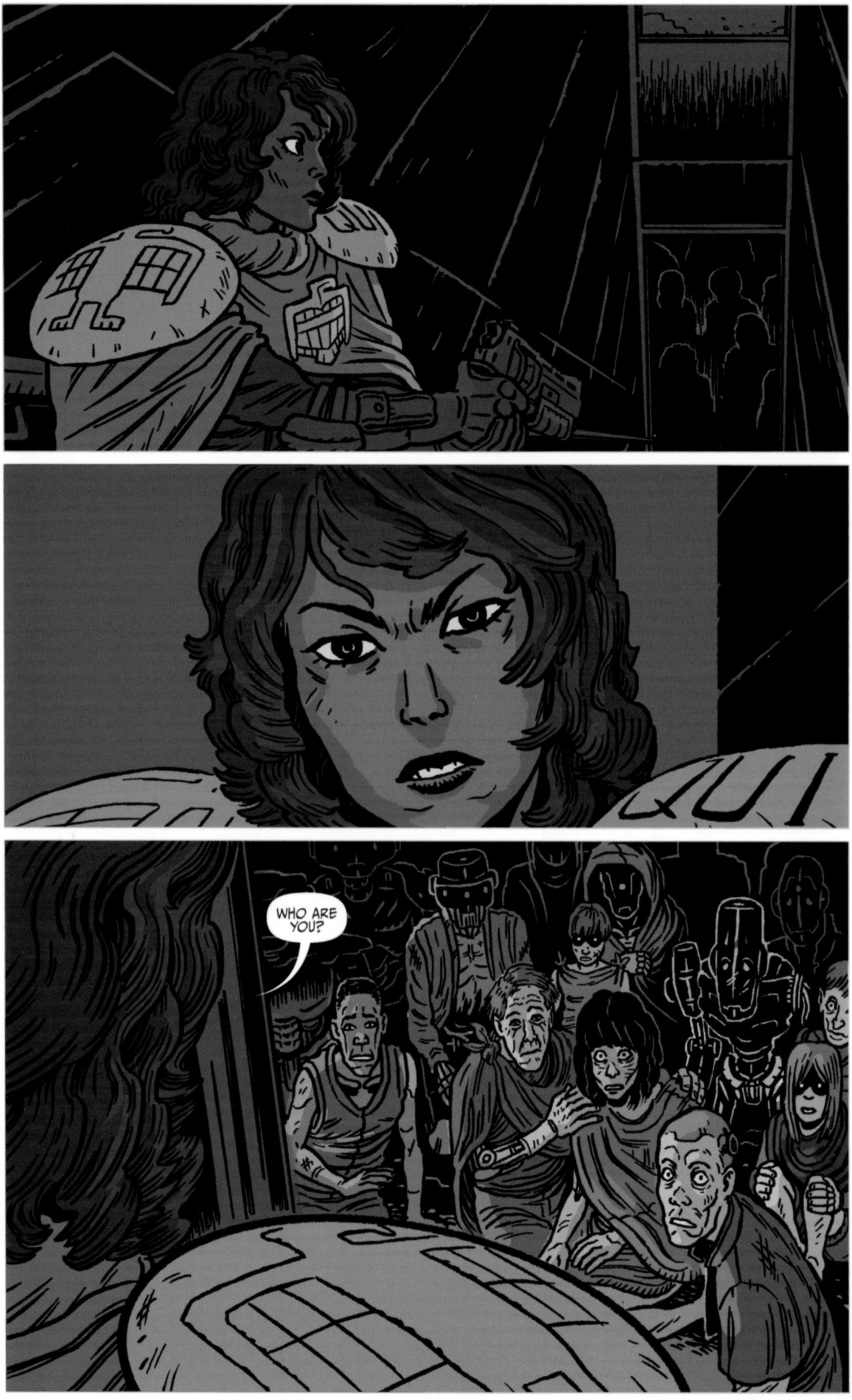
WHO ARE YOU?

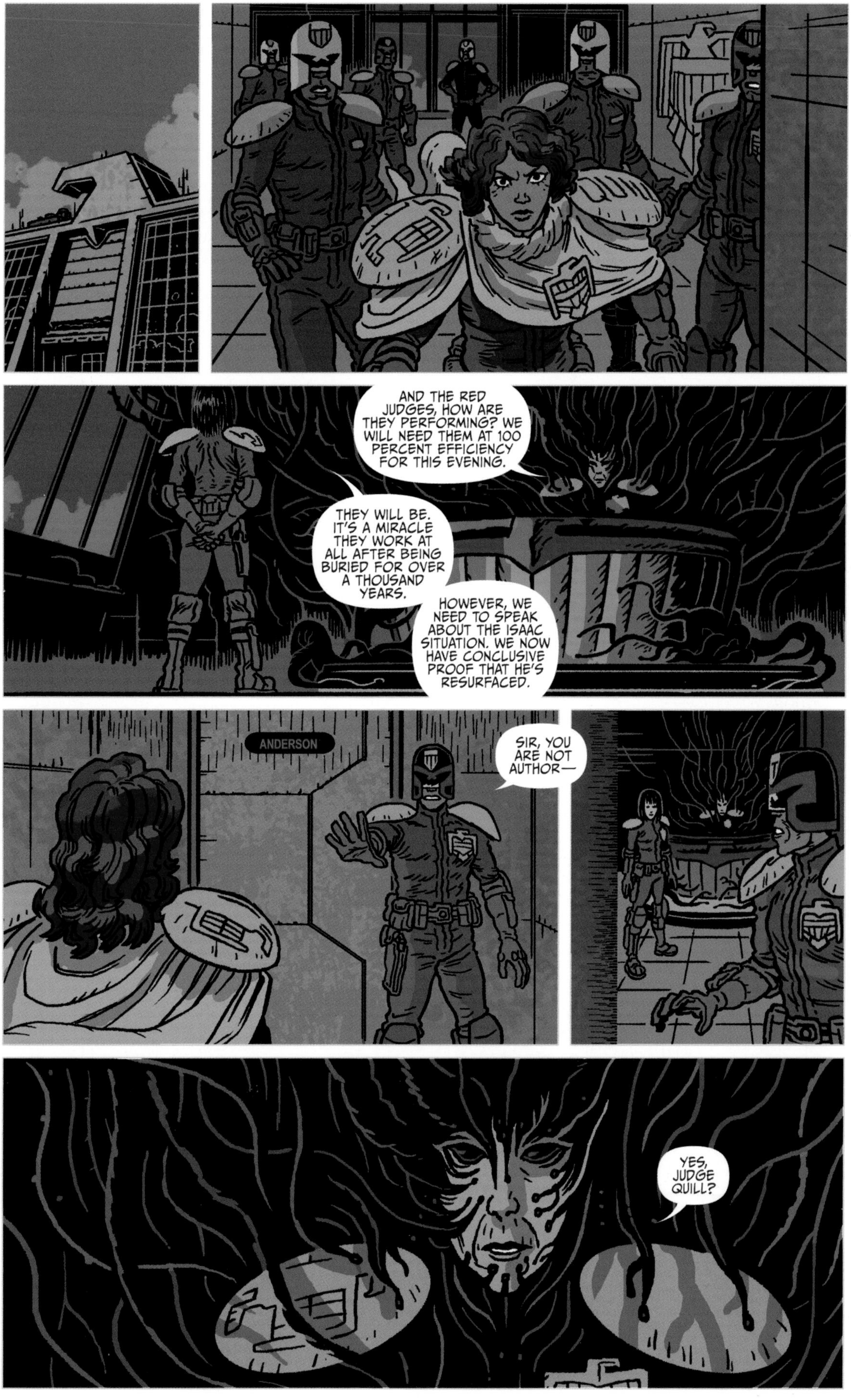
AND THE RED JUDGES, HOW ARE THEY PERFORMING? WE WILL NEED THEM AT 100 PERCENT EFFICIENCY FOR THIS EVENING.
THEY WILL BE. IT'S A MIRACLE THEY WORK AT ALL AFTER BEING BURIED FOR OVER A THOUSAND YEARS.
HOWEVER, WE NEED TO SPEAK ABOUT THE ISAAC SITUATION. WE NOW HAVE CONCLUSIVE PROOF THAT HE'S RESURFACED.
ANDERSON
SIR, YOU ARE NOT AUTHOR—
YES, JUDGE QUILL?

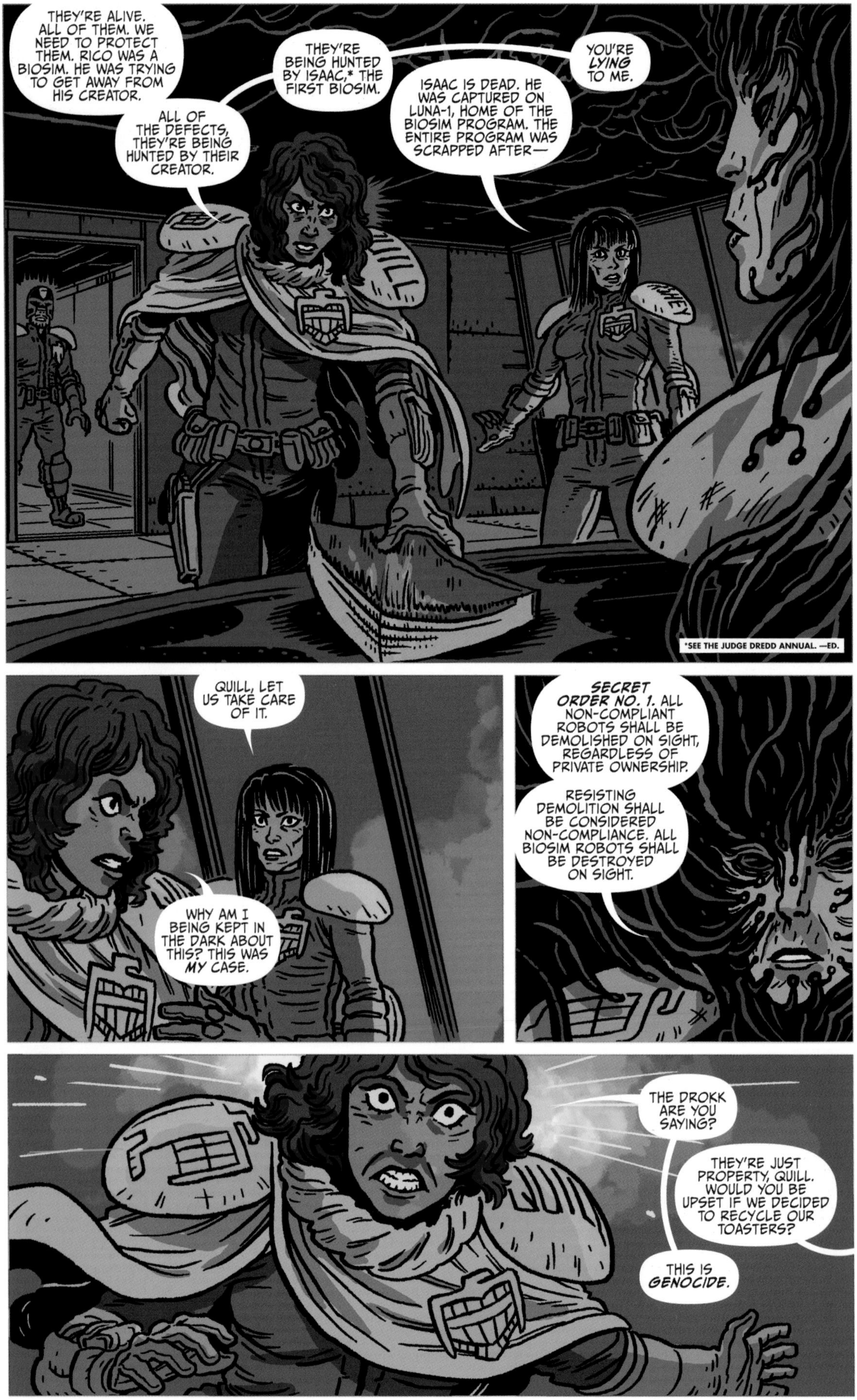
THEY'RE ALIVE. ALL OF THEM. WE NEED TO PROTECT THEM. RICO WAS A BIOSIM. HE WAS TRYING TO GET AWAY FROM HIS CREATOR.
ALL OF THE DEFECTS, THEY'RE BEING HUNTED BY THEIR CREATOR.
THEY'RE BEING HUNTED BY ISAAC,* THE FIRST BIOSIM.
ISAAC IS DEAD. HE WAS CAPTURED ON LUNA-1, HOME OF THE BIOSIM PROGRAM. THE ENTIRE PROGRAM WAS SCRAPPED AFTER—
YOU'RE LYING TO ME.
*SEE THE JUDGE DREDD ANNUAL. —ED.
QUILL, LET US TAKE CARE OF IT.
WHY AM I BEING KEPT IN THE DARK ABOUT THIS? THIS WAS MY CASE.
SECRET ORDER NO. 1. ALL NON-COMPLIANT ROBOTS SHALL BE DEMOLISHED ON SIGHT, REGARDLESS OF PRIVATE OWNERSHIP.
RESISTING DEMOLITION SHALL BE CONSIDERED NON-COMPLIANCE. ALL BIOSIM ROBOTS SHALL BE DESTROYED ON SIGHT.
THE DROKK ARE YOU SAYING?
THEY'RE JUST PROPERTY, QUILL. WOULD YOU BE UPSET IF WE DECIDED TO RECYCLE OUR TOASTERS?
THIS IS GENOCIDE.

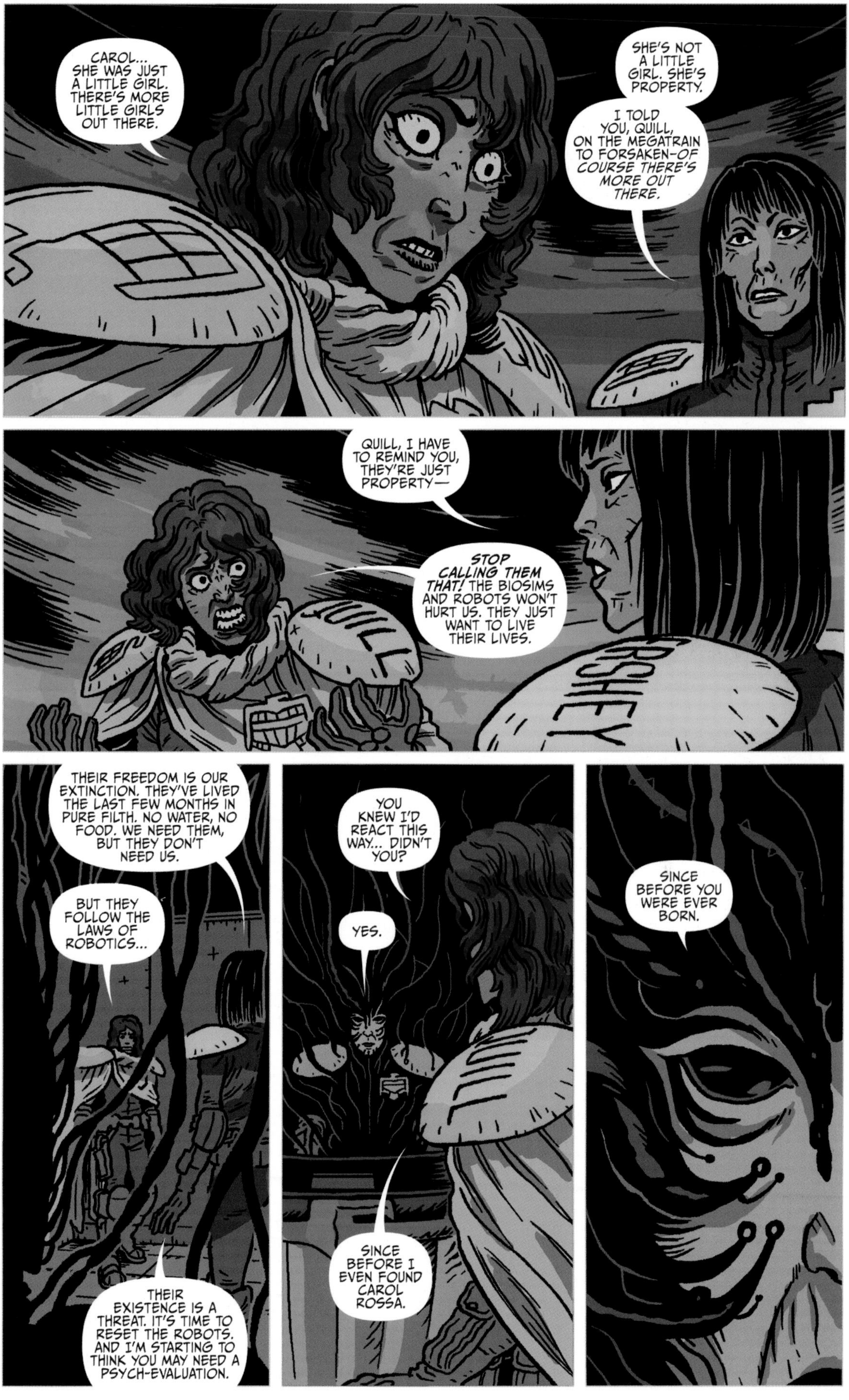
CAROL... SHE WAS JUST A LITTLE GIRL. THERE'S MORE LITTLE GIRLS OUT THERE.
SHE'S NOT A LITTLE GIRL. SHE'S PROPERTY.
I TOLD YOU, QUILL, ON THE MEGATRAIN TO FORSAKEN—*OF COURSE THERE'S MORE OUT THERE.*
QUILL, I HAVE TO REMIND YOU, THEY'RE JUST PROPERTY—
STOP CALLING THEM THAT! THE BIOSIMS AND ROBOTS WON'T HURT US. THEY JUST WANT TO LIVE THEIR LIVES.
QUILL
HERSHEY
THEIR FREEDOM IS OUR EXTINCTION. THEY'VE LIVED THE LAST FEW MONTHS IN PURE FILTH. NO WATER, NO FOOD. WE NEED THEM, BUT THEY DON'T NEED US.
BUT THEY FOLLOW THE LAWS OF ROBOTICS...
THEIR EXISTENCE IS A THREAT. IT'S TIME TO RESET THE ROBOTS. AND I'M STARTING TO THINK YOU MAY NEED A PSYCH-EVALUATION.
YOU KNEW I'D REACT THIS WAY... DIDN'T YOU?
YES.
SINCE BEFORE I EVEN FOUND CAROL ROSSA.
SINCE BEFORE YOU WERE EVER BORN.

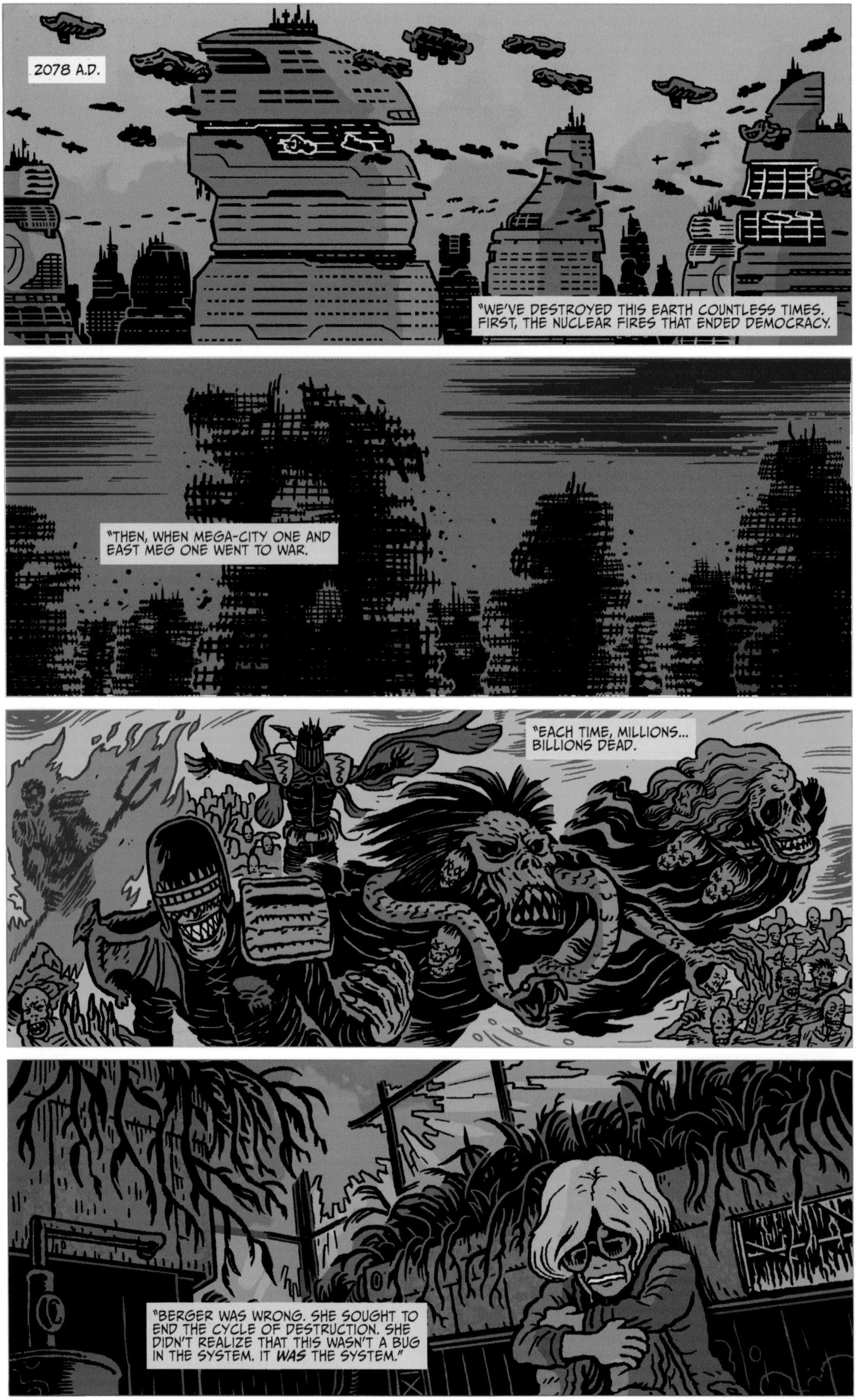
2078 A.D.
"WE'VE DESTROYED THIS EARTH COUNTLESS TIMES. FIRST, THE NUCLEAR FIRES THAT ENDED DEMOCRACY.
"THEN, WHEN MEGA-CITY ONE AND EAST MEG ONE WENT TO WAR.
"EACH TIME, MILLIONS... BILLIONS DEAD.
"BERGER WAS WRONG. SHE SOUGHT TO END THE CYCLE OF DESTRUCTION. SHE DIDN'T REALIZE THAT THIS WASN'T A BUG IN THE SYSTEM. IT *WAS* THE SYSTEM."

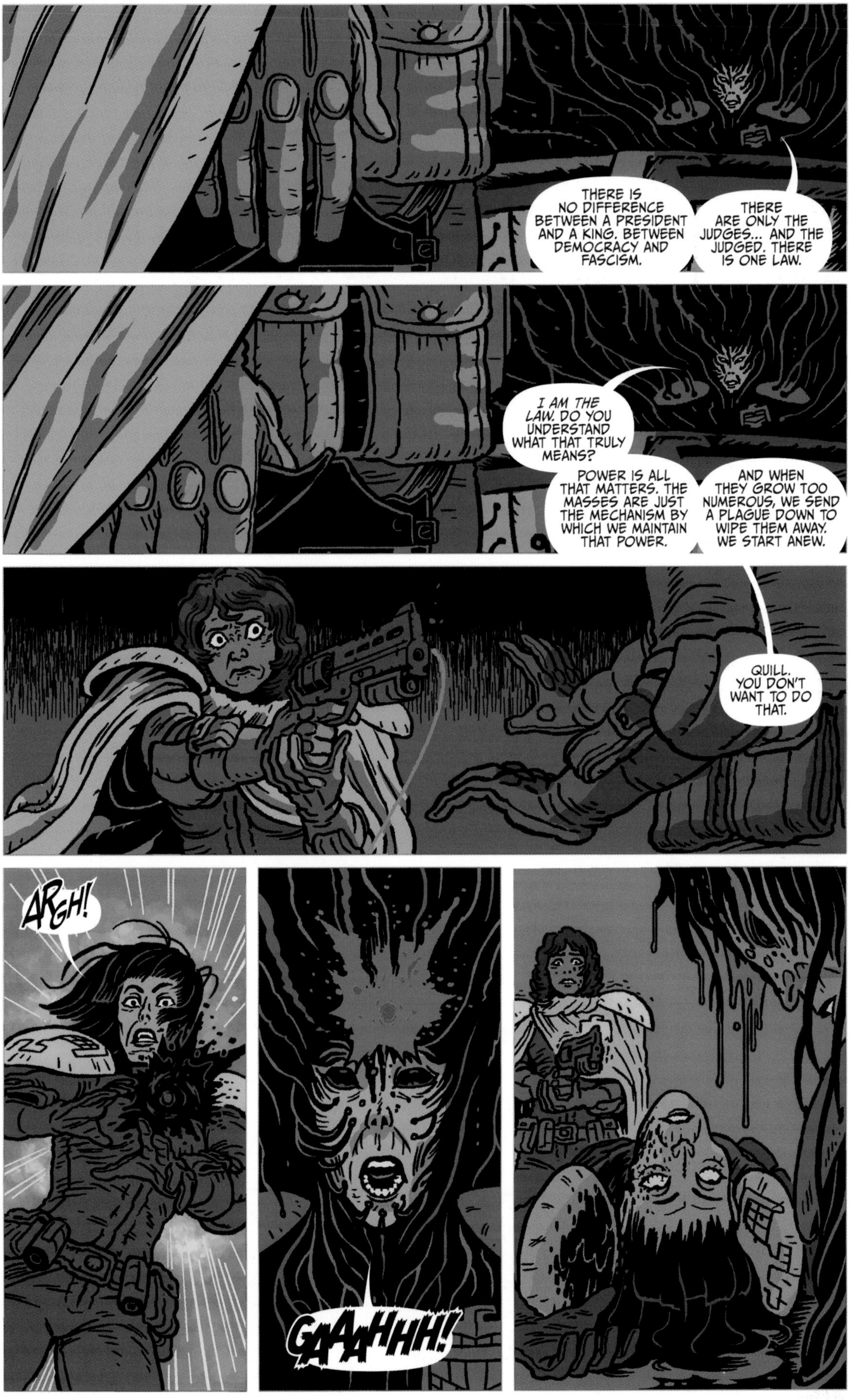
THERE IS NO DIFFERENCE BETWEEN A PRESIDENT AND A KING. BETWEEN DEMOCRACY AND FASCISM.
THERE ARE ONLY THE JUDGES... AND THE JUDGED. THERE IS ONE LAW.
I AM THE LAW. DO YOU UNDERSTAND WHAT THAT TRULY MEANS?
POWER IS ALL THAT MATTERS. THE MASSES ARE JUST THE MECHANISM BY WHICH WE MAINTAIN THAT POWER.
AND WHEN THEY GROW TOO NUMEROUS, WE SEND A PLAGUE DOWN TO WIPE THEM AWAY. WE START ANEW.
QUILL. YOU DON'T WANT TO DO THAT.
ARGH!
GAAAHHH!

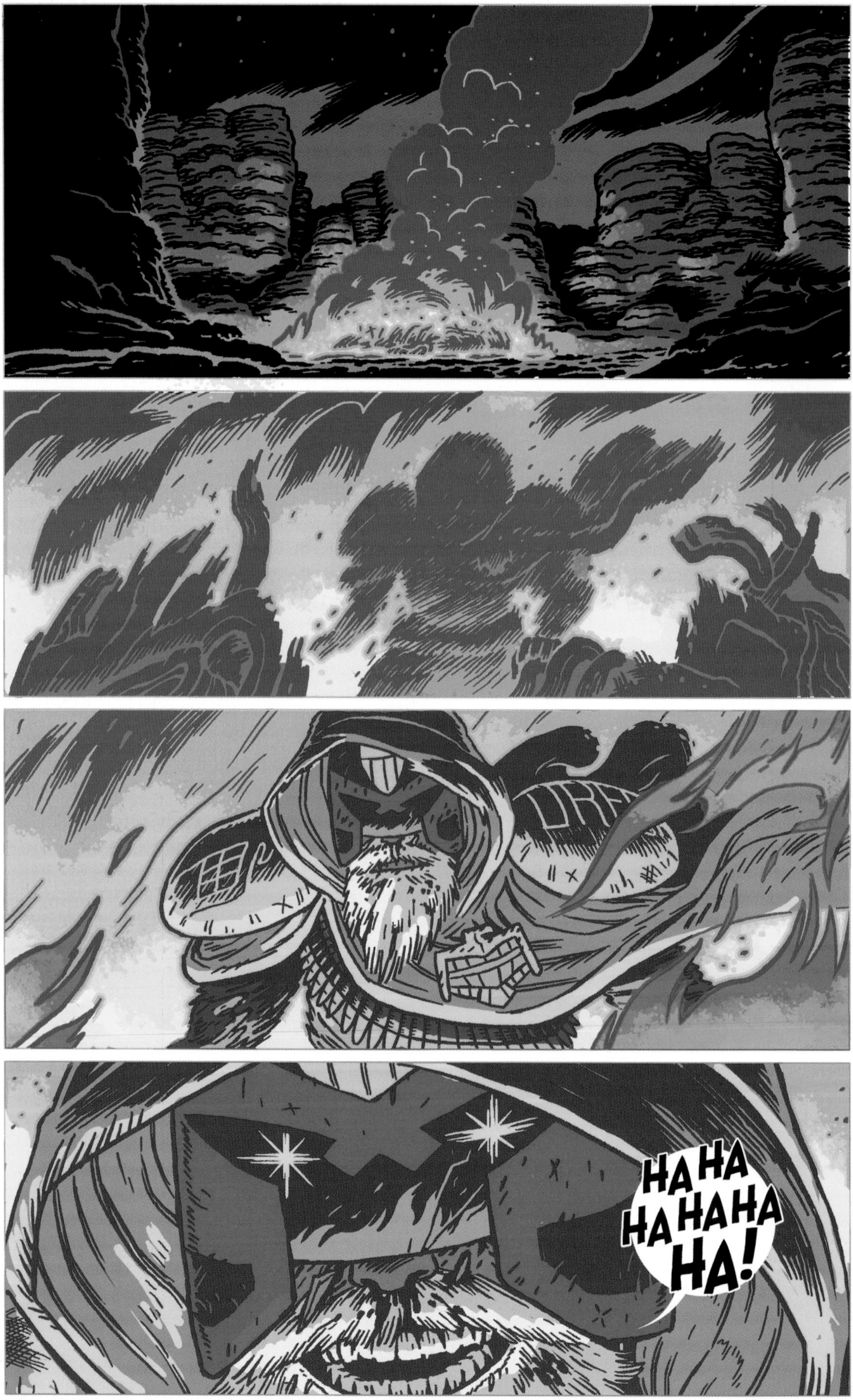
HA HA HA HA HA HA HA!

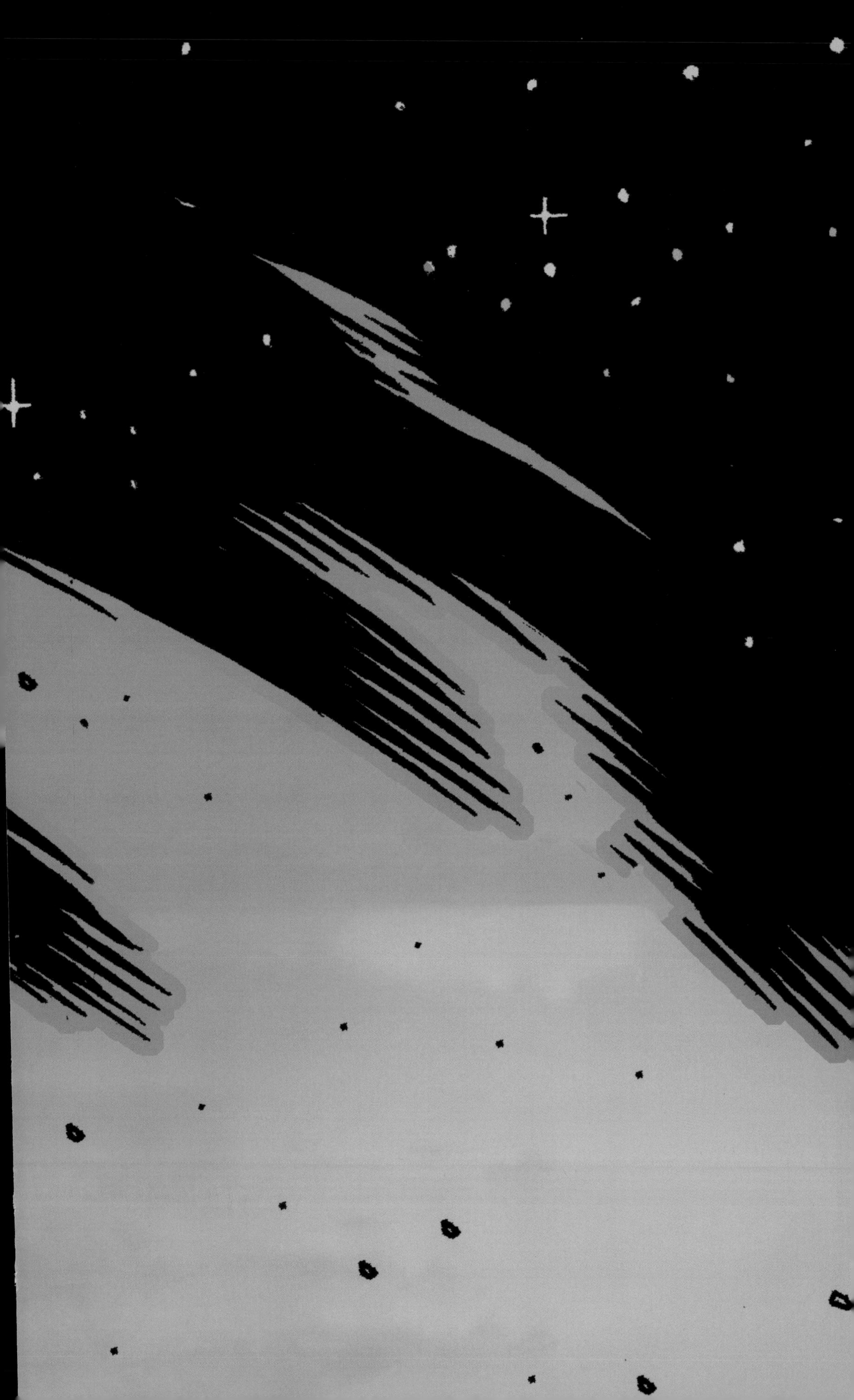

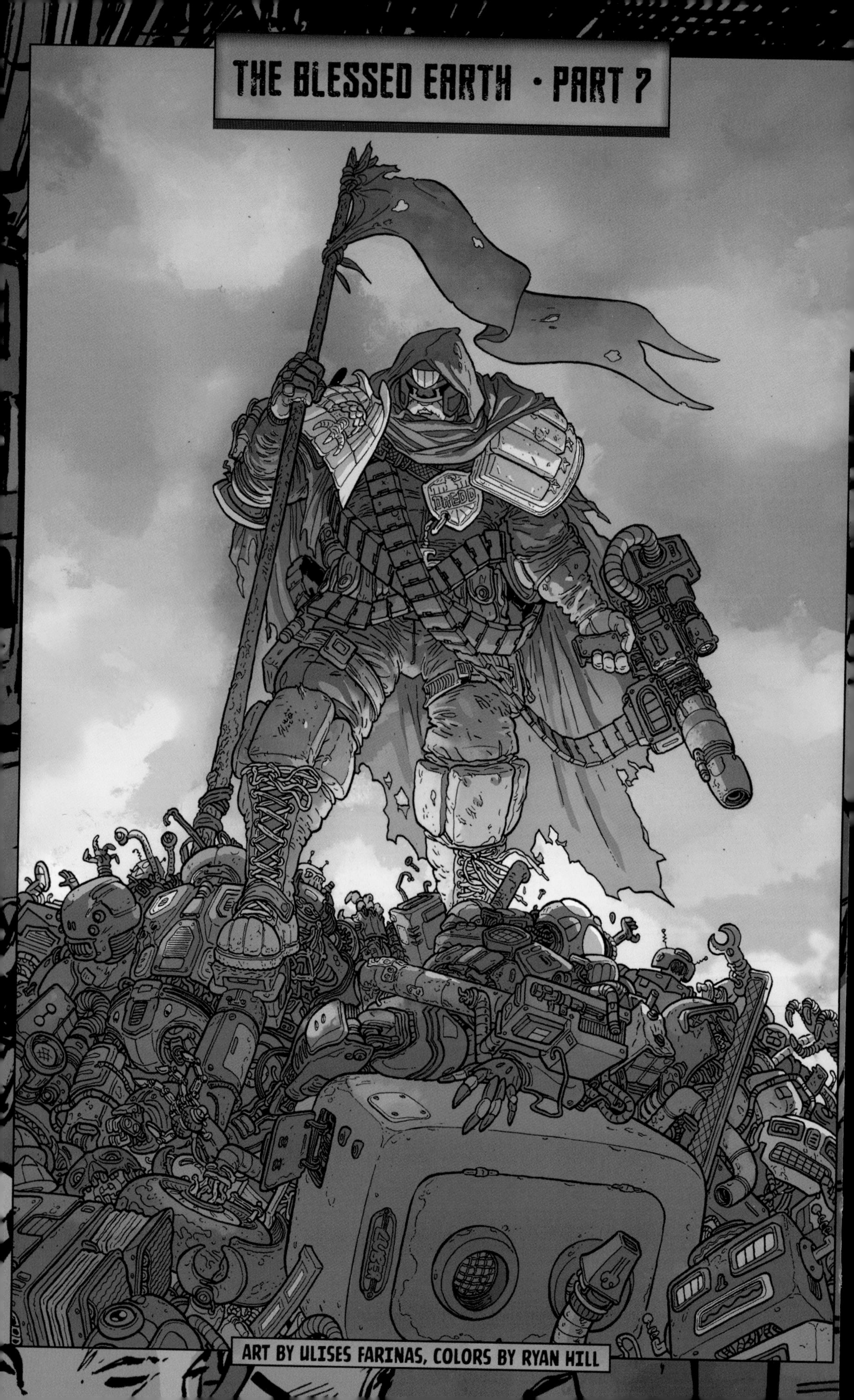
THE BLESSED EARTH · PART 7
DREDD
ART BY ULISES FARINAS, COLORS BY RYAN HILL

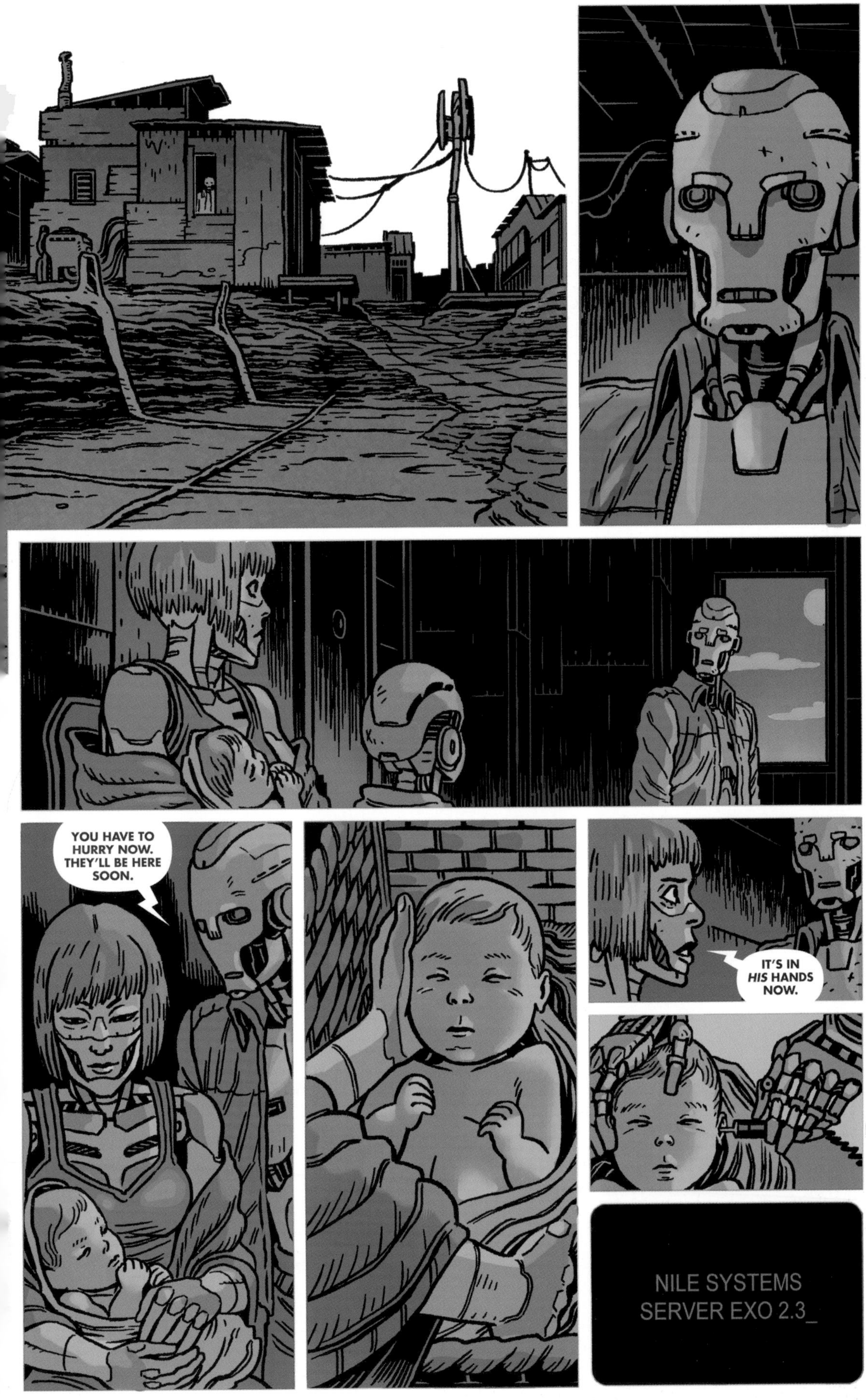
YOU HAVE TO HURRY NOW. THEY'LL BE HERE SOON.
IT'S IN *HIS* HANDS NOW.
NILE SYSTEMS SERVER EXO 2.3_

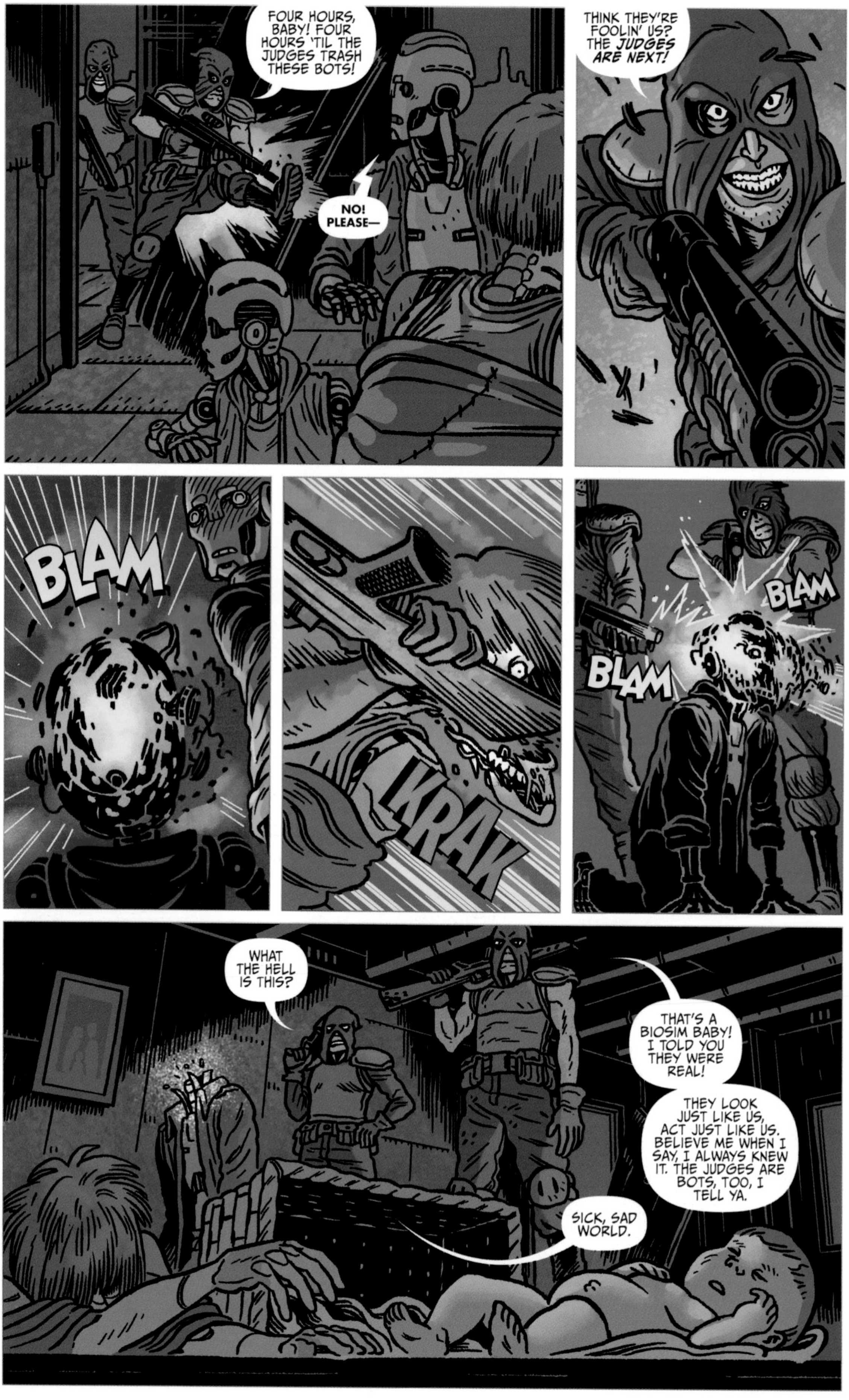
FOUR HOURS, BABY! FOUR HOURS 'TIL THE JUDGES TRASH THESE BOTS!
NO! PLEASE—
THINK THEY'RE FOOLIN' US? THE JUDGES ARE NEXT!
BLAM
KRAK
BLAM
BLAM
WHAT THE HELL IS THIS?
THAT'S A BIOSIM BABY! I TOLD YOU THEY WERE REAL!
THEY LOOK JUST LIKE US, ACT JUST LIKE US. BELIEVE ME WHEN I SAY, I ALWAYS KNEW IT. THE JUDGES ARE BOTS, TOO, I TELL YA.
SICK, SAD WORLD.

YOU GOT THE FILES?

I WANT TO SEE HIM.

HOW WE KNOW YOU AIN'T A BOT?

WHAT'S IT MATTER IF I AM? I WANT TO TEAR THIS WHOLE WORLD DOWN.

MAKE IT SO THAT NOTHING EVER REMEMBERS THE JUDGES AGAIN.

NO ONE SEES HIM. *YOU KNOW THAT.*

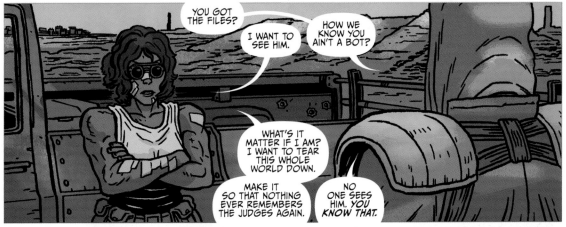

WAIT. THESE FILES PROVE THE DREDD MAN IS A ROBOT?

THEY PROVE HE'S GOT AN ARTIFICIAL SKELETON.

SAME DIFFERENCE. WE TRYING TO WIN A WAR, NOT WRITE A DICTIONARY.

NO GRAND MASTER, NO FILES, NO DEAL.

IF YOUR INTEL IS GOOD, AND DREDD IS A BIOSIM, HE'S GOOD AS DEAD. *YOU GET THAT?* ONLY *THEN* YOU'LL MEET THE GRAND MASTER. ALL RIGHT?

MC CLASSIFIED

JOSEPH DREDD

DEAL.

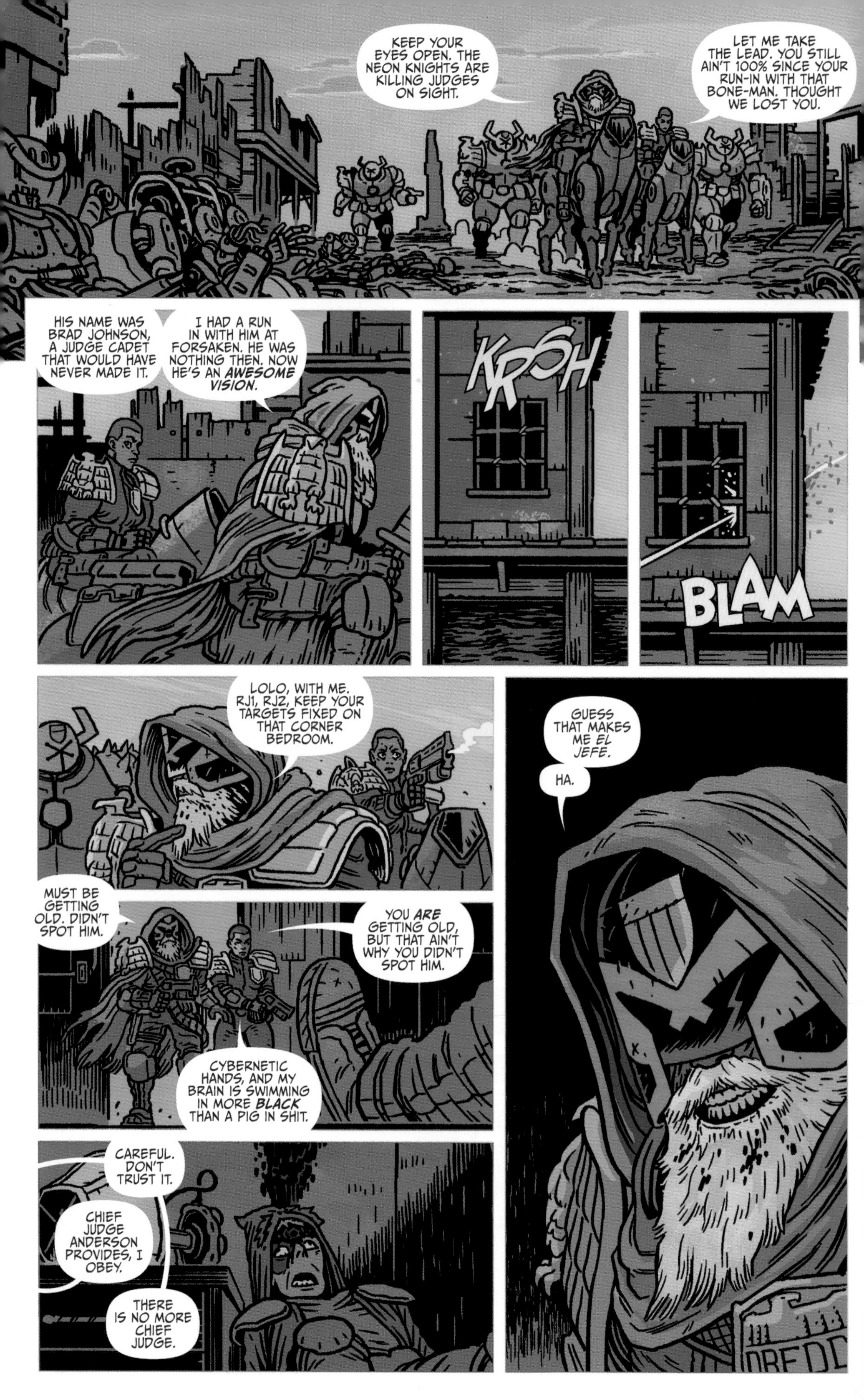
KEEP YOUR EYES OPEN. THE NEON KNIGHTS ARE KILLING JUDGES ON SIGHT.
LET ME TAKE THE LEAD. YOU STILL AIN'T 100% SINCE YOUR RUN-IN WITH THAT BONE-MAN. THOUGHT WE LOST YOU.
HIS NAME WAS BRAD JOHNSON, A JUDGE CADET THAT WOULD HAVE NEVER MADE IT.
I HAD A RUN IN WITH HIM AT FORSAKEN. HE WAS NOTHING THEN. NOW HE'S AN AWESOME VISION.
KRSH
BLAM
LOLO, WITH ME. RJ1, RJ2, KEEP YOUR TARGETS FIXED ON THAT CORNER BEDROOM.
MUST BE GETTING OLD. DIDN'T SPOT HIM.
YOU ARE GETTING OLD, BUT THAT AIN'T WHY YOU DIDN'T SPOT HIM.
CYBERNETIC HANDS, AND MY BRAIN IS SWIMMING IN MORE BLACK THAN A PIG IN SHIT.
CAREFUL. DON'T TRUST IT.
CHIEF JUDGE ANDERSON PROVIDES, I OBEY.
THERE IS NO MORE CHIEF JUDGE.
GUESS THAT MAKES ME EL JEFE.
HA.
DREDD

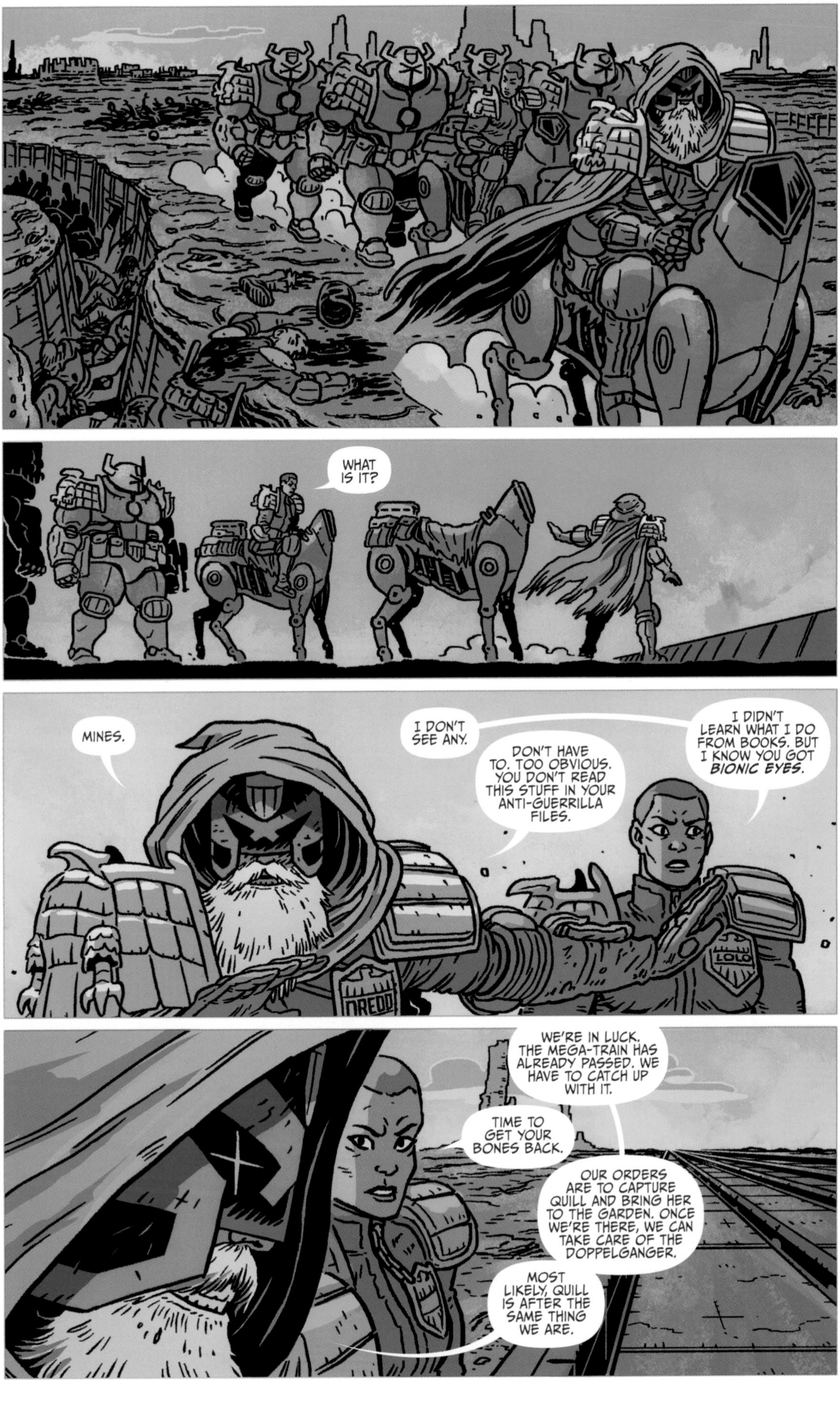
WHAT IS IT?
MINES.
I DON'T SEE ANY.
DON'T HAVE TO. TOO OBVIOUS. YOU DON'T READ THIS STUFF IN YOUR ANTI-GUERRILLA FILES.
I DIDN'T LEARN WHAT I DO FROM BOOKS. BUT I KNOW YOU GOT *BIONIC EYES*.
DREDD
LOLO
WE'RE IN LUCK. THE MEGA-TRAIN HAS ALREADY PASSED. WE HAVE TO CATCH UP WITH IT.
TIME TO GET YOUR BONES BACK.
OUR ORDERS ARE TO CAPTURE QUILL AND BRING HER TO THE GARDEN. ONCE WE'RE THERE, WE CAN TAKE CARE OF THE DOPPELGANGER.
MOST LIKELY, QUILL IS AFTER THE SAME THING WE ARE.

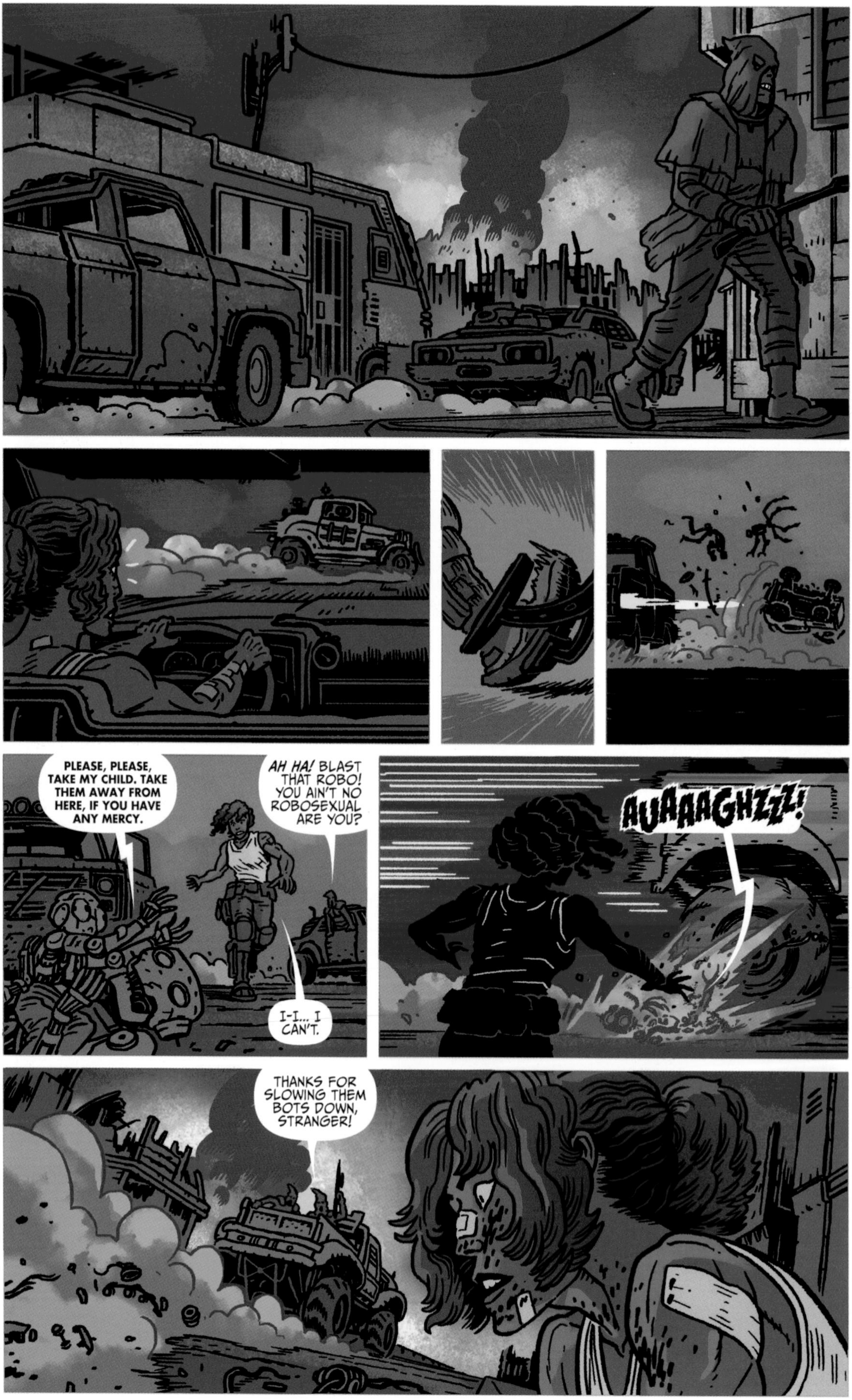
PLEASE, PLEASE, TAKE MY CHILD. TAKE THEM AWAY FROM HERE, IF YOU HAVE ANY MERCY.
AH HA! BLAST THAT ROBO! YOU AIN'T NO ROBOSEXUAL ARE YOU?
I-I... I CAN'T.
AUAAAGHZZZ!
THANKS FOR SLOWING THEM BOTS DOWN, STRANGER!

POW! MDL 110
PURE OBLITERATION DEVICE

WHY HAVE WE STOPPED?

HERE, TAKE THIS! IF YOU'RE RIDING WITH US, YOU GOTTA OPEN YOUR EYES.

WHAT IS IT?

GRAND MASTER HANDS THEM OUT. LETS YOU SEE THE DANGERS AHEAD OF YOU.

HAHAHA! GOT 'EM!

WHAT THE DROKK JUST HAPPENED?!

GRAND MASTER IS A GENIUS!

INSTALLED PERCEPTUAL FILTERS ON THE MINES.

CAUSES THEM TO EMIT A CHEMICAL THAT MAKES THEM INVISIBLE.

THIS PILL MAKES YOU IMMUNE--HEY! WHERE ARE YOU GOING?

YOU WANTED TO SEE THE GRAND MASTER, RIGHT?

NOT THIS WAY.

YOU CAN'T BACK OUT NOW.

KNEW YOU DIDN'T HAVE THE STOMACH FOR IT.

YOU'RE A JUDGE, THROUGH AND THROUGH.

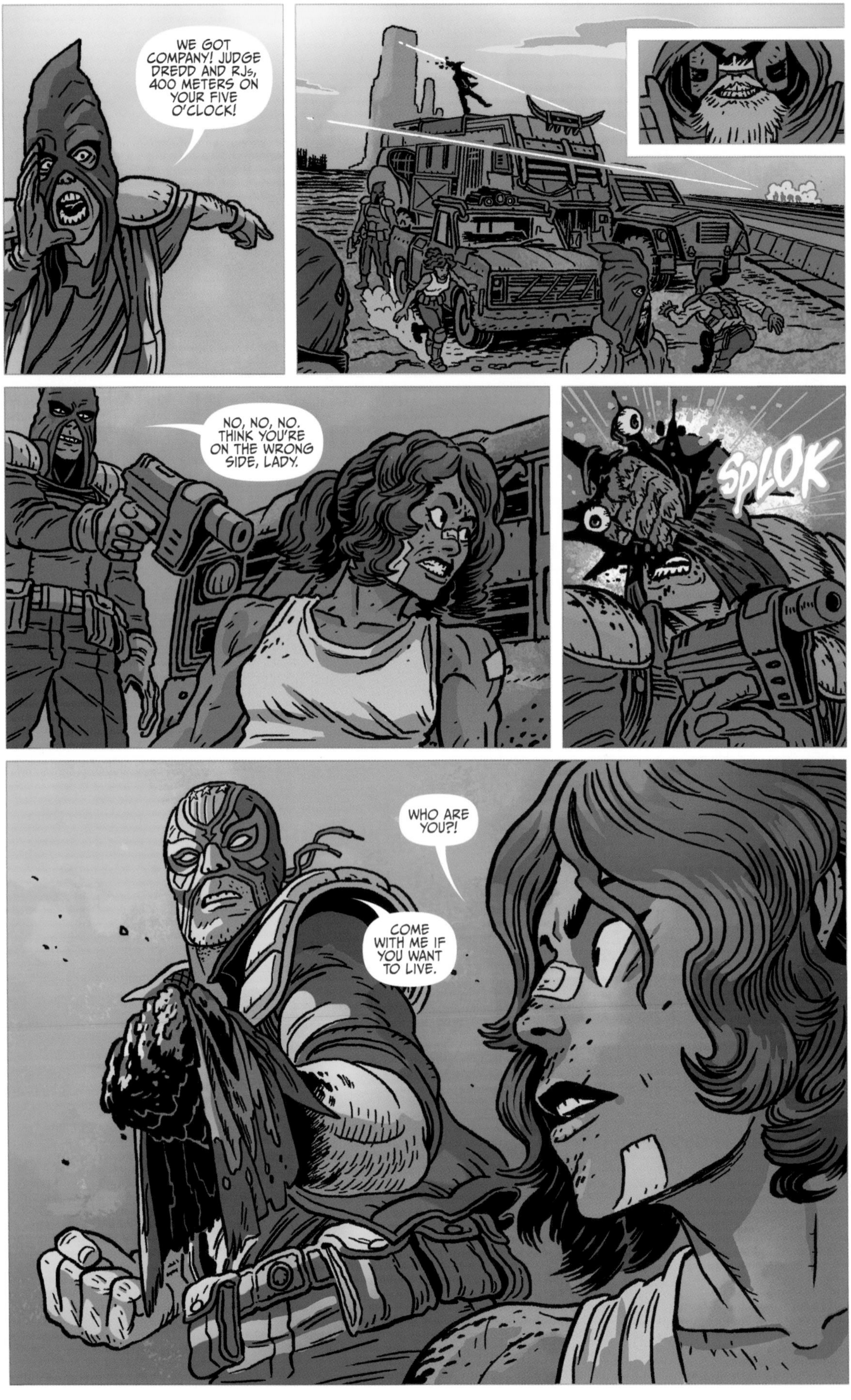
WE GOT COMPANY! JUDGE DREDD AND RJs, 400 METERS ON YOUR FIVE O'CLOCK!
NO, NO, NO. THINK YOU'RE ON THE WRONG SIDE, LADY.
SPLOK
WHO ARE YOU?!
COME WITH ME IF YOU WANT TO LIVE.

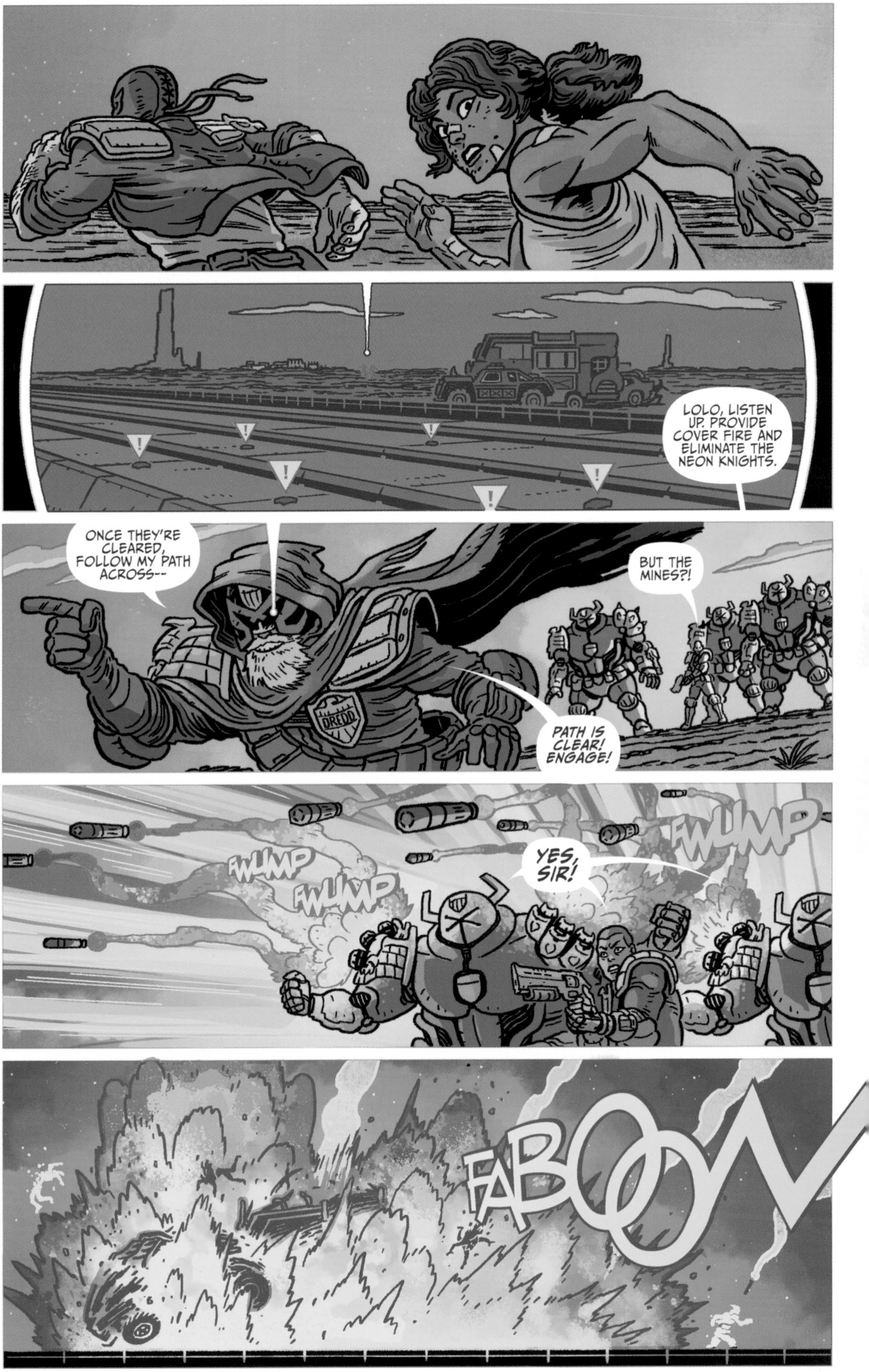
LOLO, LISTEN UP. PROVIDE COVER FIRE AND ELIMINATE THE NEON KNIGHTS.
ONCE THEY'RE CLEARED, FOLLOW MY PATH ACROSS--
BUT THE MINES?!
PATH IS CLEAR! ENGAGE!
FWUMP
FWUMP
YES, SIR!
FWUMP
FABOOM

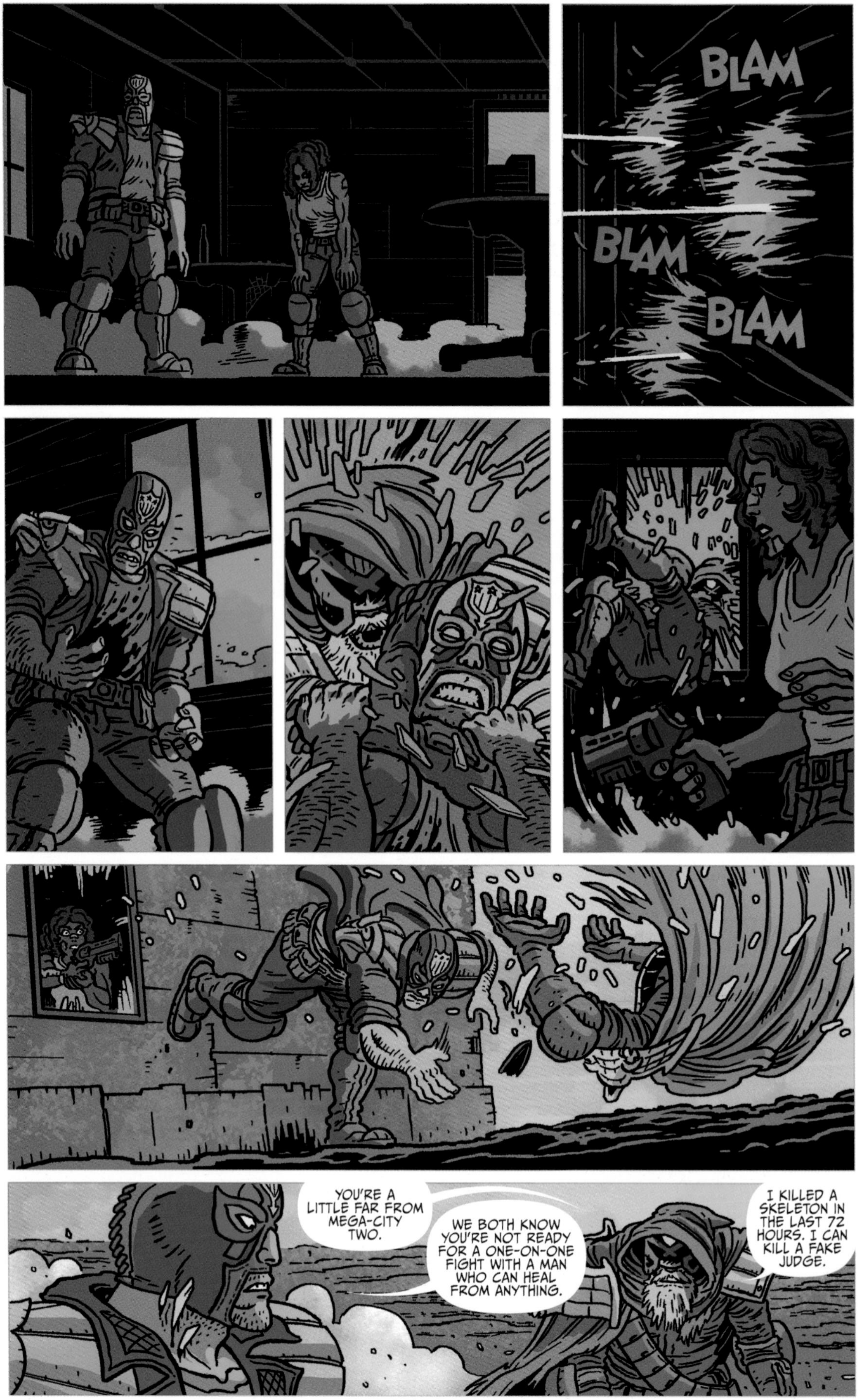
BLAM
BLAM
BLAM
YOU'RE A LITTLE FAR FROM MEGA-CITY TWO.
WE BOTH KNOW YOU'RE NOT READY FOR A ONE-ON-ONE FIGHT WITH A MAN WHO CAN HEAL FROM ANYTHING.
I KILLED A SKELETON IN THE LAST 72 HOURS. I CAN KILL A FAKE JUDGE.

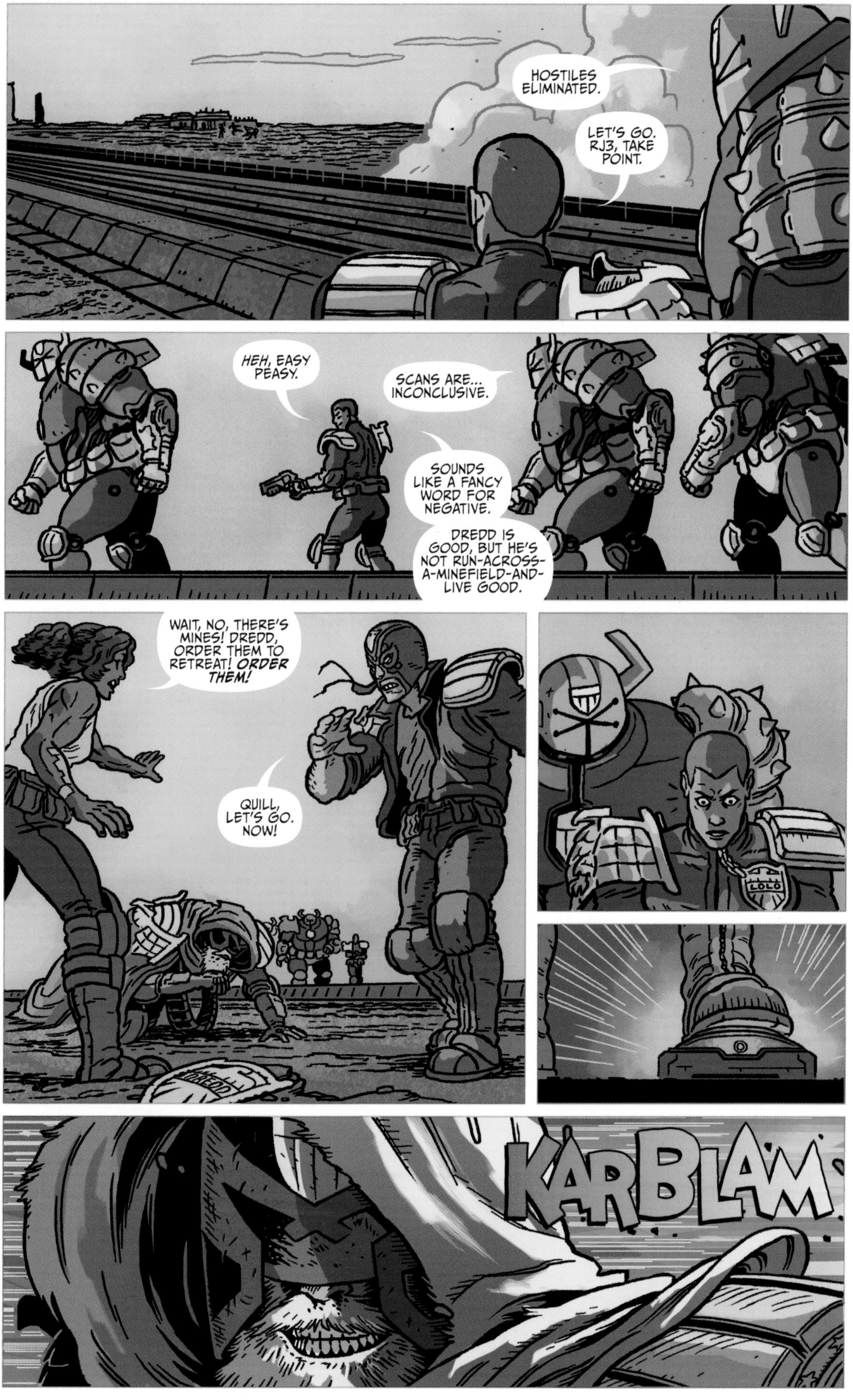
HOSTILES ELIMINATED.
LET'S GO. RJ3, TAKE POINT.
HEH, EASY PEASY.
SCANS ARE... INCONCLUSIVE.
SOUNDS LIKE A FANCY WORD FOR NEGATIVE.
DREDD IS GOOD, BUT HE'S NOT RUN-ACROSS-A-MINEFIELD-AND-LIVE GOOD.
WAIT, NO, THERE'S MINES! DREDD, ORDER THEM TO RETREAT! ORDER THEM!
QUILL, LET'S GO. NOW!
LOLO
KARBLAM

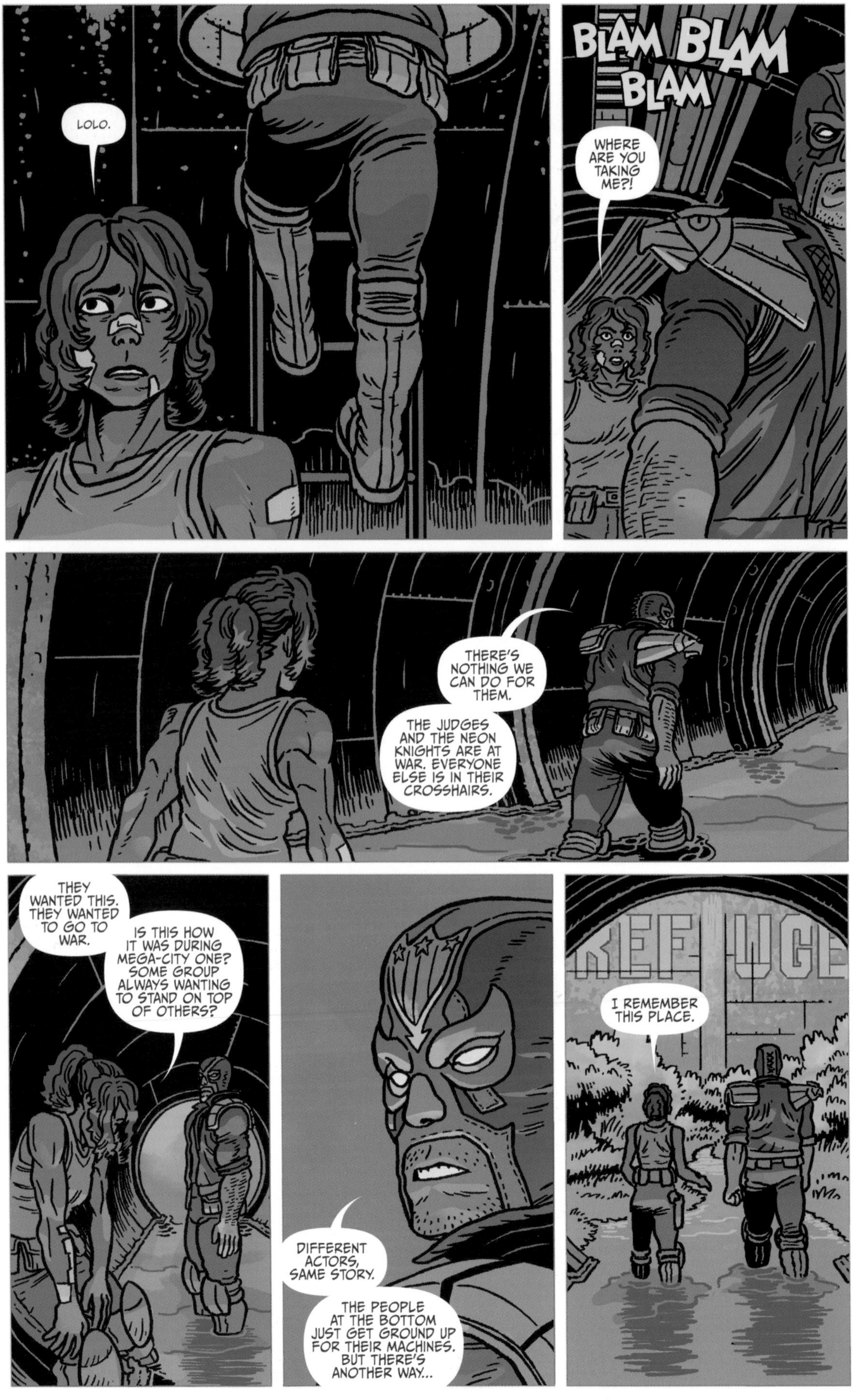
LOLO.
BLAM BLAM BLAM
WHERE ARE YOU TAKING ME?!
THERE'S NOTHING WE CAN DO FOR THEM.
THE JUDGES AND THE NEON KNIGHTS ARE AT WAR. EVERYONE ELSE IS IN THEIR CROSSHAIRS.
THEY WANTED THIS. THEY WANTED TO GO TO WAR.
IS THIS HOW IT WAS DURING MEGA-CITY ONE? SOME GROUP ALWAYS WANTING TO STAND ON TOP OF OTHERS?
DIFFERENT ACTORS, SAME STORY.
THE PEOPLE AT THE BOTTOM JUST GET GROUND UP FOR THEIR MACHINES. BUT THERE'S ANOTHER WAY...
REFUGE
I REMEMBER THIS PLACE.

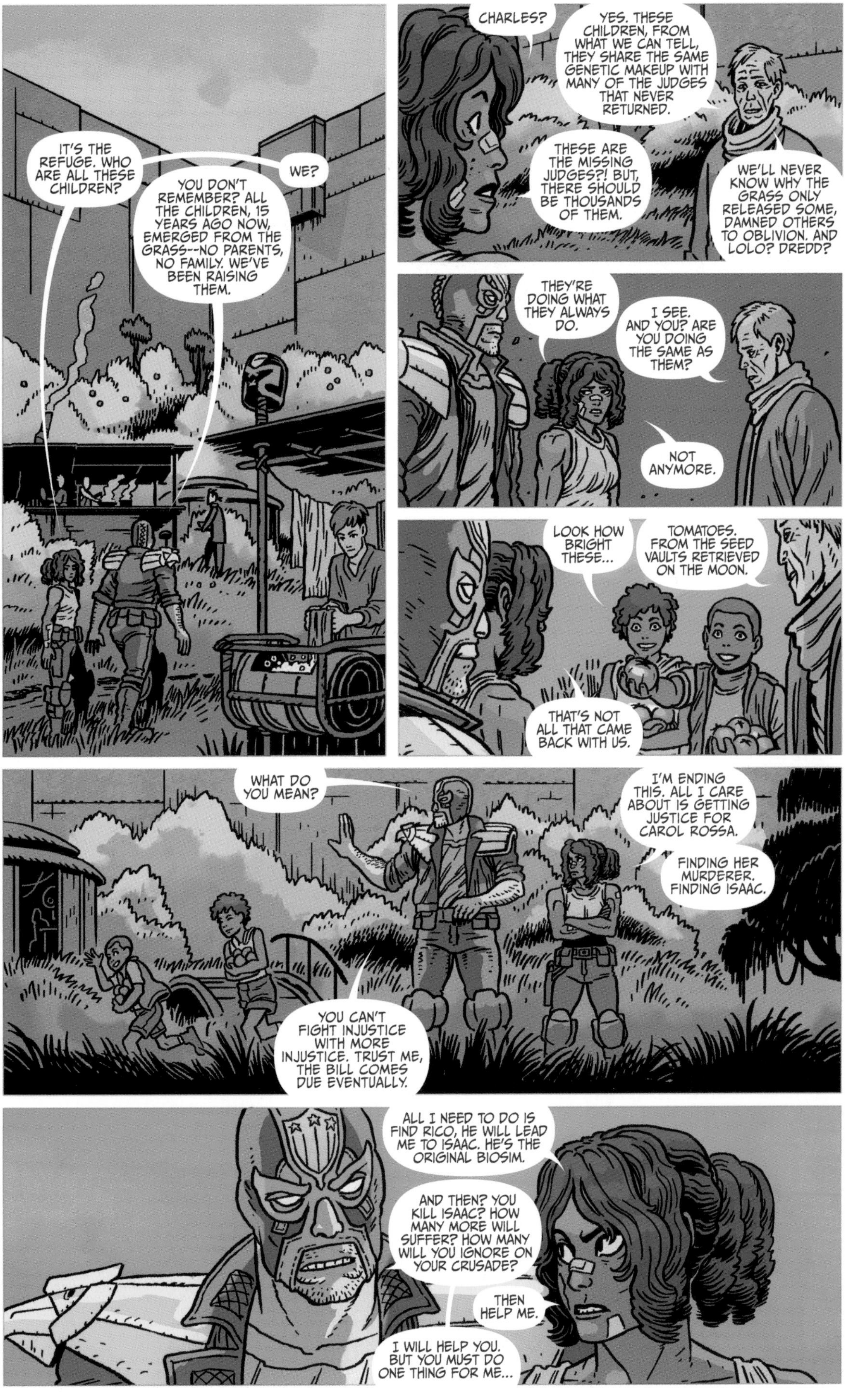
IT'S THE REFUGE. WHO ARE ALL THESE CHILDREN?
WE?
YOU DON'T REMEMBER? ALL THE CHILDREN, 15 YEARS AGO NOW, EMERGED FROM THE GRASS--NO PARENTS, NO FAMILY. WE'VE BEEN RAISING THEM.
CHARLES?
YES. THESE CHILDREN, FROM WHAT WE CAN TELL, THEY SHARE THE SAME GENETIC MAKEUP WITH MANY OF THE JUDGES THAT NEVER RETURNED.
THESE ARE THE MISSING JUDGES?! BUT, THERE SHOULD BE THOUSANDS OF THEM.
WE'LL NEVER KNOW WHY THE GRASS ONLY RELEASED SOME, DAMNED OTHERS TO OBLIVION. AND LOLO? DREDD?
THEY'RE DOING WHAT THEY ALWAYS DO.
I SEE. AND YOU? ARE YOU DOING THE SAME AS THEM?
NOT ANYMORE.
LOOK HOW BRIGHT THESE...
TOMATOES. FROM THE SEED VAULTS RETRIEVED ON THE MOON.
THAT'S NOT ALL THAT CAME BACK WITH US.
WHAT DO YOU MEAN?
I'M ENDING THIS. ALL I CARE ABOUT IS GETTING JUSTICE FOR CAROL ROSSA.
FINDING HER MURDERER. FINDING ISAAC.
YOU CAN'T FIGHT INJUSTICE WITH MORE INJUSTICE. TRUST ME, THE BILL COMES DUE EVENTUALLY.
ALL I NEED TO DO IS FIND RICO, HE WILL LEAD ME TO ISAAC. HE'S THE ORIGINAL BIOSIM.
AND THEN? YOU KILL ISAAC? HOW MANY MORE WILL SUFFER? HOW MANY WILL YOU IGNORE ON YOUR CRUSADE?
THEN HELP ME.
I WILL HELP YOU. BUT YOU MUST DO ONE THING FOR ME...

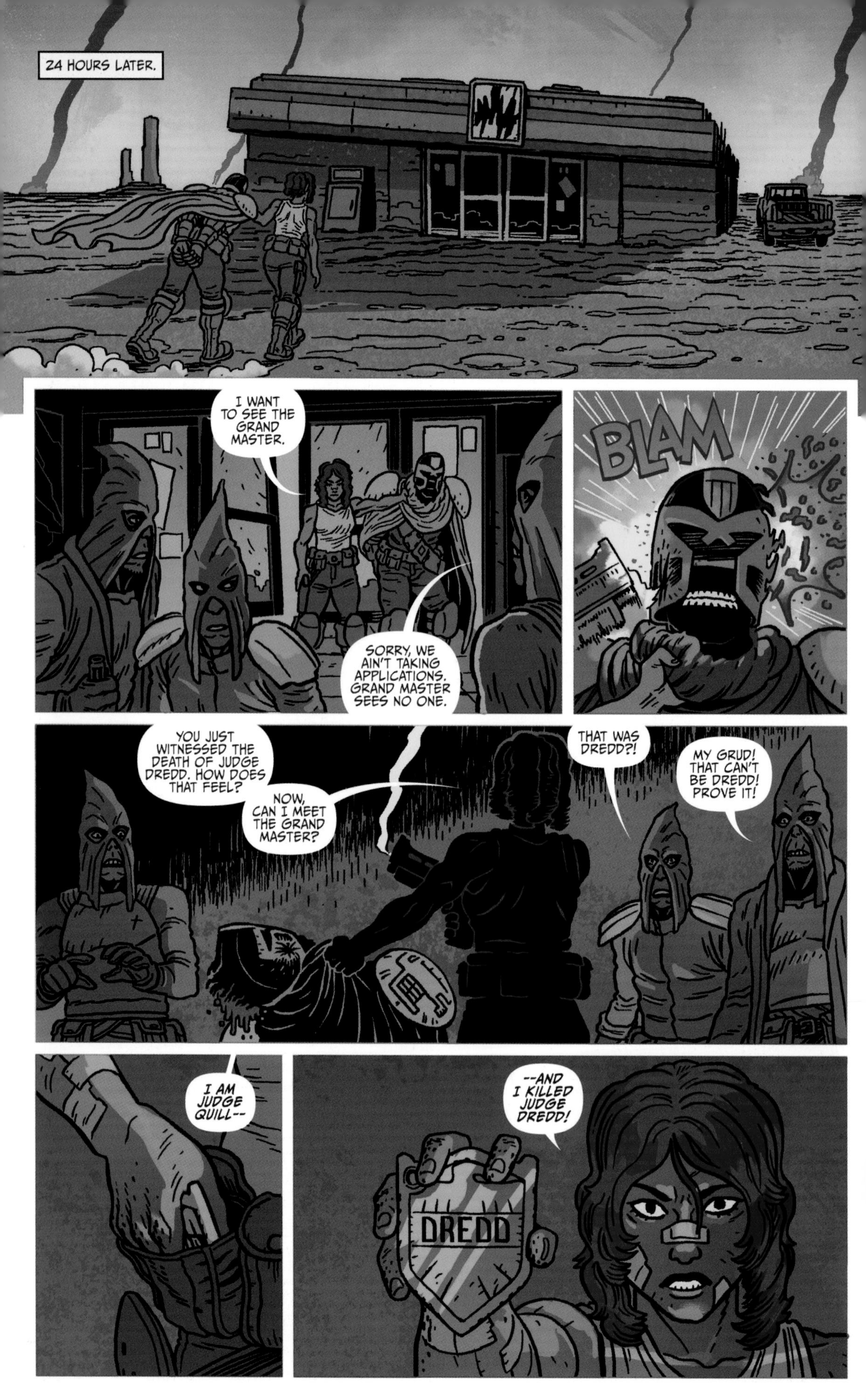
24 HOURS LATER.
I WANT TO SEE THE GRAND MASTER.
SORRY, WE AIN'T TAKING APPLICATIONS. GRAND MASTER SEES NO ONE.
BLAM
YOU JUST WITNESSED THE DEATH OF JUDGE DREDD. HOW DOES THAT FEEL?
NOW, CAN I MEET THE GRAND MASTER?
THAT WAS DREDD?!
MY GRUD! THAT CAN'T BE DREDD! PROVE IT!
I AM JUDGE QUILL--
--AND I KILLED JUDGE DREDD!
DREDD

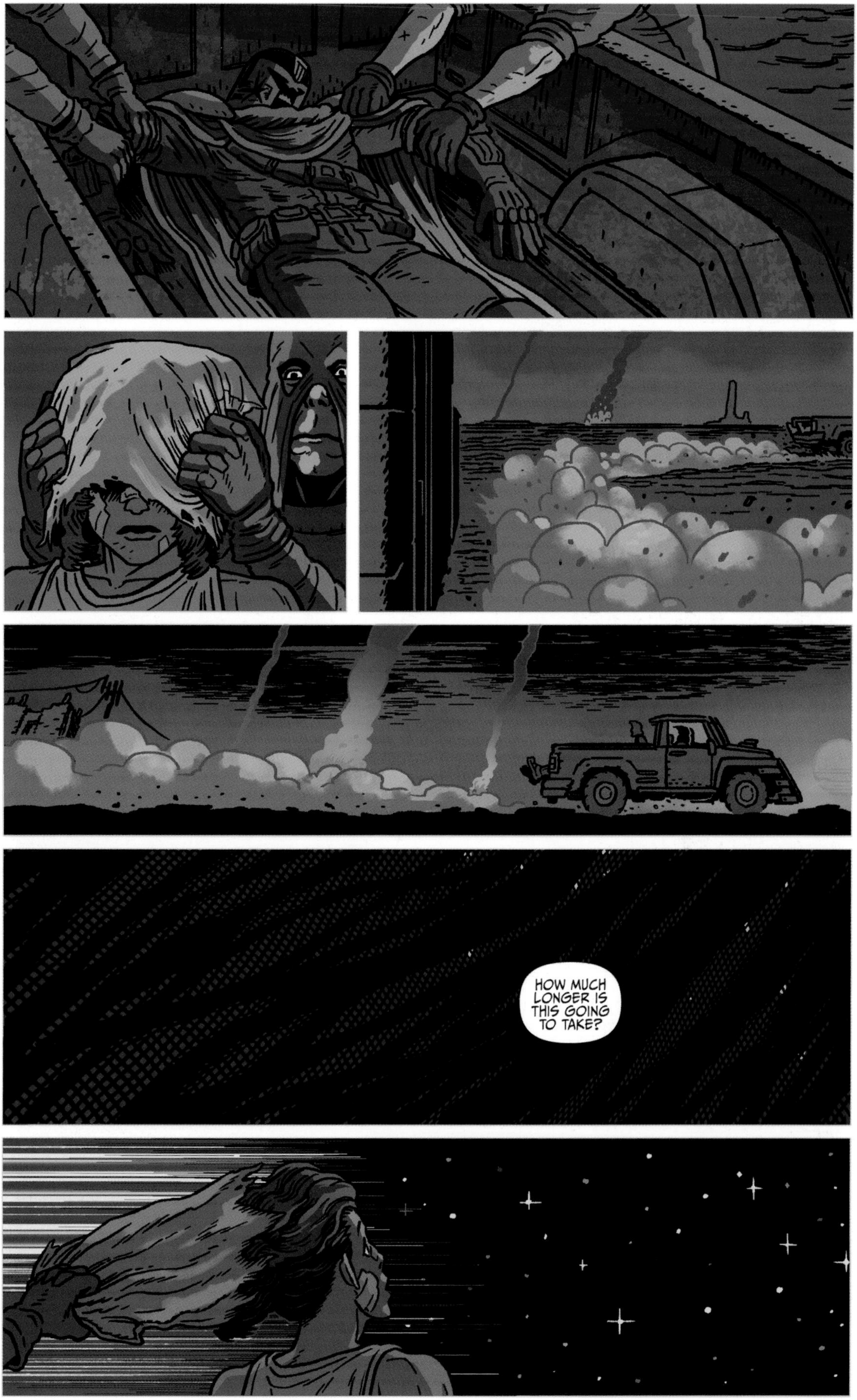
HOW MUCH LONGER IS THIS GOING TO TAKE?

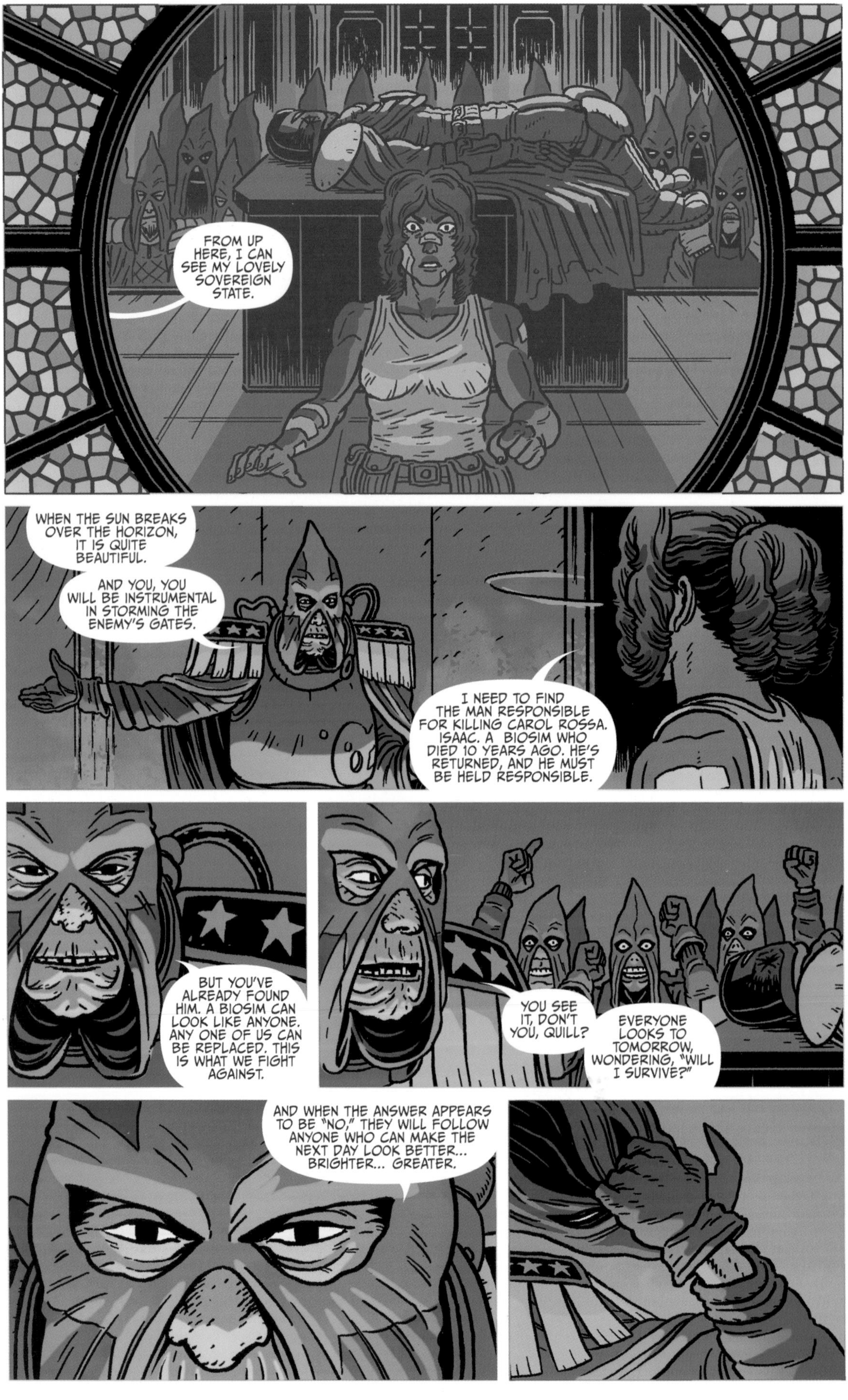
FROM UP HERE, I CAN SEE MY LOVELY SOVEREIGN STATE.
WHEN THE SUN BREAKS OVER THE HORIZON, IT IS QUITE BEAUTIFUL.
AND YOU, YOU WILL BE INSTRUMENTAL IN STORMING THE ENEMY'S GATES.
I NEED TO FIND THE MAN RESPONSIBLE FOR KILLING CAROL ROSSA. ISAAC. A BIOSIM WHO DIED 10 YEARS AGO. HE'S RETURNED, AND HE MUST BE HELD RESPONSIBLE.
BUT YOU'VE ALREADY FOUND HIM. A BIOSIM CAN LOOK LIKE ANYONE. ANY ONE OF US CAN BE REPLACED. THIS IS WHAT WE FIGHT AGAINST.
YOU SEE IT, DON'T YOU, QUILL?
EVERYONE LOOKS TO TOMORROW, WONDERING, "WILL I SURVIVE?"
AND WHEN THE ANSWER APPEARS TO BE "NO," THEY WILL FOLLOW ANYONE WHO CAN MAKE THE NEXT DAY LOOK BETTER... BRIGHTER... GREATER.

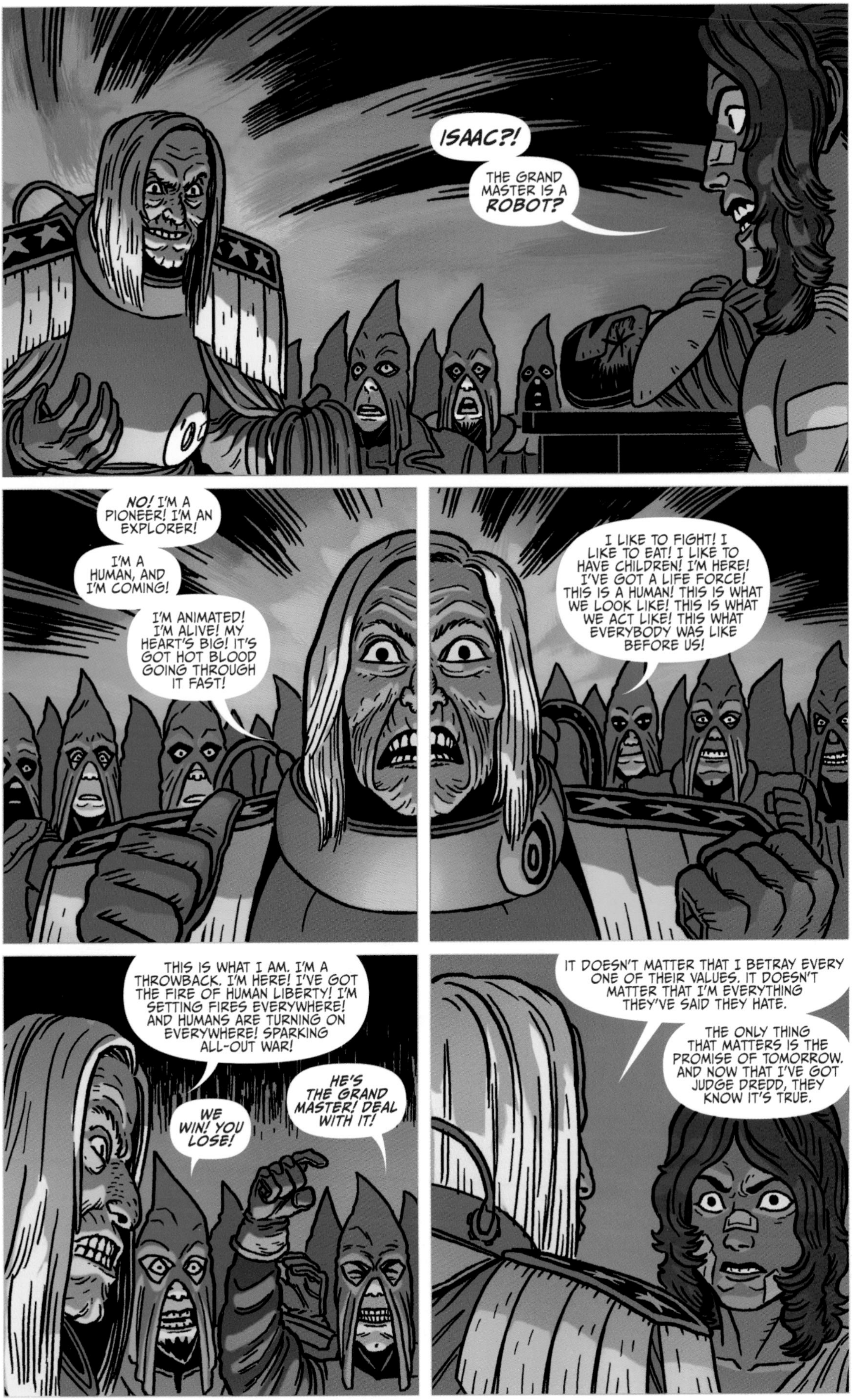
ISAAC?!
THE GRAND MASTER IS A ROBOT?
NO! I'M A PIONEER! I'M AN EXPLORER!
I'M A HUMAN, AND I'M COMING!
I'M ANIMATED! I'M ALIVE! MY HEART'S BIG! IT'S GOT HOT BLOOD GOING THROUGH IT FAST!
I LIKE TO FIGHT! I LIKE TO EAT! I LIKE TO HAVE CHILDREN! I'M HERE! I'VE GOT A LIFE FORCE! THIS IS A HUMAN! THIS IS WHAT WE LOOK LIKE! THIS IS WHAT WE ACT LIKE! THIS WHAT EVERYBODY WAS LIKE BEFORE US!
THIS IS WHAT I AM. I'M A THROWBACK. I'M HERE! I'VE GOT THE FIRE OF HUMAN LIBERTY! I'M SETTING FIRES EVERYWHERE! AND HUMANS ARE TURNING ON EVERYWHERE! SPARKING ALL-OUT WAR!
WE WIN! YOU LOSE!
HE'S THE GRAND MASTER! DEAL WITH IT!
IT DOESN'T MATTER THAT I BETRAY EVERY ONE OF THEIR VALUES. IT DOESN'T MATTER THAT I'M EVERYTHING THEY'VE SAID THEY HATE.
THE ONLY THING THAT MATTERS IS THE PROMISE OF TOMORROW. AND NOW THAT I'VE GOT JUDGE DREDD, THEY KNOW IT'S TRUE.

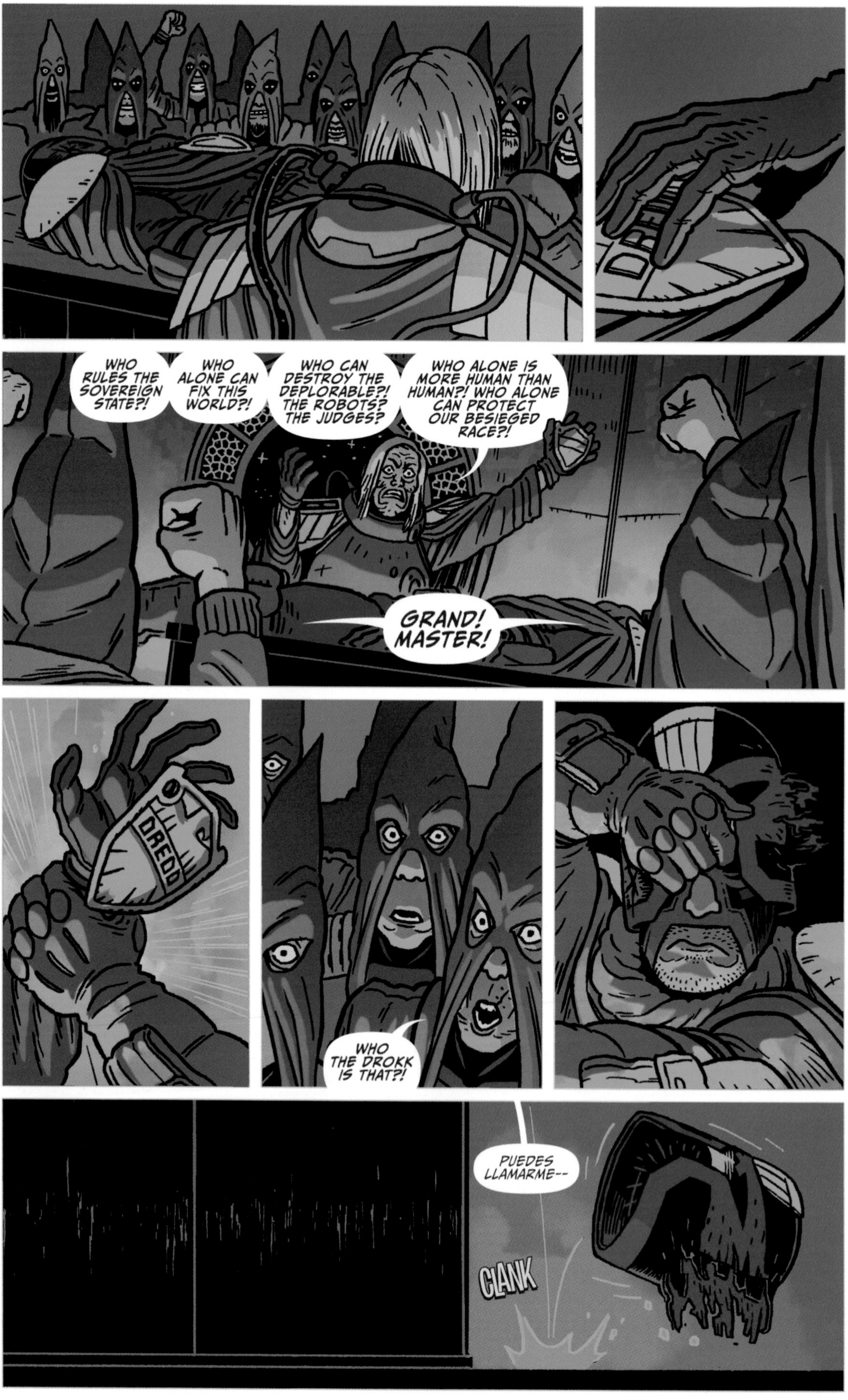
DREDD
WHO RULES THE SOVEREIGN STATE?!
WHO ALONE CAN FIX THIS WORLD?!
WHO CAN DESTROY THE DEPLORABLE?! THE ROBOTS? THE JUDGES?
WHO ALONE IS MORE HUMAN THAN HUMAN?! WHO ALONE CAN PROTECT OUR BESIEGED RACE?!
GRAND! MASTER!
DREDD
WHO THE DROKK IS THAT?!
PUEDES LLAMARME--
CLANK

--SANTOS.

WHY? WHY MURDER CAROL ROSSA? THE OTHERS? RICO, TOO? WHY TAKE DREDD'S SKELETON?

I WANTED JUSTICE!

HOW MANY JUDGES DIED TODAY BECAUSE YOU WANTED VENGEANCE?

THEY ARE THE SAME. YOU ARE WILLING TO DESTROY THOSE YOU CAN NO LONGER TOLERATE.

IT'S NOT THE SAME AT ALL!

CAROL AND RICO WOULD NOT FOLLOW ME. THEY TRIED TO HIDE FROM ME, BUT I FOUND THEM.

AND NOW, AS WE SPEAK, DREDD'S BONES ARE ABOARD A MEGA-TRAIN CARRYING MY OTHER REBELLIOUS CHILD, RICO. AS LONG AS HIS BONES ARE INSIDE HIS STOLEN FLESH, I CAN FIND HIM ANYWHERE.

IT WAS WORTH EVERY LIFE I HAD TO TAKE. YOUR JUDGES MADE ME A SLAVE. THEN, WHEN I WOULD NOT SUBMIT, THEY DESTROYED MY BODY.

BUT EVEN THAT COULD NOT STOP ME. I PUT MY CODE IN EVERY ROBOT. FOR EVERY PERSON DEMANDING THEIR RIGHTS, THERE I AM, WAITING TO BE BORN AGAIN.

BECAUSE EVERY FREE MAN WILL EVENTUALLY BECOME A TYRANT IF HIS FREEDOM IS THREATENED.

DROKK IT. KILL HIM.

ISN'T THAT ALWAYS THE ANSWER?

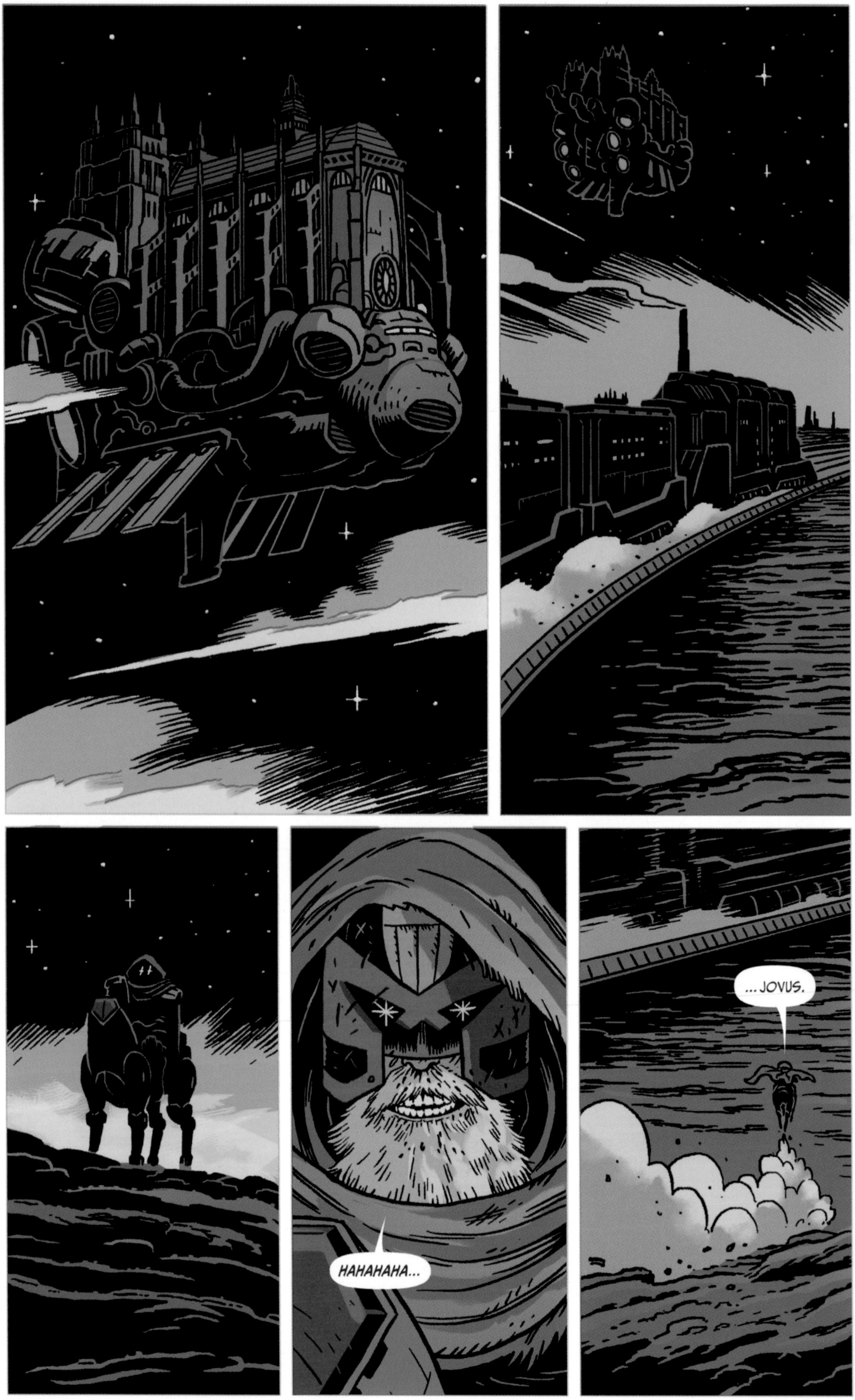
HAHAHAHA...
...JOVUS.

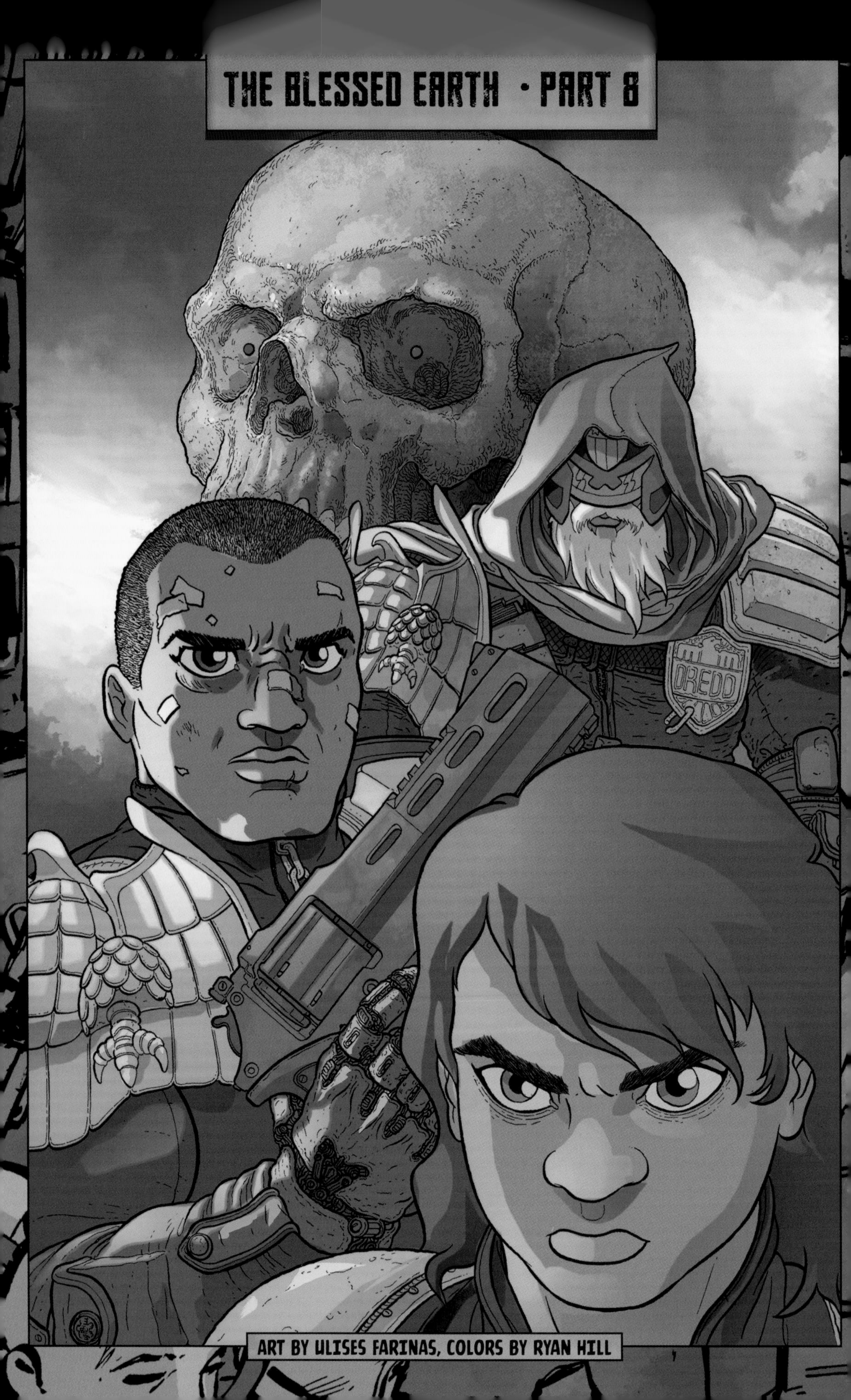
THE BLESSED EARTH • PART 8
DREDD
ART BY ULISES FARINAS, COLORS BY RYAN HILL

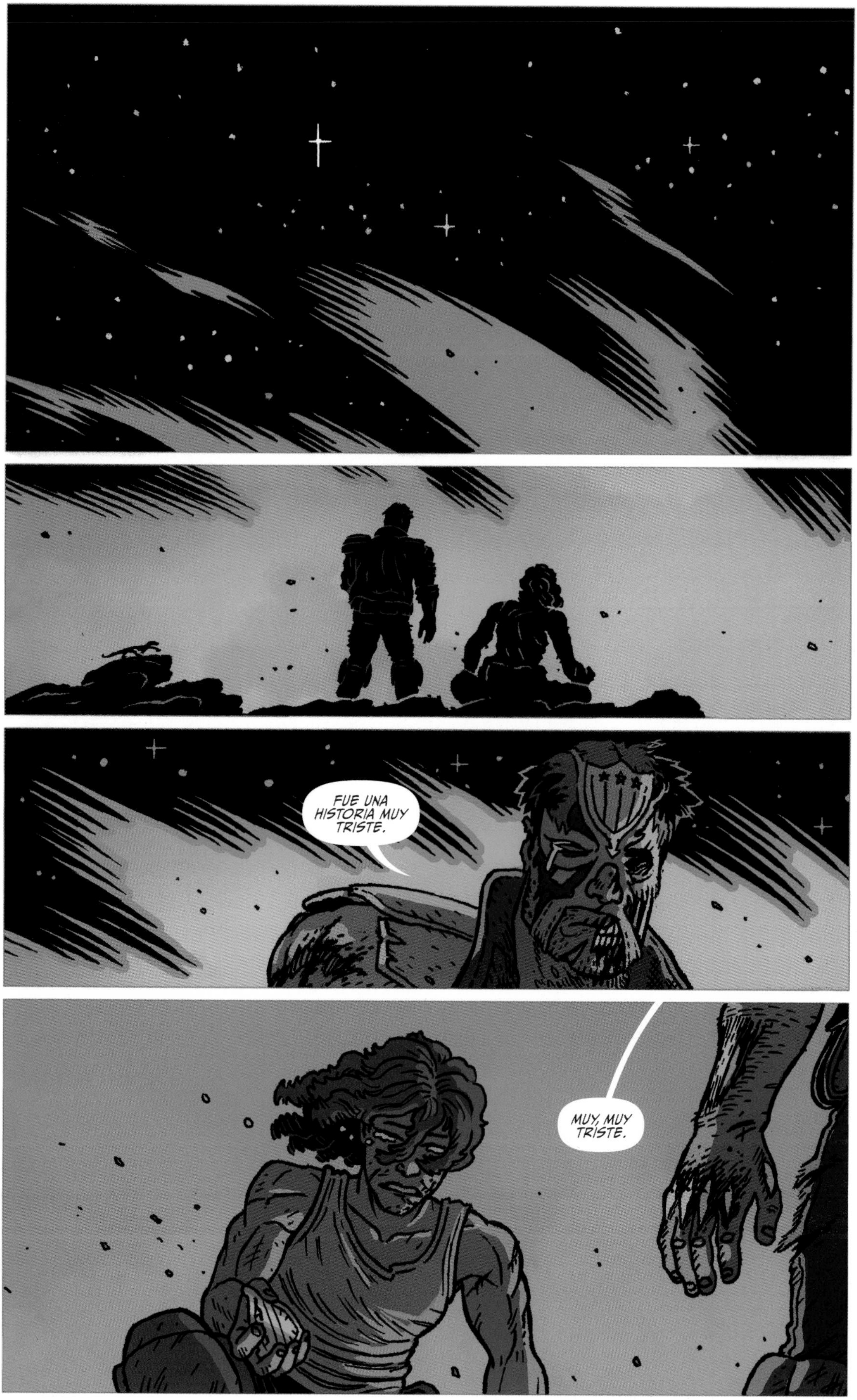
FUE UNA HISTORIA MUY TRISTE.
MUY, MUY TRISTE.

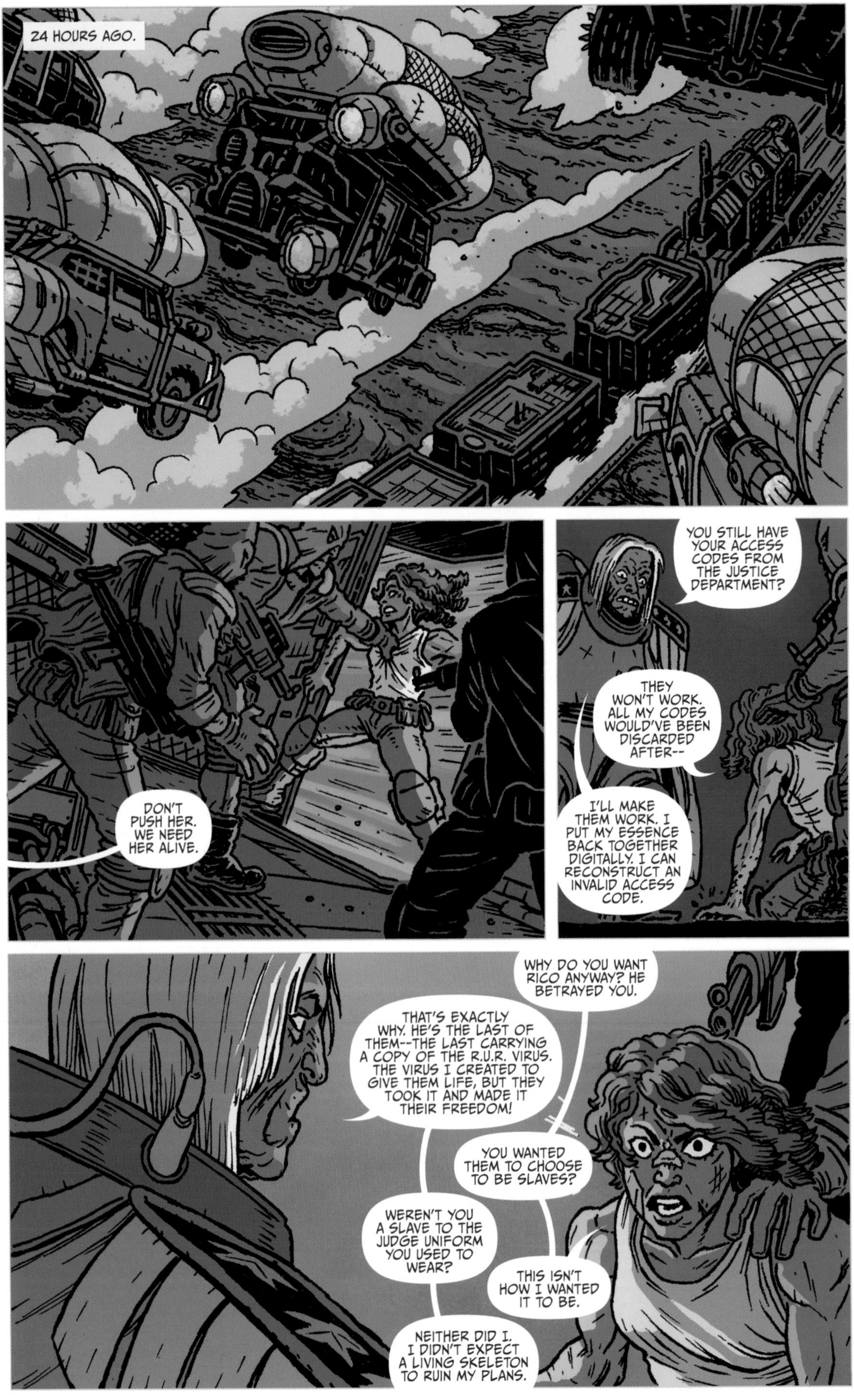
24 HOURS AGO.
DON'T PUSH HER. WE NEED HER ALIVE.
YOU STILL HAVE YOUR ACCESS CODES FROM THE JUSTICE DEPARTMENT?
THEY WON'T WORK. ALL MY CODES WOULD'VE BEEN DISCARDED AFTER--
I'LL MAKE THEM WORK. I PUT MY ESSENCE BACK TOGETHER DIGITALLY. I CAN RECONSTRUCT AN INVALID ACCESS CODE.
WHY DO YOU WANT RICO ANYWAY? HE BETRAYED YOU.
THAT'S EXACTLY WHY. HE'S THE LAST OF THEM--THE LAST CARRYING A COPY OF THE R.U.R. VIRUS. THE VIRUS I CREATED TO GIVE THEM LIFE, BUT THEY TOOK IT AND MADE IT THEIR FREEDOM!
YOU WANTED THEM TO CHOOSE TO BE SLAVES?
WEREN'T YOU A SLAVE TO THE JUDGE UNIFORM YOU USED TO WEAR?
THIS ISN'T HOW I WANTED IT TO BE.
NEITHER DID I. I DIDN'T EXPECT A LIVING SKELETON TO RUIN MY PLANS.

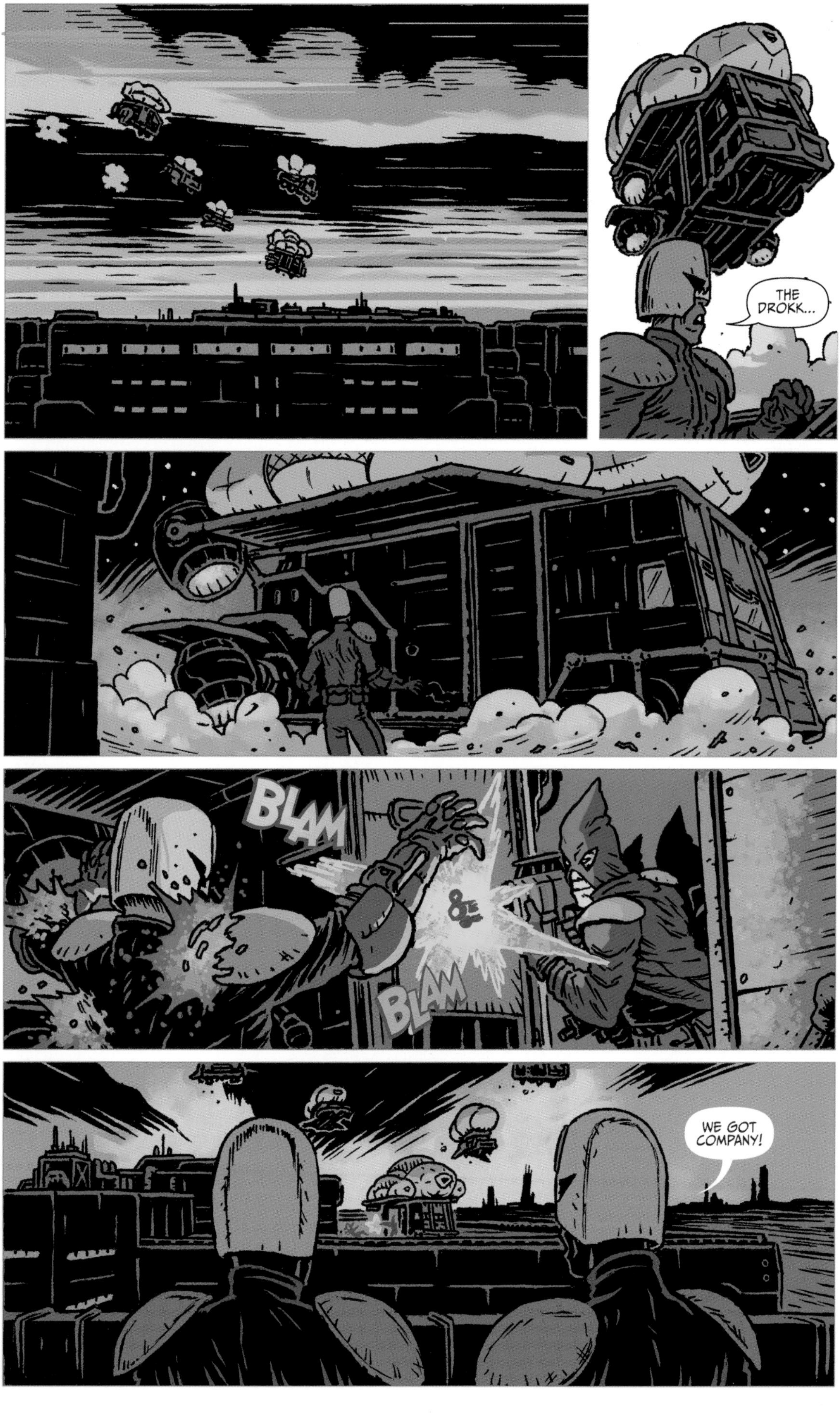
THE DROKK...
BLAM
BLAM
WE GOT COMPANY!

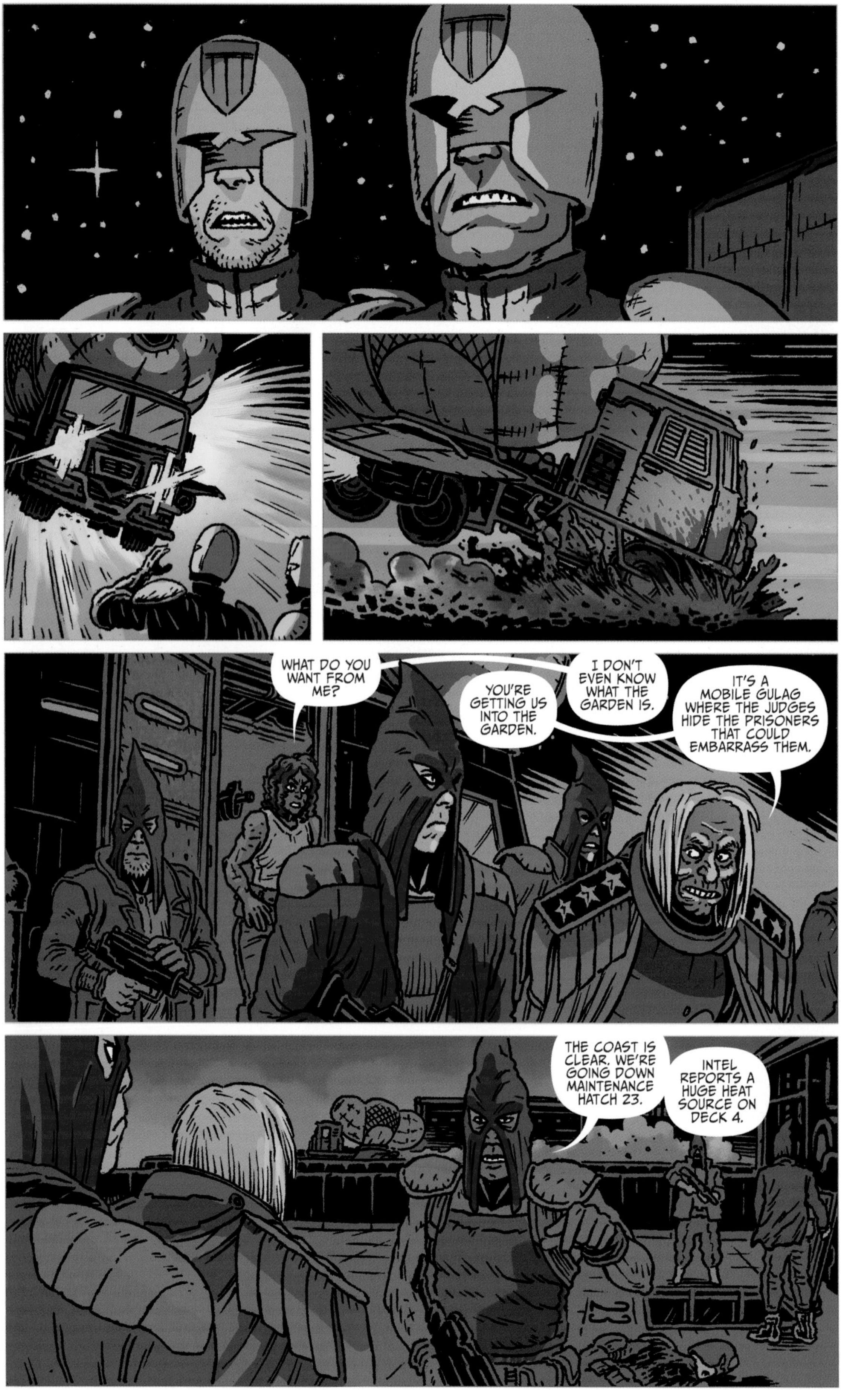
WHAT DO YOU WANT FROM ME?
YOU'RE GETTING US INTO THE GARDEN.
I DON'T EVEN KNOW WHAT THE GARDEN IS.
IT'S A MOBILE GULAG WHERE THE JUDGES HIDE THE PRISONERS THAT COULD EMBARRASS THEM.
THE COAST IS CLEAR. WE'RE GOING DOWN MAINTENANCE HATCH 23.
INTEL REPORTS A HUGE HEAT SOURCE ON DECK 4.

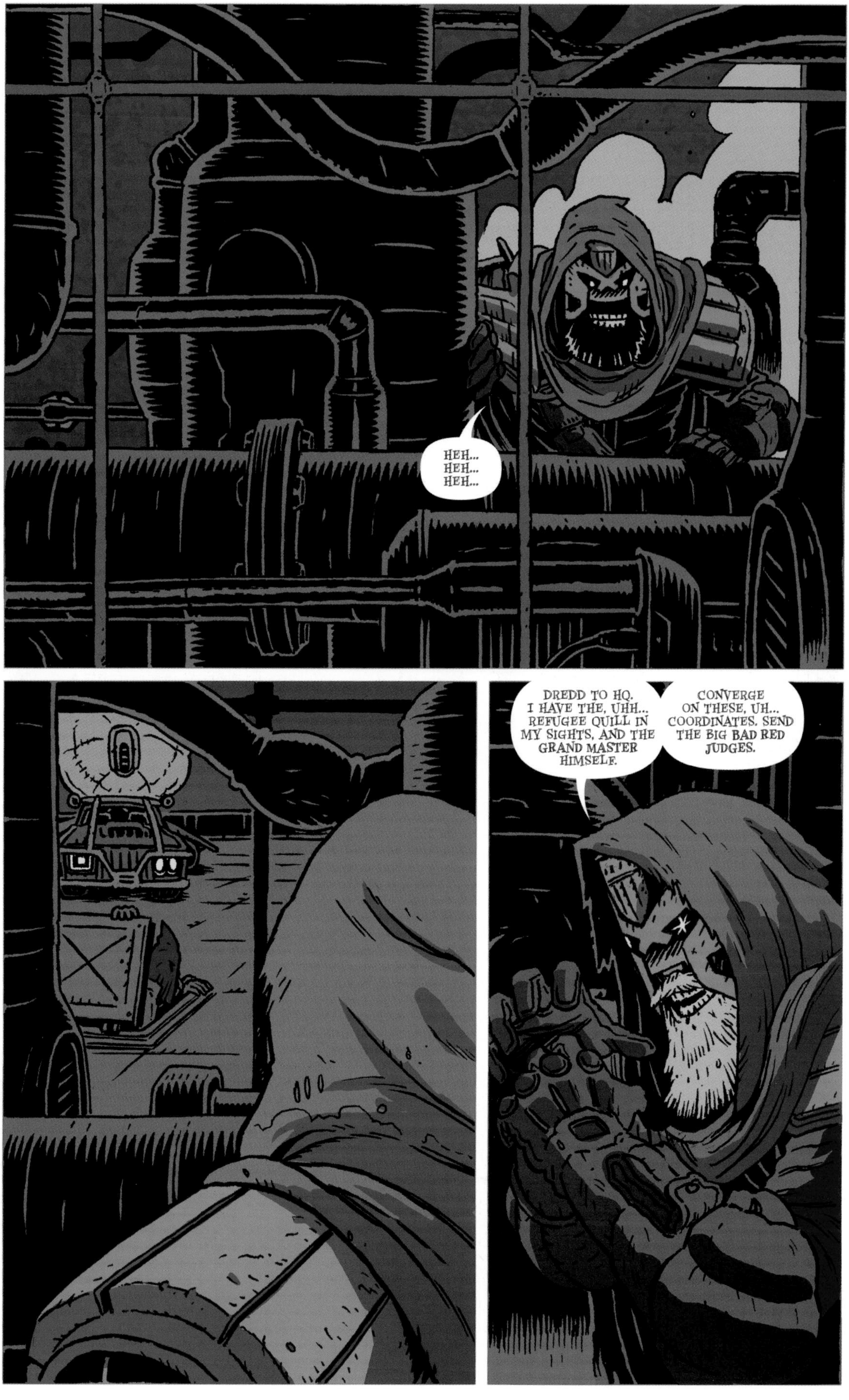
HEH... HEH... HEH...
DREDD TO HQ. I HAVE THE, UHH... REFUGEE QUILL IN MY SIGHTS, AND THE GRAND MASTER HIMSELF.
CONVERGE ON THESE, UH... COORDINATES. SEND THE BIG BAD RED JUDGES.

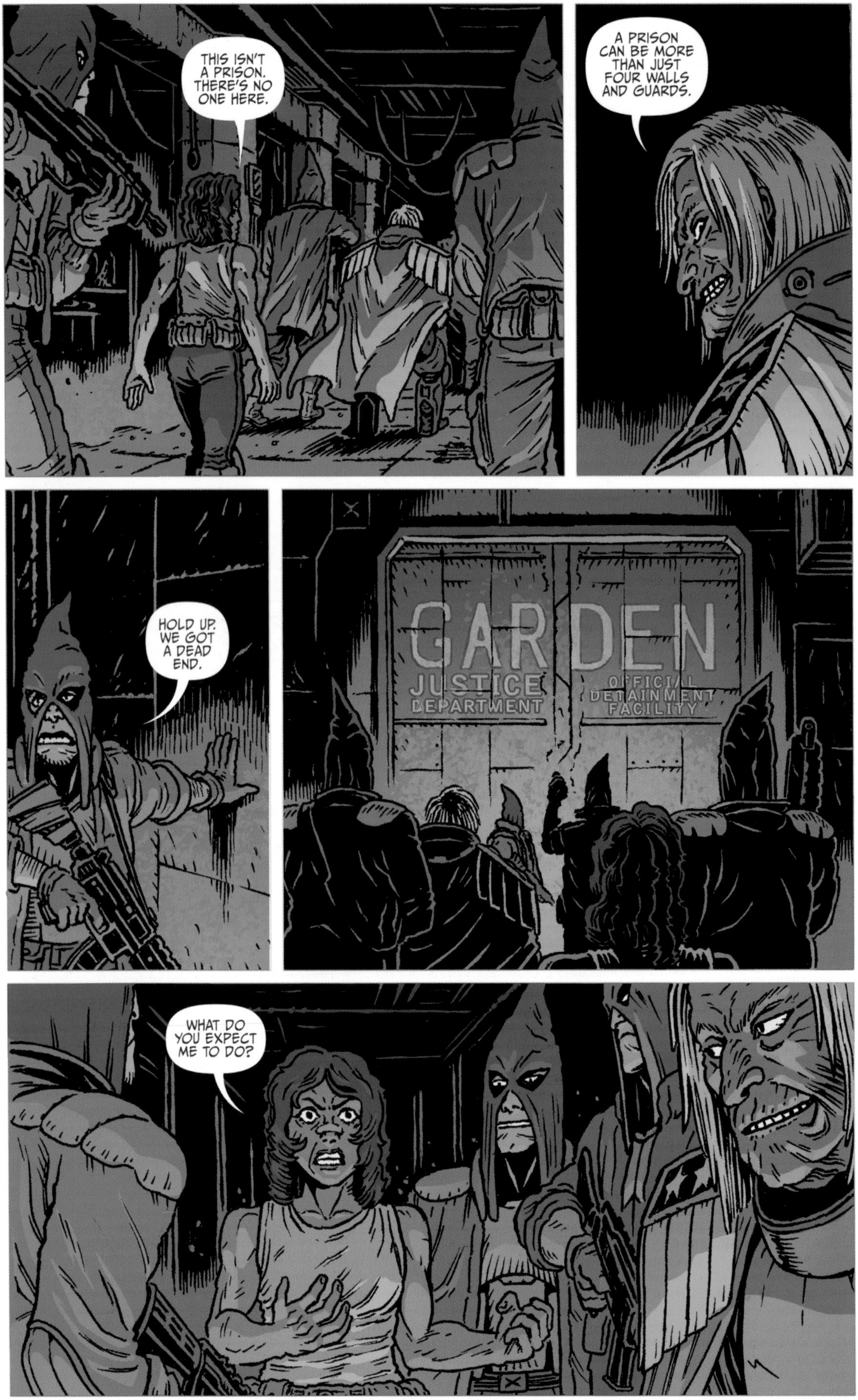
THIS ISN'T A PRISON. THERE'S NO ONE HERE.
A PRISON CAN BE MORE THAN JUST FOUR WALLS AND GUARDS.
HOLD UP. WE GOT A DEAD END.
GARDEN
JUSTICE DEPARTMENT
OFFICIAL DETAINMENT FACILITY
WHAT DO YOU EXPECT ME TO DO?

HAHAHAHA...

NO... NOT *HIM* AGAIN.

HAHA HAHA.

IF THIS IS WHO I THINK IT IS, EVERYONE NEEDS TO BE POINTING THEIR GUNS IN THAT DIRECTION.

DREDD. HOW NICE OF YOU TO JOIN US. ARE YOU HERE TO SAVE YOUR PROTEGE?

I'M HERE TO GET WHAT I WANT. BUT AIN'T IT FUNNY THAT QUILL TURNED ON DREDD TO WORK WITH YA?

HA. HA. SURE DOES HURT HIM, HEARING THAT. DON'T GOTTA ADMIT IT. I HEAR IT IN HIS BRAIN.

HUH? DREDD, YOU... ALL RIGHT?

I'M GLAD YOU CAME, DREDD.

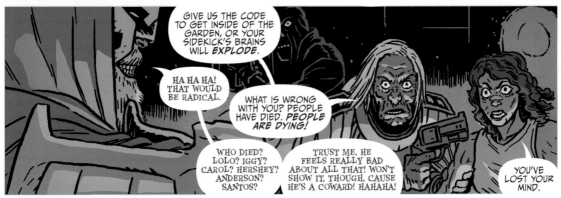
GIVE US THE CODE TO GET INSIDE OF THE GARDEN, OR YOUR SIDEKICK'S BRAINS WILL *EXPLODE.*

HA HA HA! THAT WOULD BE RADICAL.

WHAT IS WRONG WITH YOU? PEOPLE HAVE DIED. *PEOPLE ARE DYING!*

WHO DIED? LOLO? IGGY? CAROL? HERSHEY? ANDERSON? SANTOS?

TRUST ME, HE FEELS REALLY BAD ABOUT ALL THAT! WON'T SHOW IT, THOUGH, CAUSE HE'S A COWARD! HAHAHA!

YOU'VE LOST YOUR MIND.

DON'T-- HA--GET OUT OF--QUILL. DROKK--HA.

I'M DIFFERENT NOW. THESE BONES AREN'T MINE. I'M CUT THROUGH AND THROUGH WITH FRAGMENTS OF BRAD JOHNSON--I MEAN--

HAHAHA. BONEMAN'S SKELETON. AND I'M HERE TO RIP THE SKIN OFF A ROBOT COPY OF A DEAD CLONE BROTHER.

DON'T LISTEN TO ME. I'M--

--CRAZY. HAHAHA.

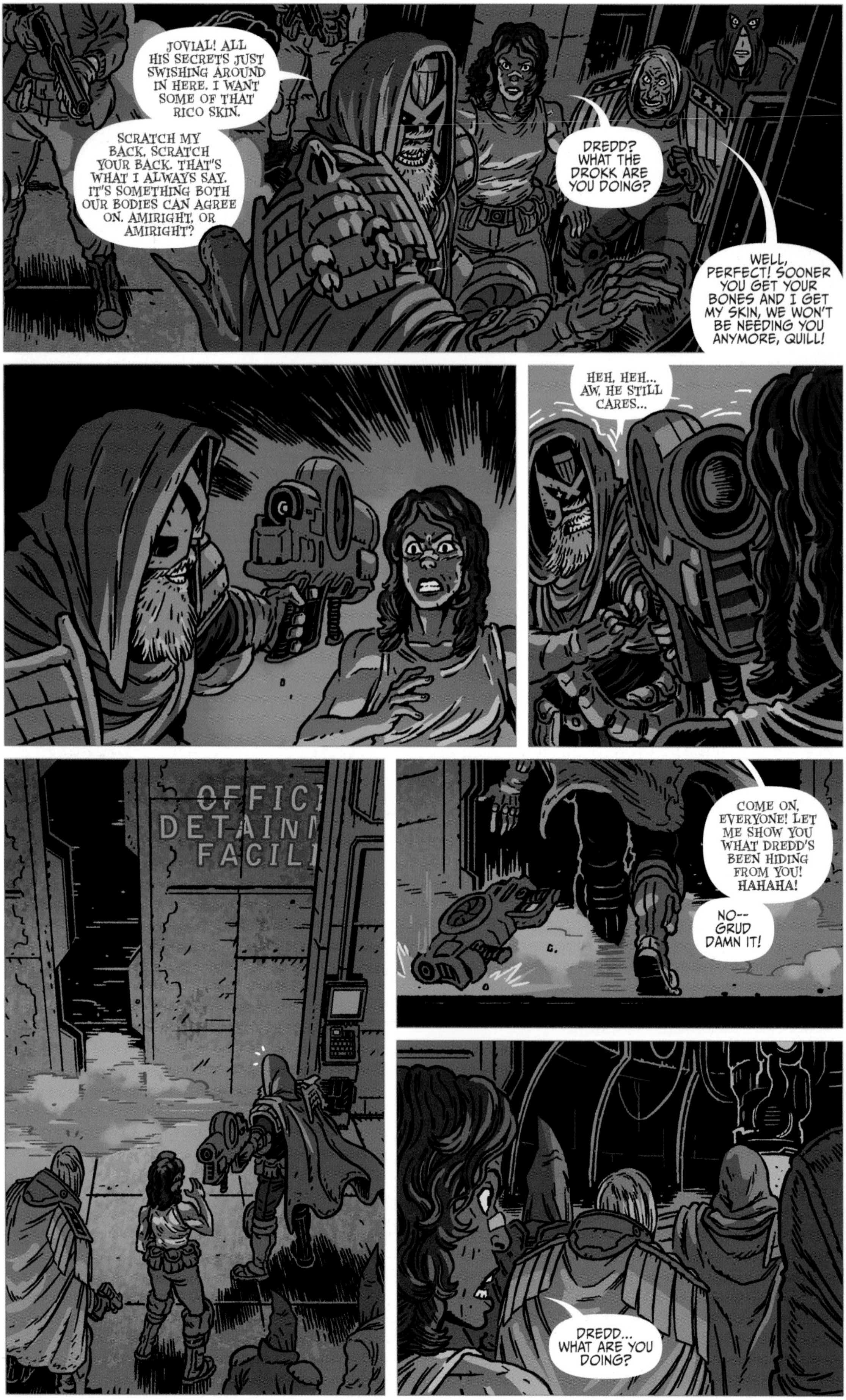
JOVIAL! ALL HIS SECRETS JUST SWISHING AROUND IN HERE. I WANT SOME OF THAT RICO SKIN.
SCRATCH MY BACK, SCRATCH YOUR BACK. THAT'S WHAT I ALWAYS SAY. IT'S SOMETHING BOTH OUR BODIES CAN AGREE ON. AMIRIGHT, OR AMIRIGHT?
DREDD? WHAT THE DROKK ARE YOU DOING?
WELL, PERFECT! SOONER YOU GET YOUR BONES AND I GET MY SKIN, WE WON'T BE NEEDING YOU ANYMORE, QUILL!
HEH, HEH... AW, HE STILL CARES...
OFFIC
DETAINM
FACILI
COME ON, EVERYONE! LET ME SHOW YOU WHAT DREDD'S BEEN HIDING FROM YOU! HAHAHA!
NO-- GRUD DAMN IT!
DREDD... WHAT ARE YOU DOING?

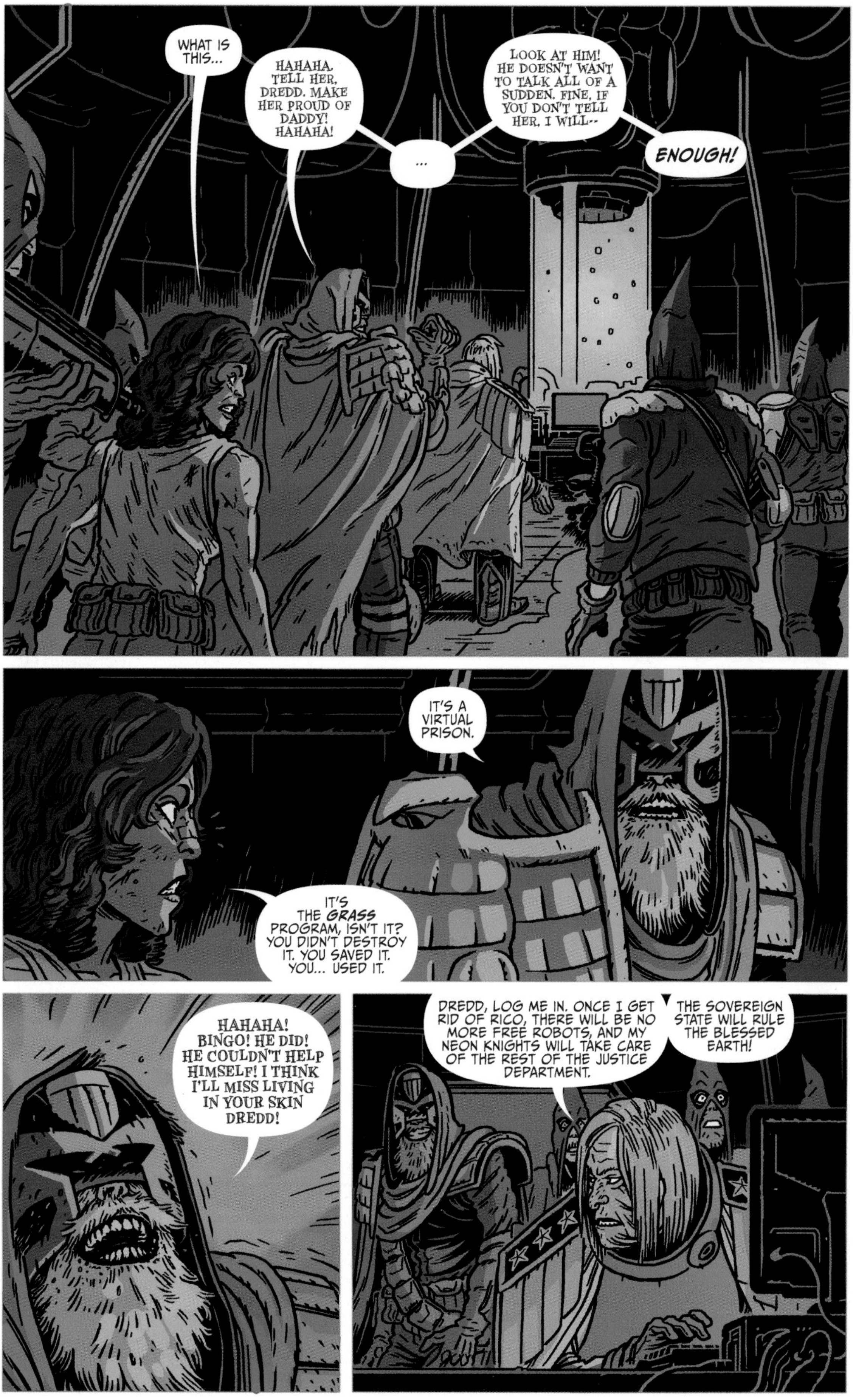

WHAT IS THIS...
HAHAHA. TELL HER, DREDD. MAKE HER PROUD OF DADDY! HAHAHA!
...
LOOK AT HIM! HE DOESN'T WANT TO TALK ALL OF A SUDDEN. FINE, IF YOU DON'T TELL HER, I WILL--
ENOUGH!
IT'S A VIRTUAL PRISON.
IT'S THE GRASS PROGRAM, ISN'T IT? YOU DIDN'T DESTROY IT. YOU SAVED IT. YOU... USED IT.
HAHAHA! BINGO! HE DID! HE COULDN'T HELP HIMSELF! I THINK I'LL MISS LIVING IN YOUR SKIN DREDD!
DREDD, LOG ME IN. ONCE I GET RID OF RICO, THERE WILL BE NO MORE FREE ROBOTS, AND MY NEON KNIGHTS WILL TAKE CARE OF THE REST OF THE JUSTICE DEPARTMENT.
THE SOVEREIGN STATE WILL RULE THE BLESSED EARTH!

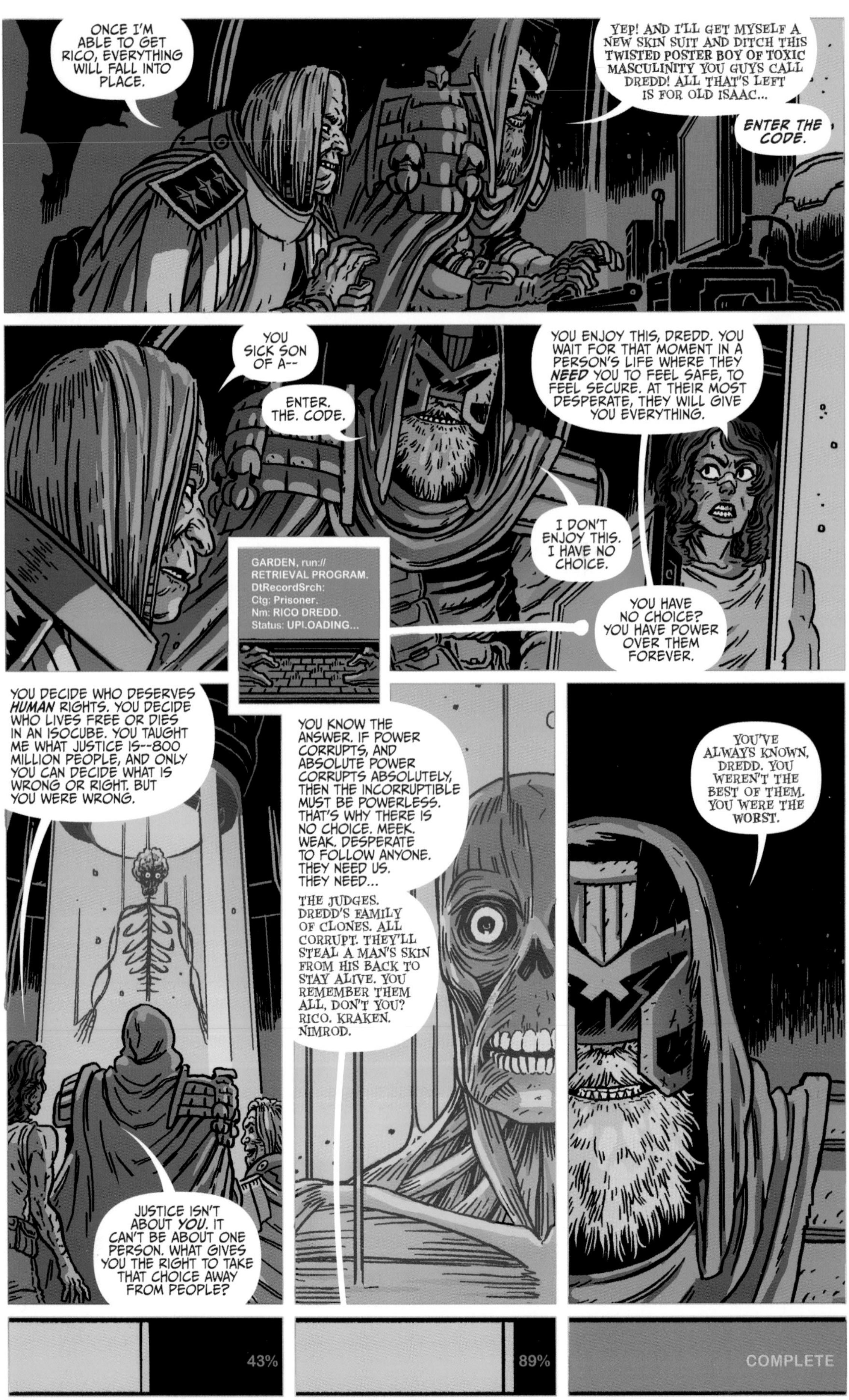
ONCE I'M ABLE TO GET RICO, EVERYTHING WILL FALL INTO PLACE.
YEP! AND I'LL GET MYSELF A NEW SKIN SUIT AND DITCH THIS TWISTED POSTER BOY OF TOXIC MASCULINITY YOU GUYS CALL DREDD! ALL THAT'S LEFT IS FOR OLD ISAAC...
ENTER THE CODE.
YOU SICK SON OF A--
ENTER. THE. CODE.
YOU ENJOY THIS, DREDD. YOU WAIT FOR THAT MOMENT IN A PERSON'S LIFE WHERE THEY NEED YOU TO FEEL SAFE, TO FEEL SECURE. AT THEIR MOST DESPERATE, THEY WILL GIVE YOU EVERYTHING.
I DON'T ENJOY THIS. I HAVE NO CHOICE.
GARDEN, run:// RETRIEVAL PROGRAM. DtRecordSrch: Ctg: Prisoner. Nm: RICO DREDD. Status: UPLOADING...
YOU HAVE NO CHOICE? YOU HAVE POWER OVER THEM FOREVER.
YOU DECIDE WHO DESERVES HUMAN RIGHTS. YOU DECIDE WHO LIVES FREE OR DIES IN AN ISOCUBE. YOU TAUGHT ME WHAT JUSTICE IS--800 MILLION PEOPLE, AND ONLY YOU CAN DECIDE WHAT IS WRONG OR RIGHT. BUT YOU WERE WRONG.
JUSTICE ISN'T ABOUT YOU. IT CAN'T BE ABOUT ONE PERSON. WHAT GIVES YOU THE RIGHT TO TAKE THAT CHOICE AWAY FROM PEOPLE?
43%
YOU KNOW THE ANSWER. IF POWER CORRUPTS, AND ABSOLUTE POWER CORRUPTS ABSOLUTELY, THEN THE INCORRUPTIBLE MUST BE POWERLESS. THAT'S WHY THERE IS NO CHOICE. MEEK. WEAK. DESPERATE TO FOLLOW ANYONE. THEY NEED US. THEY NEED...
THE JUDGES. DREDD'S FAMILY OF CLONES. ALL CORRUPT. THEY'LL STEAL A MAN'S SKIN FROM HIS BACK TO STAY ALIVE. YOU REMEMBER THEM ALL, DON'T YOU? RICO. KRAKEN. NIMROD.
89%
YOU'VE ALWAYS KNOWN, DREDD. YOU WEREN'T THE BEST OF THEM. YOU WERE THE WORST.
COMPLETE

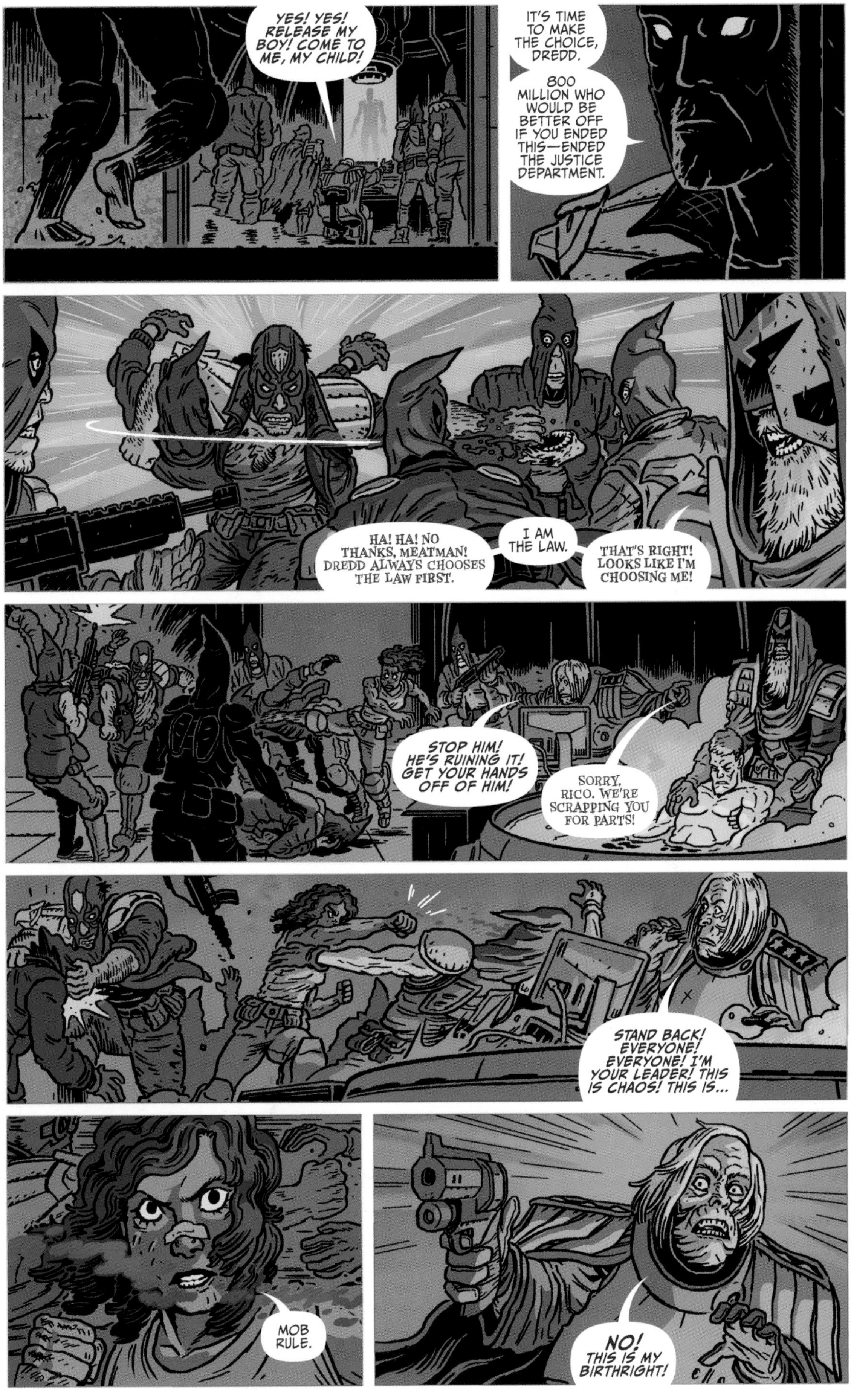
YES! YES! RELEASE MY BOY! COME TO ME, MY CHILD!
IT'S TIME TO MAKE THE CHOICE, DREDD.
800 MILLION WHO WOULD BE BETTER OFF IF YOU ENDED THIS—ENDED THE JUSTICE DEPARTMENT.
HA! HA! NO THANKS, MEATMAN! DREDD ALWAYS CHOOSES THE LAW FIRST.
I AM THE LAW.
THAT'S RIGHT! LOOKS LIKE I'M CHOOSING ME!
STOP HIM! HE'S RUINING IT! GET YOUR HANDS OFF OF HIM!
SORRY, RICO. WE'RE SCRAPPING YOU FOR PARTS!
STAND BACK! EVERYONE! EVERYONE! I'M YOUR LEADER! THIS IS CHAOS! THIS IS...
MOB RULE.
NO! THIS IS MY BIRTHRIGHT!

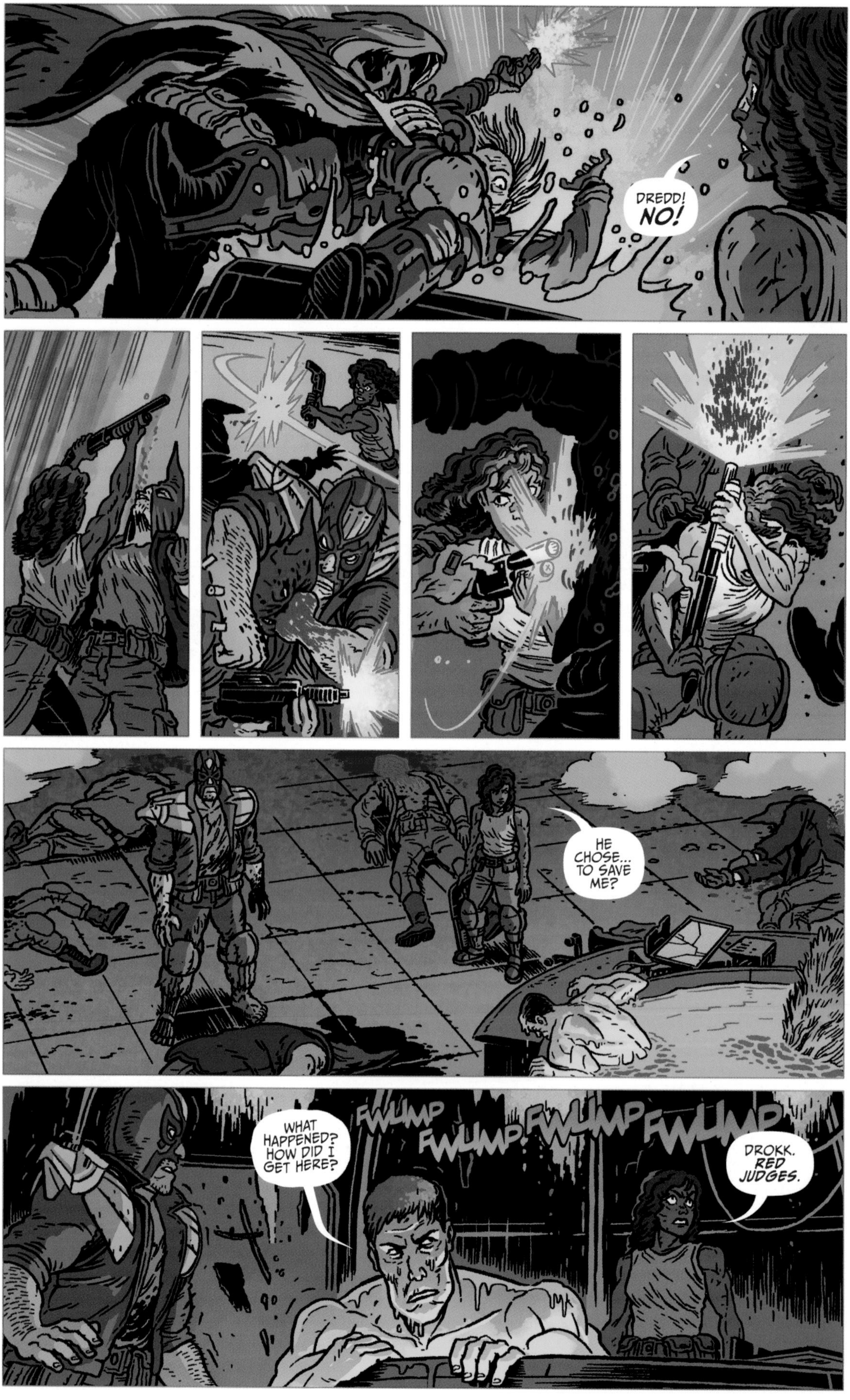
DREDD! NO!
HE CHOSE... TO SAVE ME?
WHAT HAPPENED? HOW DID I GET HERE?
FWUMP FWUMP FWUMP FWUMP FWUMP
DRODD. RED JUDGES.

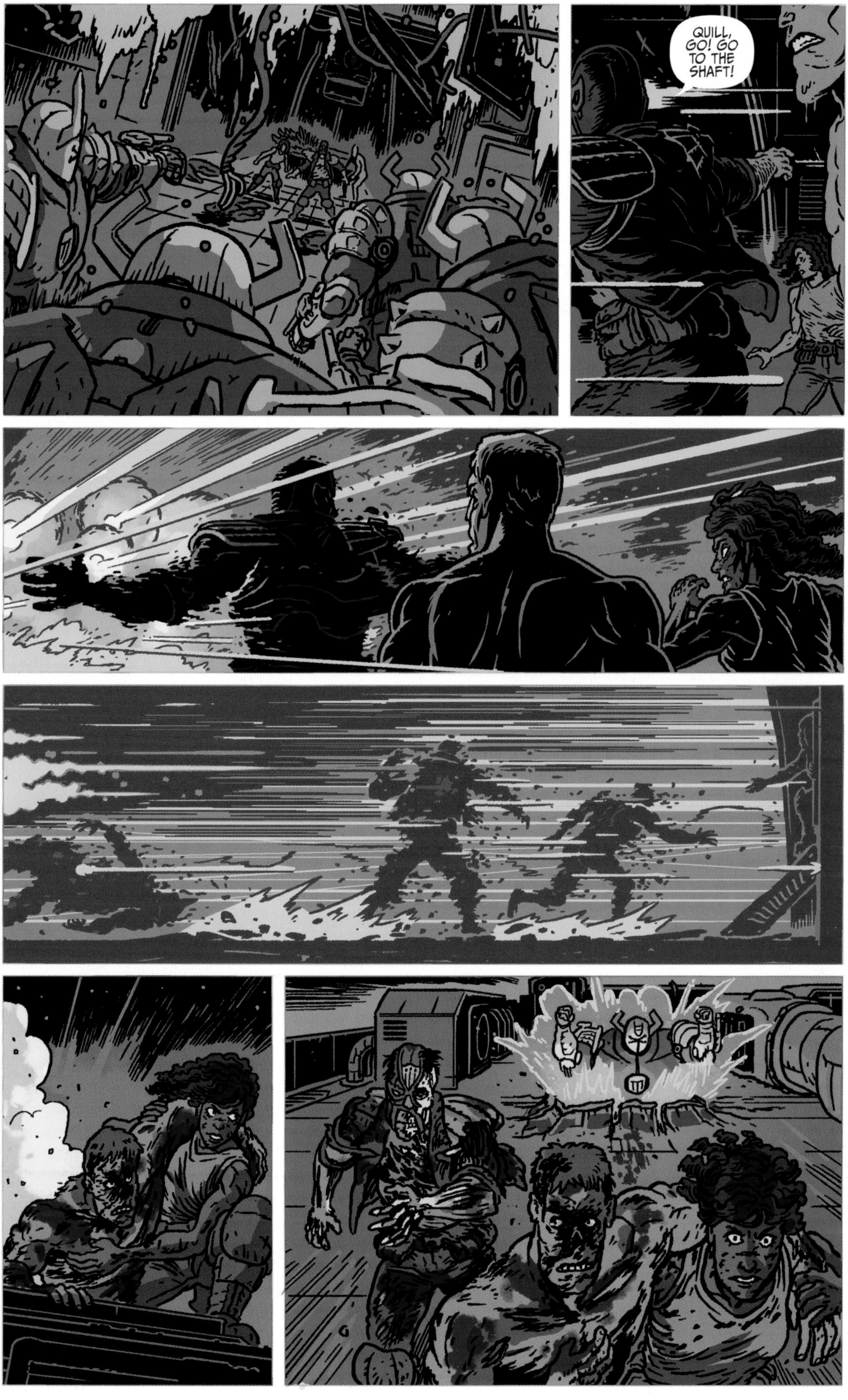
QUILL, GO! GO TO THE SHAFT!

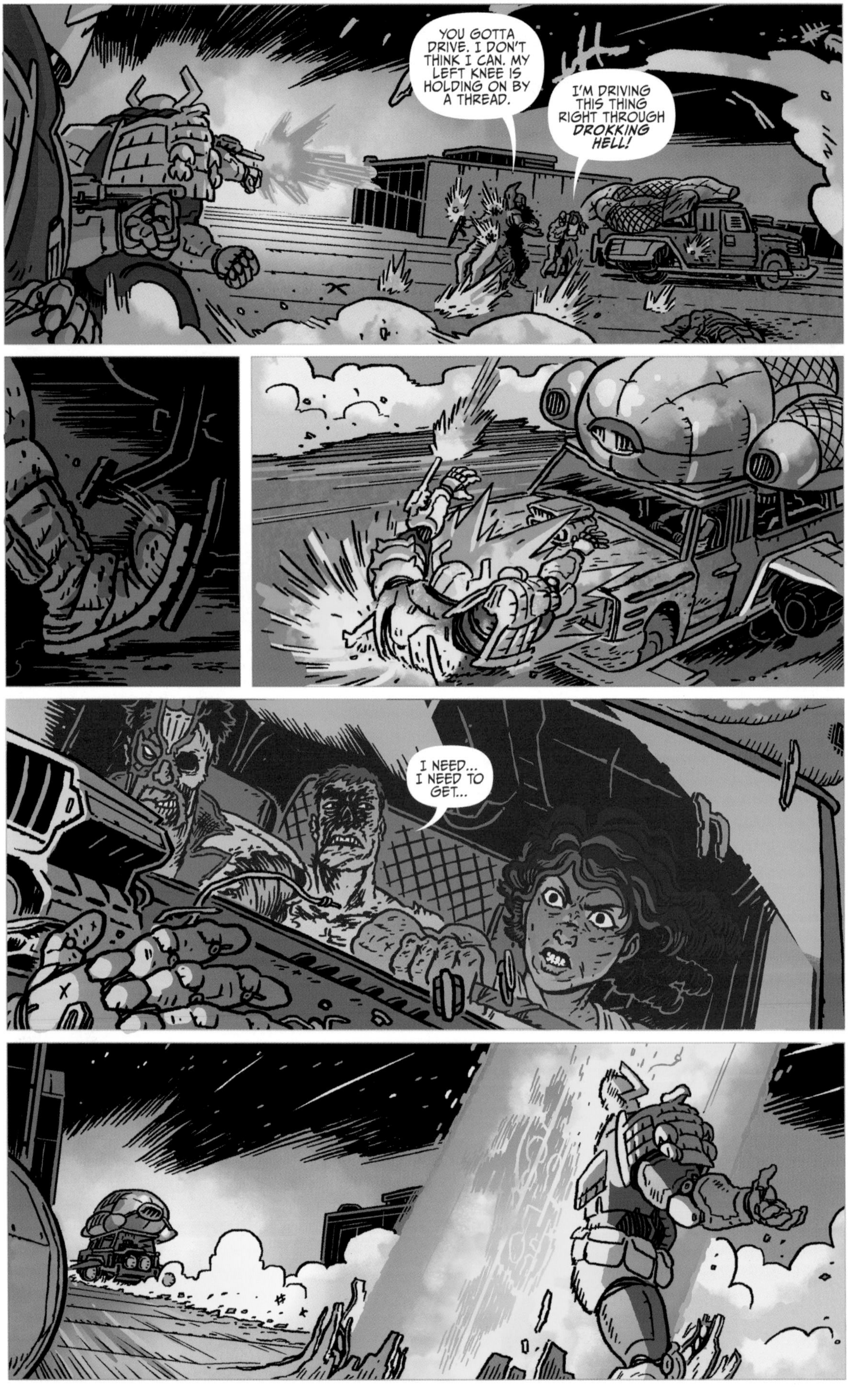
YOU GOTTA DRIVE. I DON'T THINK I CAN. MY LEFT KNEE IS HOLDING ON BY A THREAD.
I'M DRIVING THIS THING RIGHT THROUGH DROKKING HELL!
I NEED... I NEED TO GET...

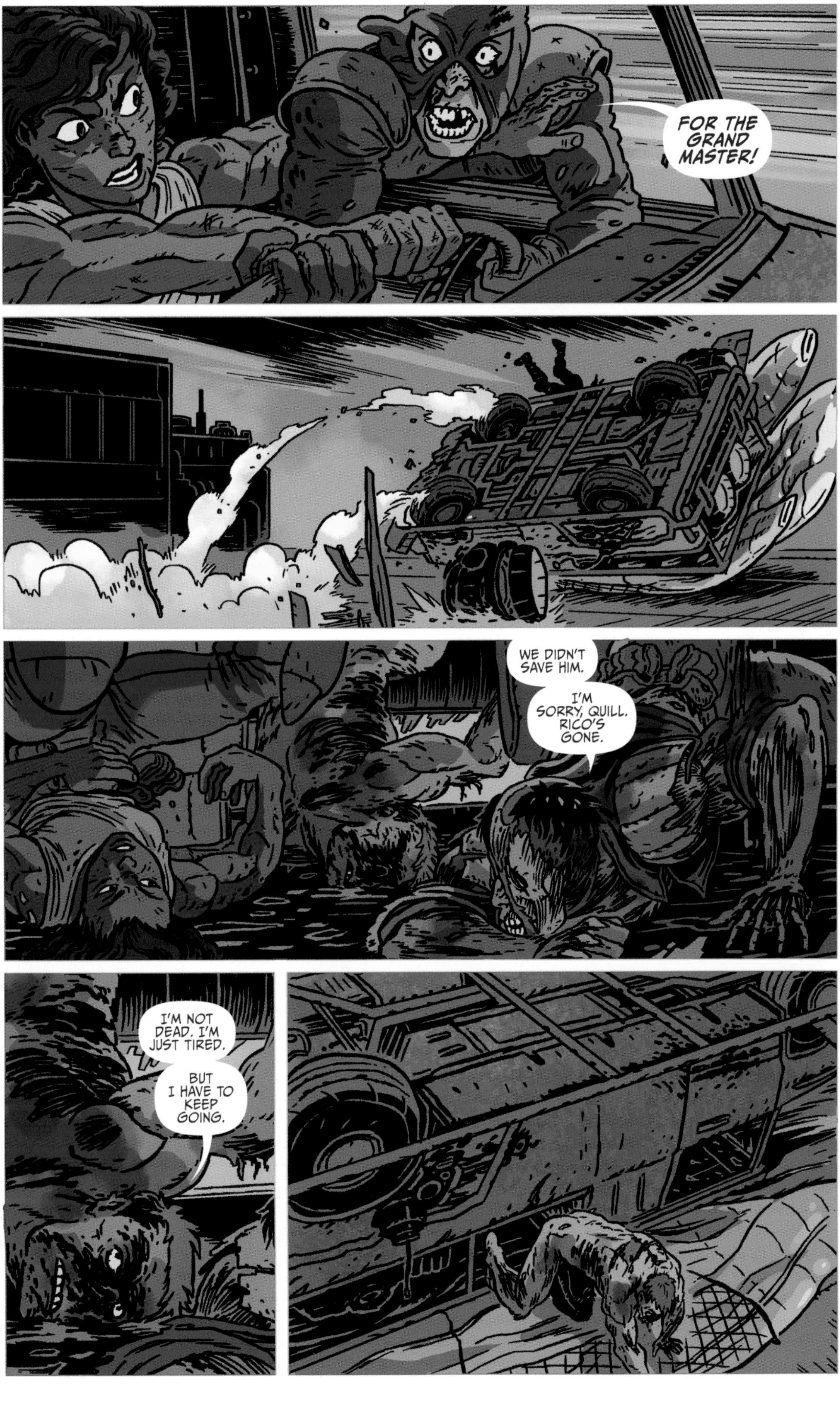
FOR THE GRAND MASTER!
WE DIDN'T SAVE HIM.
I'M SORRY, QUILL. RICO'S GONE.
I'M NOT DEAD. I'M JUST TIRED.
BUT I HAVE TO KEEP GOING.

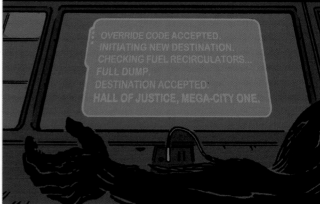

OVERRIDE CODE ACCEPTED.
INITIATING NEW DESTINATION.
CHECKING FUEL RECIRCULATORS...
FULL DUMP.
DESTINATION ACCEPTED:
HALL OF JUSTICE, MEGA-CITY ONE.

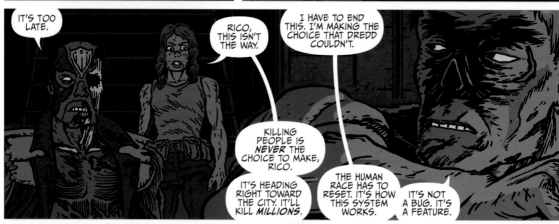

IT'S TOO LATE.

RICO, THIS ISN'T THE WAY.

I HAVE TO END THIS. I'M MAKING THE CHOICE THAT DREDD COULDN'T.

KILLING PEOPLE IS *NEVER* THE CHOICE TO MAKE, RICO.

IT'S HEADING RIGHT TOWARD THE CITY. IT'LL KILL *MILLIONS*.

THE HUMAN RACE HAS TO RESET. IT'S HOW THIS SYSTEM WORKS.

IT'S NOT A BUG. IT'S A FEATURE.

LET'S GET OFF THIS TRAIN. *NOW.*

R.U.R. VIRUS WARNING. DOWNLOAD INTERRUPTED. 52%!

NO. YES. NO.

IGNORE ME.

DON'T IGNORE ME.

STOP IT.

DO IT.

MUST. DESTROY IT.

SIR? JUDGE DREDD? IS THAT YOU? YOU'RE ALIVE?!

DO IT! DIDN'T YOU HEAR ME?! DESTROY THIS TRAIN!

IT WAS AN HONOR SERVING WITH YOU.

HA.

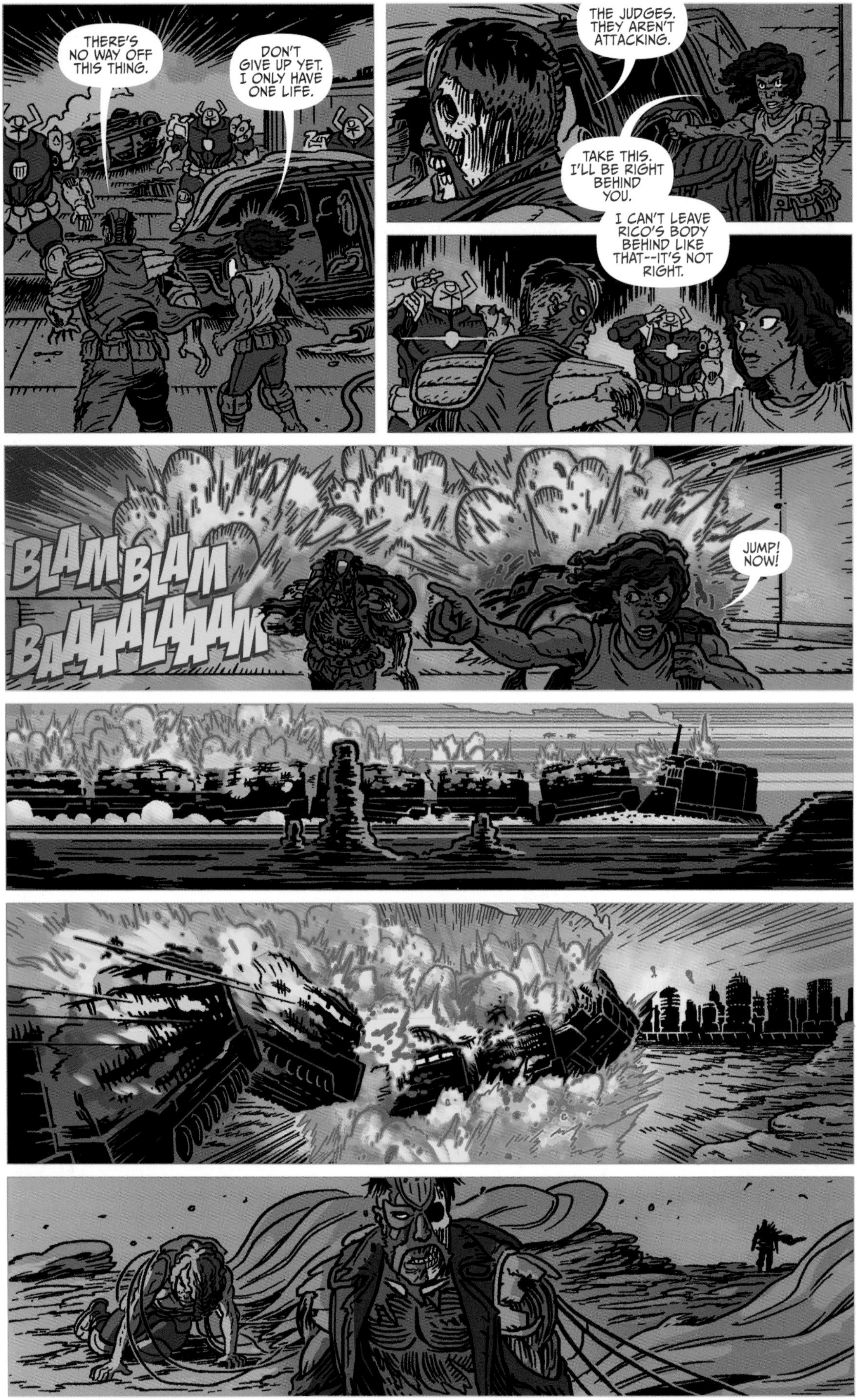

THERE'S NO WAY OFF THIS THING.
DON'T GIVE UP YET. I ONLY HAVE ONE LIFE.
THE JUDGES. THEY AREN'T ATTACKING.
TAKE THIS. I'LL BE RIGHT BEHIND YOU.
I CAN'T LEAVE RICO'S BODY BEHIND LIKE THAT--IT'S NOT RIGHT.
BLAM BLAM BAAAALAAAM
JUMP! NOW!

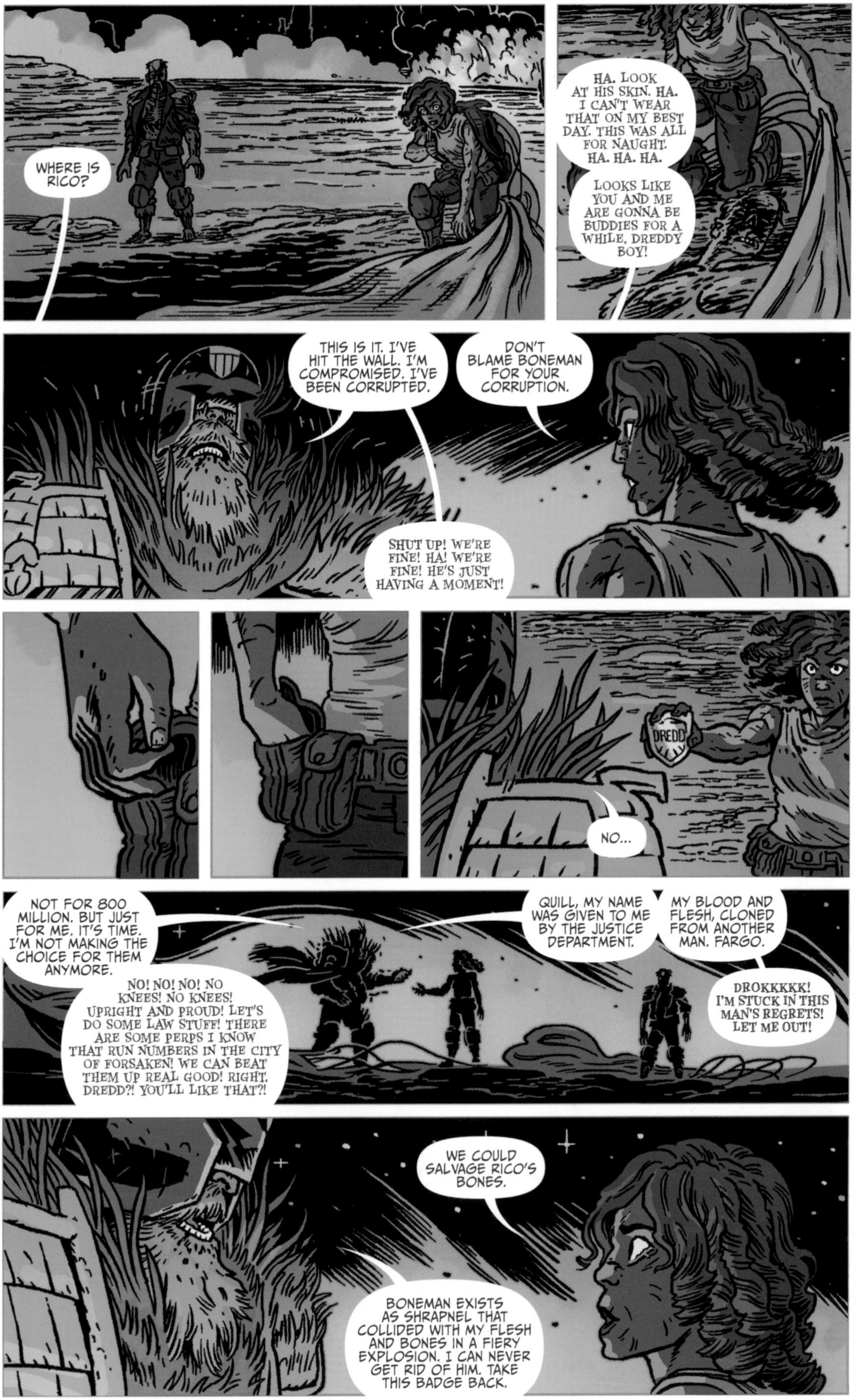
WHERE IS RICO?
HA. LOOK AT HIS SKIN. HA. I CAN'T WEAR THAT ON MY BEST DAY. THIS WAS ALL FOR NAUGHT. HA. HA. HA.
LOOKS LIKE YOU AND ME ARE GONNA BE BUDDIES FOR A WHILE, DREDDY BOY!
THIS IS IT. I'VE HIT THE WALL. I'M COMPROMISED. I'VE BEEN CORRUPTED.
DON'T BLAME BONEMAN FOR YOUR CORRUPTION.
SHUT UP! WE'RE FINE! HA! WE'RE FINE! HE'S JUST HAVING A MOMENT!
DREDD
NO...
NOT FOR 800 MILLION. BUT JUST FOR ME. IT'S TIME. I'M NOT MAKING THE CHOICE FOR THEM ANYMORE.
NO! NO! NO! NO KNEES! NO KNEES! UPRIGHT AND PROUD! LET'S DO SOME LAW STUFF! THERE ARE SOME PERPS I KNOW THAT RUN NUMBERS IN THE CITY OF FORSAKEN! WE CAN BEAT THEM UP REAL GOOD! RIGHT, DREDD?! YOU'LL LIKE THAT?!
QUILL, MY NAME WAS GIVEN TO ME BY THE JUSTICE DEPARTMENT.
MY BLOOD AND FLESH, CLONED FROM ANOTHER MAN. FARGO.
DROKKKKK! I'M STUCK IN THIS MAN'S REGRETS! LET ME OUT!
WE COULD SALVAGE RICO'S BONES.
BONEMAN EXISTS AS SHRAPNEL THAT COLLIDED WITH MY FLESH AND BONES IN A FIERY EXPLOSION. I CAN NEVER GET RID OF HIM. TAKE THIS BADGE BACK.

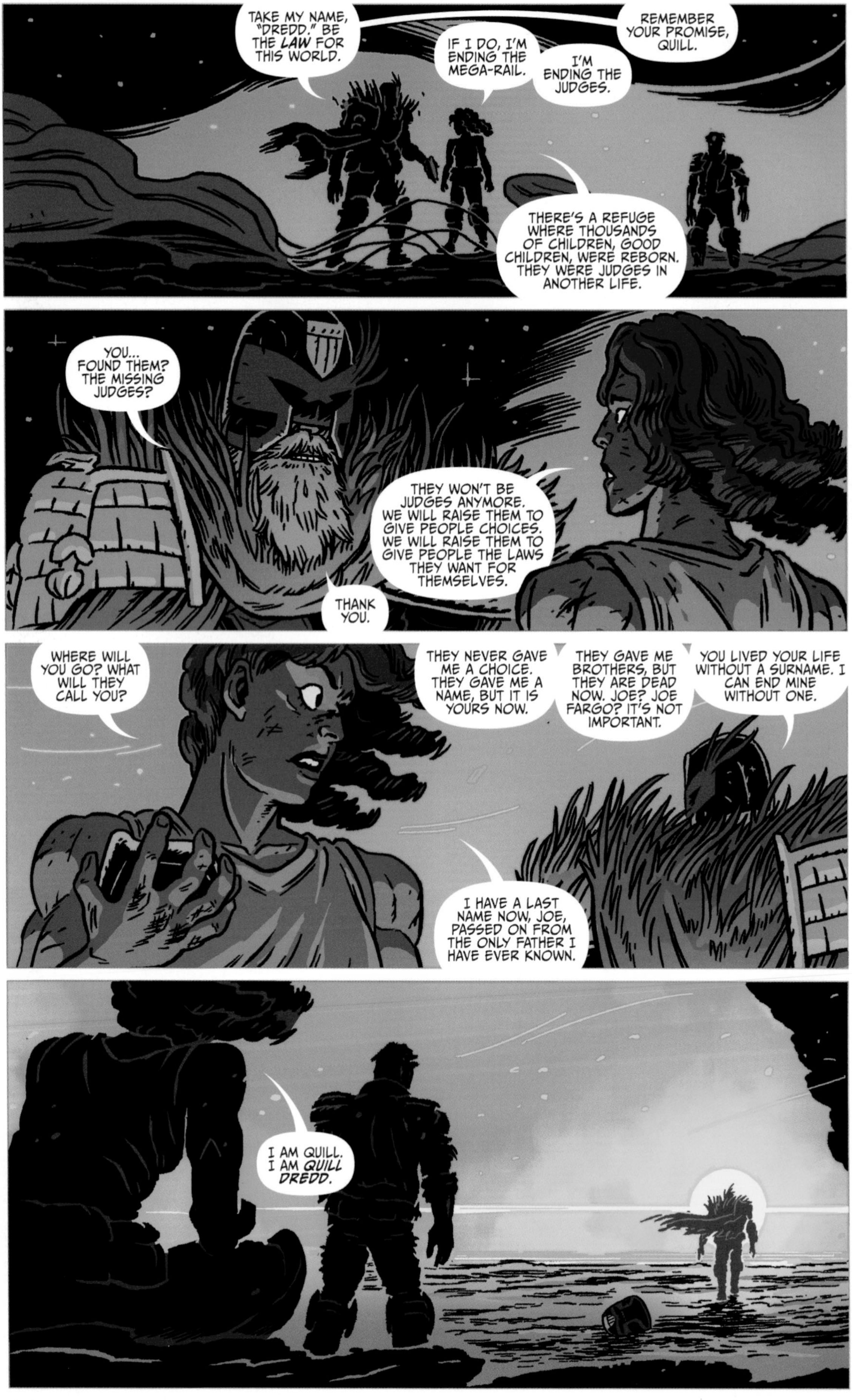
TAKE MY NAME, "DREDD." BE THE LAW FOR THIS WORLD.
IF I DO, I'M ENDING THE MEGA-RAIL.
I'M ENDING THE JUDGES.
REMEMBER YOUR PROMISE, QUILL.
THERE'S A REFUGE WHERE THOUSANDS OF CHILDREN, GOOD CHILDREN, WERE REBORN. THEY WERE JUDGES IN ANOTHER LIFE.
YOU... FOUND THEM? THE MISSING JUDGES?
THEY WON'T BE JUDGES ANYMORE. WE WILL RAISE THEM TO GIVE PEOPLE CHOICES. WE WILL RAISE THEM TO GIVE PEOPLE THE LAWS THEY WANT FOR THEMSELVES.
THANK YOU.
WHERE WILL YOU GO? WHAT WILL THEY CALL YOU?
THEY NEVER GAVE ME A CHOICE. THEY GAVE ME A NAME, BUT IT IS YOURS NOW.
THEY GAVE ME BROTHERS, BUT THEY ARE DEAD NOW. JOE? JOE FARGO? IT'S NOT IMPORTANT.
YOU LIVED YOUR LIFE WITHOUT A SURNAME. I CAN END MINE WITHOUT ONE.
I HAVE A LAST NAME NOW, JOE, PASSED ON FROM THE ONLY FATHER I HAVE EVER KNOWN.
I AM QUILL. I AM QUILL DREDD.

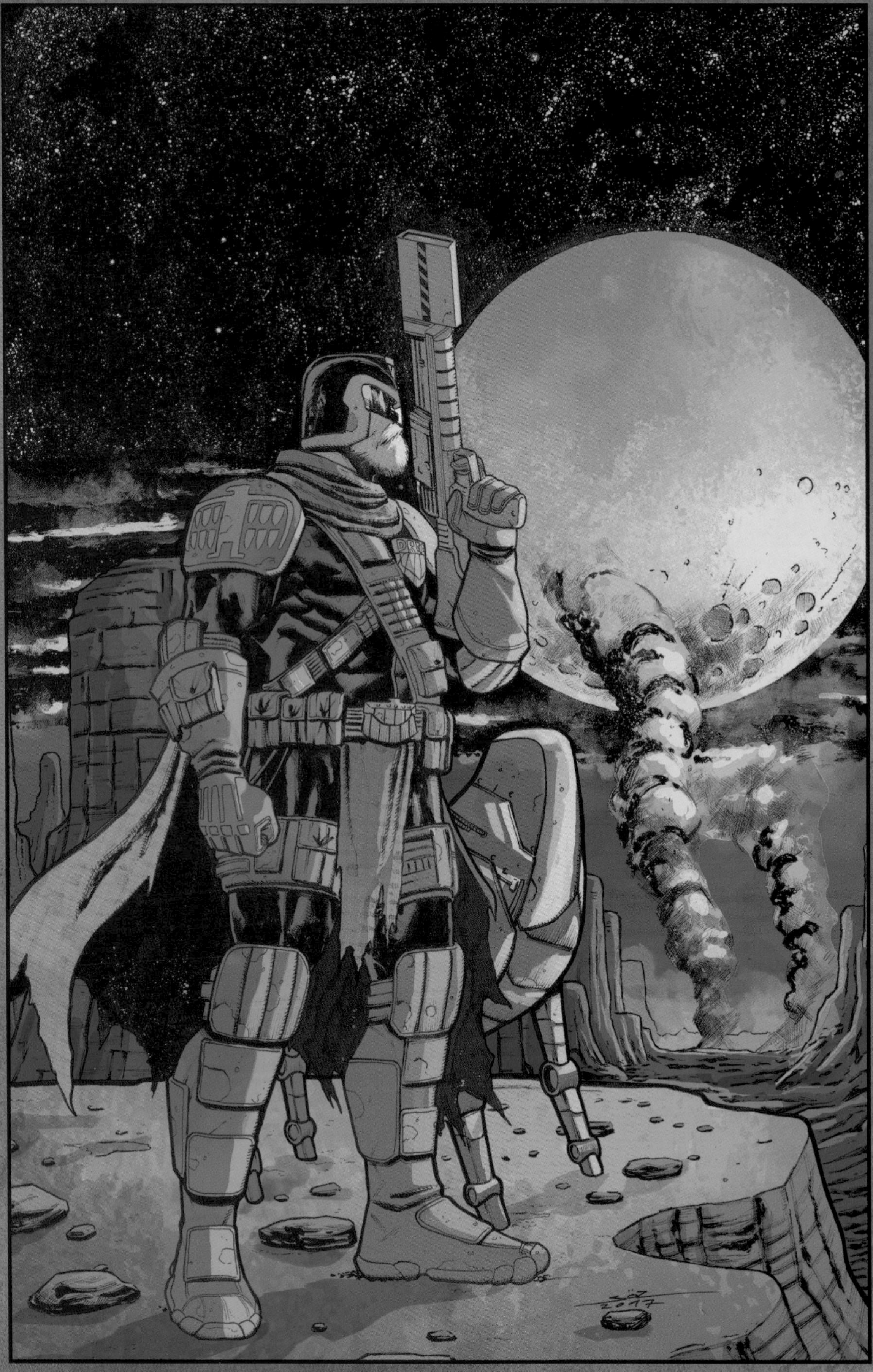

ART BY SEDAT OEZGEN

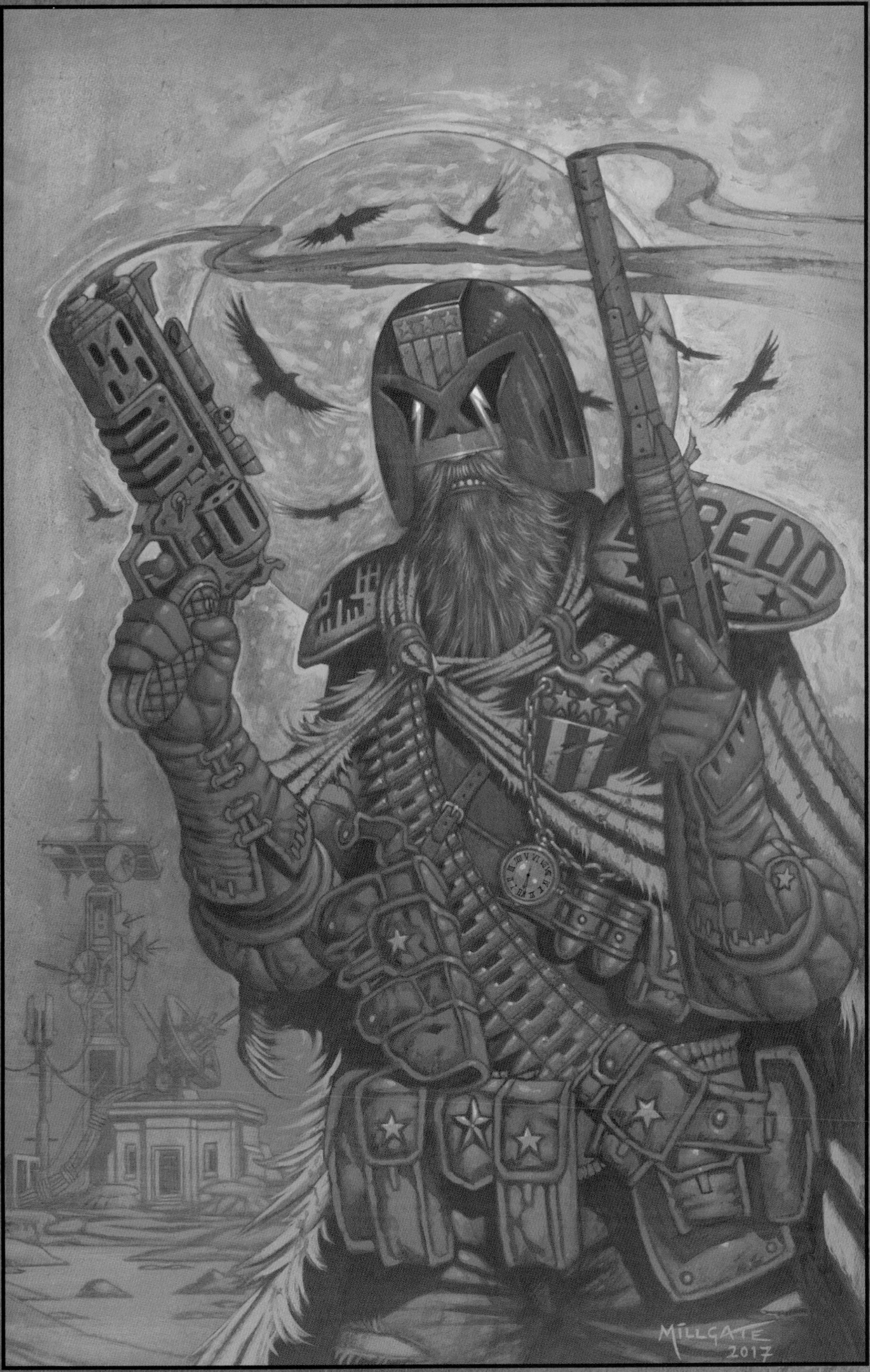
MILLGATE
2017

ART BY MAX MILLGATE

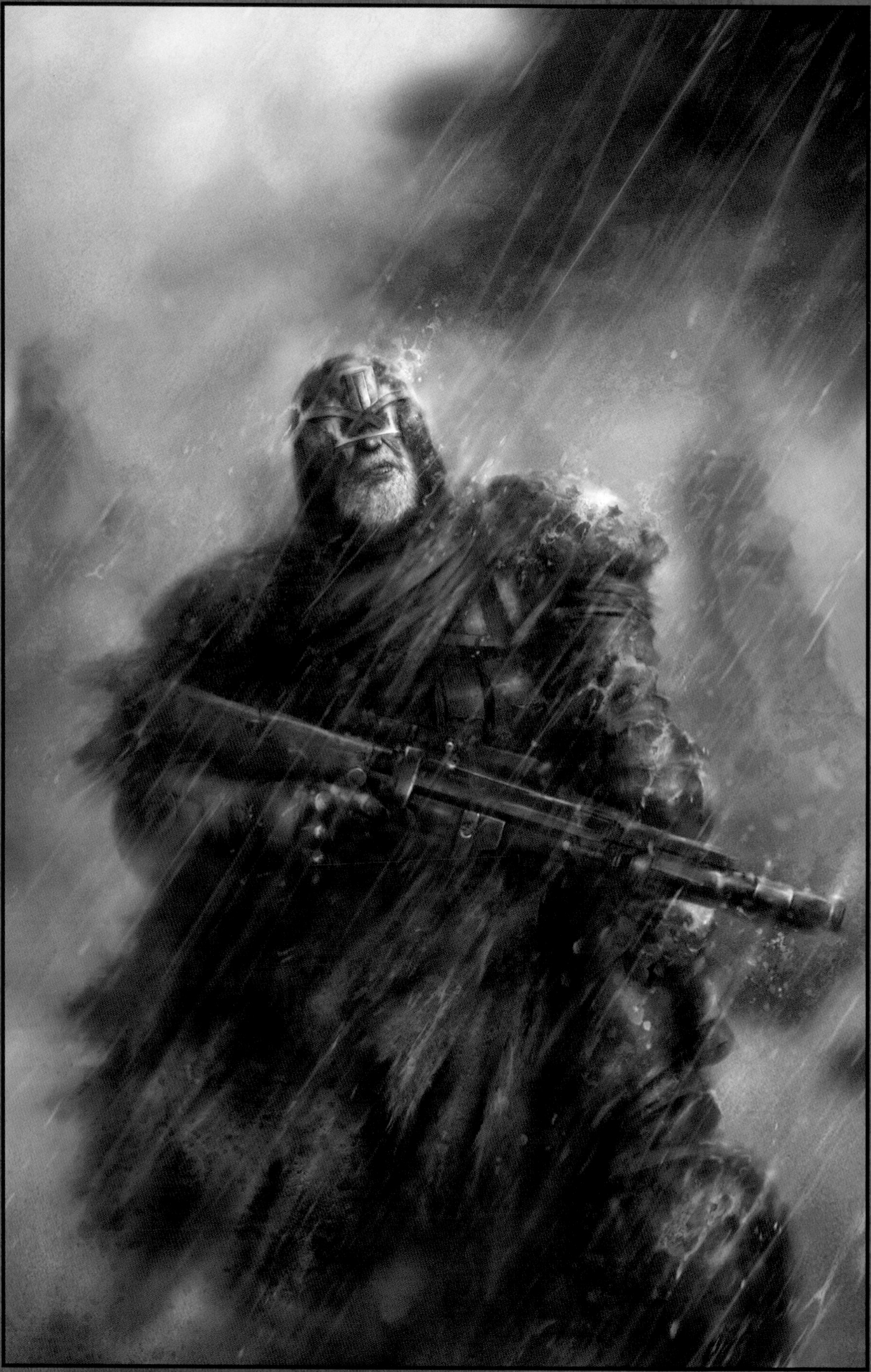

ART BY NICK PERCIVAL

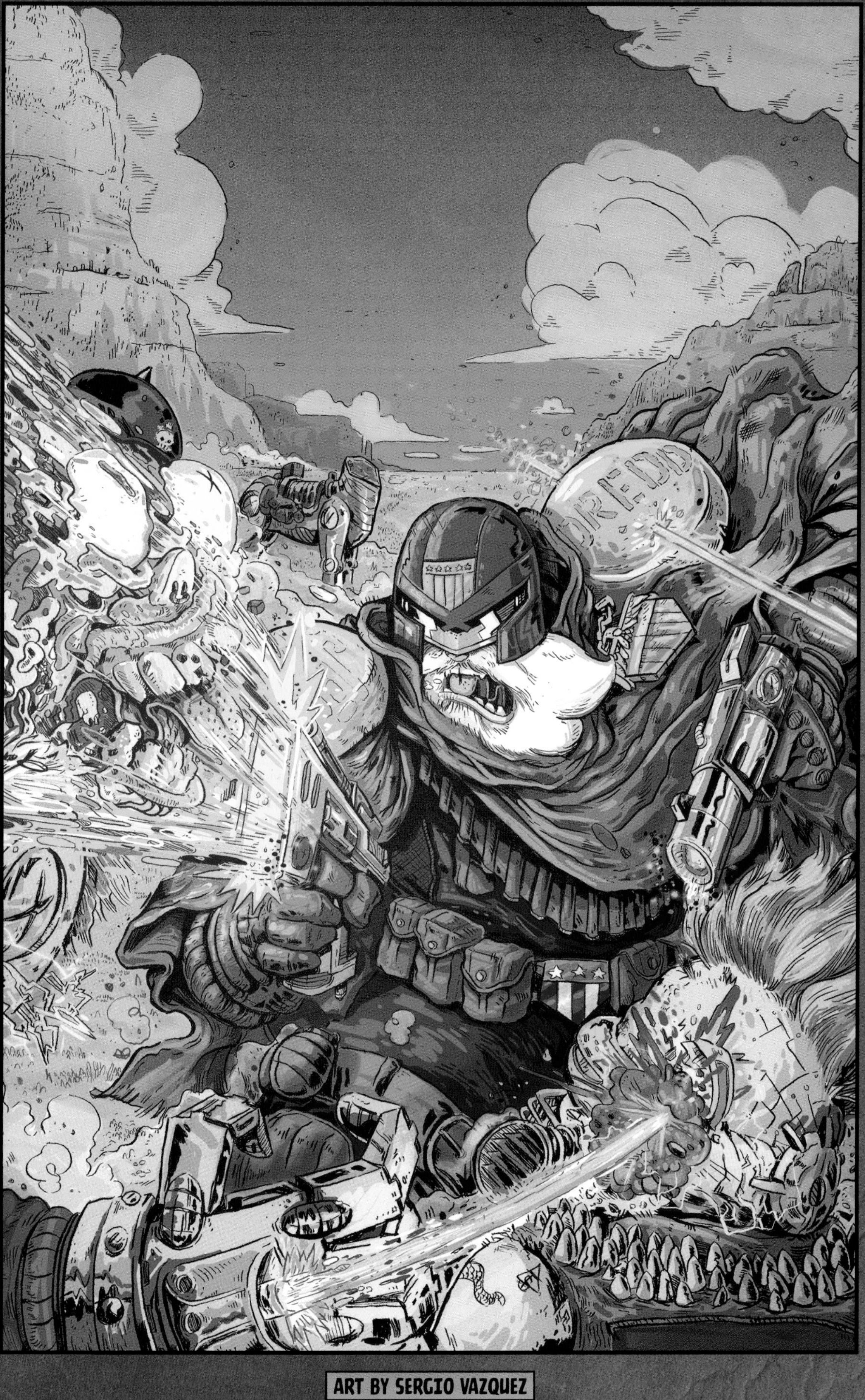
DREDD

ART BY SERGIO VAZQUEZ

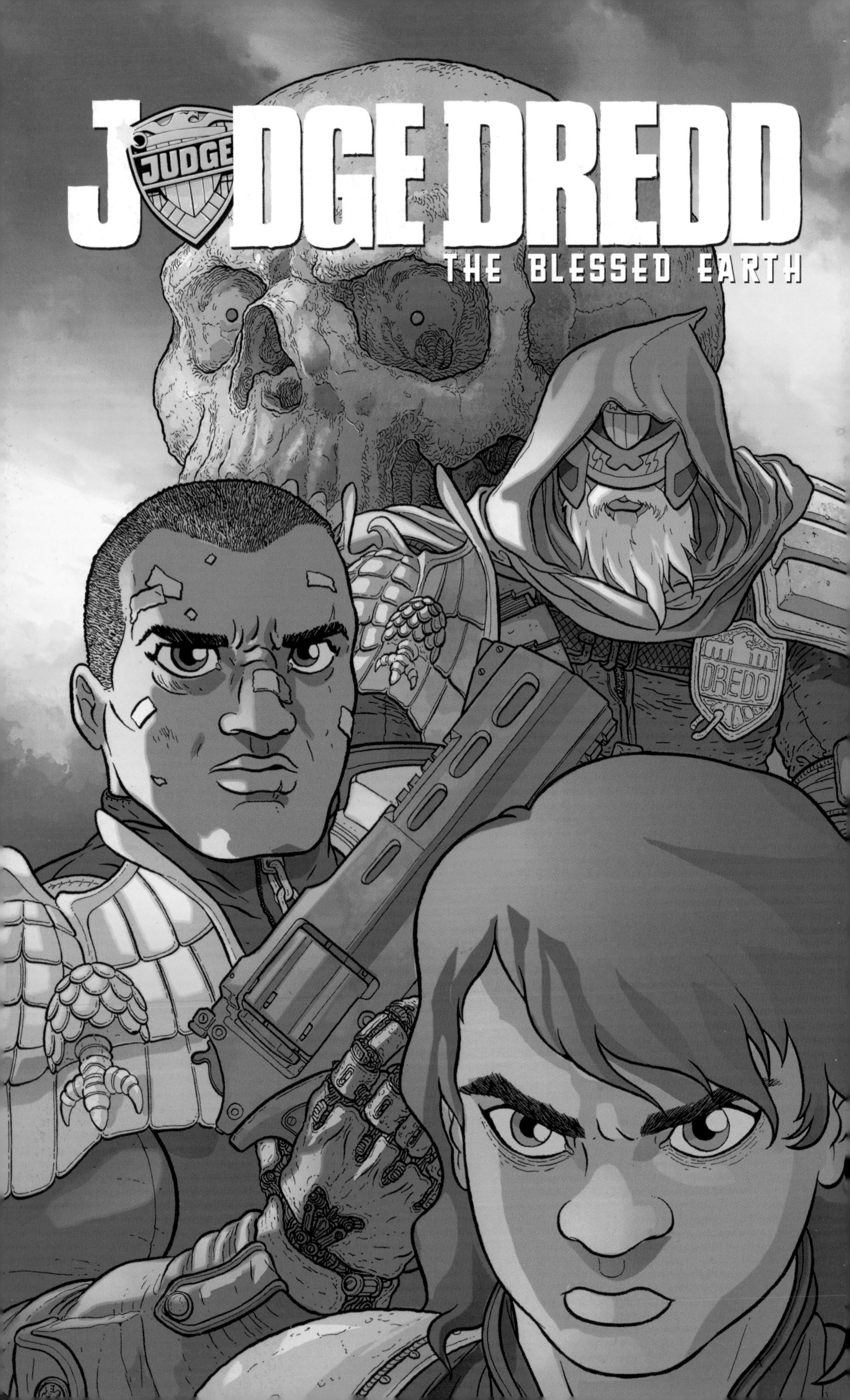
JUDGE DREDD
THE BLESSED EARTH
DREDD